British Political Biography

Edited by
Chris Cook

BRITISH POLITICAL BIOGRAPHY

ROBERT TAYLOR

LORD SALISBURY

ALLEN LANE

009589

DA
564
.52T39
1975

TO ANN
WHOSE PATIENCE AND ENCOURAGEMENT
MADE THIS BOOK POSSIBLE

CONTENTS

PREFACE

This book does not pretend to be in any way a definitive biography of Lord Salisbury. We must still wait for a full-scale Life to be written. My purpose has been more limited – to provide a short account of Salisbury's public career. I have decided to concentrate on a number of hitherto neglected aspects of Salisbury's long period at the forefront of British politics. His foreign policy has received extensive coverage from the historians. This is why I have not paid overdue attention to Salisbury's diplomatic achievements. Instead, I have devoted more space to his career in domestic politics and in particular his ideas and activities over parliamentary reform, Ireland and social reform. My sources have been both primary and secondary material. A full bibliography can be found at the end of the book. Lack of space meant lack of footnotes, but my extensive quotations are clearly dated for reference purposes.

September 1973   R. G. T.

INTRODUCTION

Men felt to him as to the pilot who had weath-
ered an appalling storm, the physician who had mastered a terrible
malady. They recognized his ability, and were glad in a moment of
danger to have such a counsellor at hand; but they do not appear
to have been drawn to him by the bonds of that intense personal
devotion which has united so many great statesmen with their
political supporters. Therefore his influence died with his own death.
He was the head of a powerful party in momentous times; he led a
nation to the highest pinnacle of renown; he laid down landmarks of
policy which have lasted through many revolutions of opinion and
are respected still. But he did not found a school. His name contained
no spell to bind together after his death those whom he had influenced
in life; none of the tender reverence gathered round his memory with
which disciples recall the deeds and treasure up the sayings of a
departed master.

Lord Robert Cecil on Castlereagh,
Quarterly Review, January 1862.
It can also stand as an eloquent epitaph
to Salisbury's life.

Of Lord Robert
I have no hesitation in saying
that if he will work,
and he has a working look,
I will make a man of him.
Disraeli to the Second Marquis of Salisbury,
8 April 1854

1

THE ISHMAELITE
FROM
STAMFORD

February 1830–October 1865

Robert Arthur Talbot Gascoyne Cecil, third son
of the Second Marquis of Salisbury, was born at the family's country
seat at Hatfield, Hertfordshire, on 3 February 1830. He was a weak,
sickly child 'with a passionate temper and a craving for affection'.
His boyhood was lonely and friendless. Cecil's mother died when he
was only ten. It was a loss which his daughter Lady Gwendolen
judged to have been 'irreplaceable' for 'a child of his temperament'.
For a short time, he was tutored privately by a local clergyman. This
was followed with a brief spell in a preparatory school close to Hatfield. Cecil disliked his stay there. He described his experience as 'an
existence among devils'. At the age of ten, Cecil was sent to Eton.

The future Indian Viceroy, Lord Dufferin, then an Etonian, remembered him at the time as 'a thin, frail, little lower-school boy even then writing clever essays'. Cecil was both delicate and precocious. He loathed physical sport of any kind. He shone at academic subjects, notably at theology, the classics, history and modern languages. Such intellectual distinction tended to set Lord Robert apart from the other boys. He became the hapless victim of incessant bullying, which he was never to forget. This left an indelible mark on his personality. Although he was to send his own sons to Eton, Cecil refused to visit the school again in later life. It was Eton which reinforced his fear of mixing with his fellow men. During the school holidays, he used to walk the streets in dread of bumping into fellow Etonians. That worry over personal recognition was to remain a persistent obsession. As Lady Gwendolen recalled:

To take a walk with him through a frequented place – excepting London where everyone is safe from undesired observation – was to realize with some accuracy what must be the feelings of a criminal escaping from justice. One went in constant terror of recognition and of its possible consequences, knowing that any overt expression of admiration from some passing group would cast him into the profoundest gloom and spoil all further enjoyment for the afternoon.

Cecil kept his personal contact with other people to the barest minimum. He was to take no interest in the gossipy world of clubland in later life. Nor did he make a habit of frequenting country-house weekend parties. Cecil could be a witty dinner-companion with a mordant sense of humour, but he used to endure the occasional social evening at Hatfield more from a sense of duty than for actual personal pleasure.

Cecil's time at Eton was almost a complete waste. But at least those years turned him into a life-long opponent of corporal punishment in public schools. He was later to castigate Eton's teaching methods as nothing more than 'the treadmill of classical versification'. Cecil's father took him away from the school when he was fifteen. During his next two years he was tutored at Hatfield. Cecil looked back on that period of his life as one of the most enjoyable. He was allowed a good deal of time by himself, which he spent either reading voraciously in the family library, or walking in the Hertfordshire countryside, where he acquired a lasting interest in botany.

In January 1848 – the year of European revolutions – Cecil went up to Christ Church, Oxford, to read mathematics. He was seventeen. Unfortunately his undergraduate days were cut short by physical and mental illness and he was compelled to leave the University after only two years of study, taking an honorary fourth-class degree. Cecil's stay at Christ Church was not entirely fruitless. He joined the Oxford Union, where he became secretary and later treasurer. To his fellow undergraduates Cecil appeared a stern, unbending Tory with a trenchant oratorical style in debate and a sarcastic turn of phrase. He was said to speak with 'a deadly earnestness', and was already the pessimist, the prophet of national decay, who cast a withering eye over the complacencies of mid-Victorian progress. Sir Robert Peel's liberal Conservatism made no appeal to him. He spoke out strongly against any extension of the parliamentary franchise, against the removal of civil disabilities on the Jews, against Free Trade, against any internal reform of the Church of England. At that time Cecil's favourite hero was the Earl of Strafford, Charles I's first minister, who ended his life on the block. Yet not all Cecil's opinions were predictably high Tory. His friends in the exclusive Pythic Society in Oxford were often surprised and alarmed at the breadth and independence of some of his judgements. He believed, for instance, that able working-class boys should be entitled to places in the University.

On coming down from Oxford Cecil lapsed into acute melancholia. He read for the Bar in a desultory fashion, but he remained uncertain of what he should do with his life. It was under doctor's orders that he was packed off on a long sea-voyage to the Antipodes. He left for Cape Colony aboard the sailing ship *Maidstone* on 9 July 1851. Cecil spent several months at the Cape, where he was befriended by the Puseyite Bishop of Cape Town. He then journeyed on to Australia, arriving in Adelaide on 30 January 1852, at the height of the gold rush, where he was impressed by the order and civility of the diggers whom he met in the shanty towns of the outback. He recorded his experiences in a small pocket diary, where he reflected on the cupidity of the middle classes and the more absurd manifestations of colonial rule. After a brief visit to New Zealand, Cecil sailed back to England. He did so without enthusiasm. The prospect of being 'stewed and bored at dinners and parties' filled him with 'great horror'. The years abroad had done much to revive his health, but they had failed to provide him with any clearer idea of what to do. He did not really want to practise law. In his view a barrister was, at best, 'a tolerated evil'. Cecil confessed to his father that the House of Commons was 'undoubtedly the sphere in which a man can be most useful', but he believed his chance of entering politics was 'practically none'. He felt that he would probably end up doing nothing in particular and trying to eke out a living from writing articles for the newspapers.

Yet within a few months of his return from the Antipodes Cecil entered Parliament. The Stamford division of Lincolnshire fell vacant on the death of the sitting member. The seat was in the pocket of the Marquis of Exeter, Cecil's cousin. Cecil's father was successful in acquiring the nomination for him. On 18 August 1853 he presented himself to the borough electors outside Stamford Corn Market 'with the band playing and the church bells ringing'. No one bothered to contest his election. Cecil was returned unopposed to Westminster. To his undoubted relief, he never had to endure any fight on the hustings during his fifteen years as Stamford's M.P. In the autumn of 1853 Cecil achieved another, unexpected, honour. Much to his own surprise, he was elected a Fellow of All Souls College, Oxford.

Cecil's neurotic moods and tempers were not to vanish with his arrival in national politics. Indeed, it was uncertain for some time whether he would ever be able to withstand the rough and tumble of parliamentary life. He seriously contemplated leaving politics in 1858, when Lord Derby refused to give him a post in his short-lived ministry. He thought of taking a job with the Inland Revenue. His father made an unsuccessful attempt to provide him with a clerkship of the Privy Council. Cecil was offered the governorship of Moreton Bay, later Queensland, in Australia, but turned it down. His depressions were a continual worry to his family through those years. As Lady Gwendolen explained:

He remained through life liable to attacks which he used to speak of as nerve-storms. They operated in that borderline between mind and body whose boundaries medical science has hitherto failed to delimitate. Sometimes they seemed to have their origin in mental worry, sometimes in physical exhaustion; they would be accompanied by an overwhelming depression of spirits and also by a great bodily lassitude and by a morbid acuteness of the senses of touch and hearing. The slightest noise or physical contact became painful to him when in this state.

None the less Cecil did not become a complete neurotic. His highly successful marriage and a firm, unwavering belief in the truths of the Christian faith both had a steadying influence. It is perhaps not surprising that the young Cecil found it difficult to establish normal friendly relations with women. A tall, stooping, myopic intellectual recluse, he was also an untidy, unprepossessing man. However in 1856 he met Miss Georgina Alderson, the eldest daughter of a Norfolk judge. Despite his father's strong objections, Cecil married her, on 11 July 1857. His wife became his most important 'counsellor and confidant' through his political life until her death in October 1899. She possessed many of the personal qualities which Cecil lacked himself. Her cheerful optimism, her sociability, her knack for judging character, her capacity for individual human sympathy – all those attributes provided compensation for his own contrasting qualities.

Cecil was always sceptical about established truths. In his study of the sciences, history, even politics he had what his daughter called 'an innate yearning after heterodoxy in all its forms'. However, in his religious convictions, Cecil was never to question 'the love and trust of the living Christ'. Although his writings and speeches do not reveal the depths of his Christian belief, it lay at the core of his political thought. As Lady Gwendolen explained, 'his creed was essentially the inspiration and background of a life of action – not an object for continued investigation and analysis'. In Cecil's opinion, the Anglican form of Christianity could not be the object of either any precise definitions nor a rigorous *a priori* analysis. The mysteries of the Faith were beyond the realm of rational speculation. Cecil once remarked that 'God is all-powerful and God is all-loving, and the world is what it is! How are you going to explain that?' Cecil believed in the doctrine of the Incarnation and the story of the Gospels. Lady Gwendolen recalls that his personal vision provided 'a large serenity – over which his humour – often cynically expressed but essentially indulgent – played with a constantly enlivening ripple'. It was his religious belief which gave Cecil an inner self-confidence. Viscountess Milner later wrote of Salisbury in the 1890s: 'He has as much right as Gladstone to be regarded as a great Christian statesman'.

> Although he was a Churchman and an observer of all religious duties, he never gave the impression of being intellectually mastered by the creed he followed and fundamentally believed in . . . I never quite understood how it happened that Lord Salisbury came to be so conventional on this one subject. He was both sceptical and unconventional on every other.

During his early years in politics, Cecil found himself in dire financial straits. He turned to journalism as a means of making money to support himself and his family. His often lengthy articles in the *Quarterly Review* and the *Saturday Review* provide a rich source for an understanding of Cecil's political thought during the 1850s and early 1860s. During that period Cecil was a somewhat solitary figure on the Conservative back benches. He shared very little in common with the leaders of the weak and divided party. Neither Lord Derby nor Disraeli were forceful enough Tories for Cecil's liking. At the same time, he shared no sympathy with the middle-class members of the party. Nor was he a representative figure of rural Toryism. Cecil once compared the back-bench squirearchy to 'red-hot cannon-balls', which he claimed they resembled 'in density, if not in weight'. He stood for the Conservatism of the clever man. Cecil was no diehard resister of all change. He was never to display much affection for the forms of Conservatism, and he was conscious of the ephemeral nature of political issues. Cecil wrote in April 1861:

The axioms of the last age are the fallacies of the present. The principles which may save one generation may be the ruin of the next. There is nothing abiding in political science but the necessity for truth, purity and justice. The evils by which the body politic is threatened are in a state of constant change and with them the remedies by which those evils must be cured.

None the less, Cecil was a firm believer in the virtue of what he called 'constitutional government', that legacy of the 1832 Reform Act, which he claimed was held together by the 'discretion and patriotism' of the ruling class. In his opinion, such a system, which was neither a tyranny nor a democracy, was the most effective in reconciling the defence of individual freedom with the established social and political order. Cecil was convinced that the benevolent rule of a civic-minded and responsible élite was the nearest approximation to the Aristotelian ideal of a balanced system of government. As he wrote:

Every community has natural leaders to whom, if they are not misled by the insane passion for equality, they will instinctively defer. Always wealth, in some countries birth, in all intellectual power and culture, mark out the men to whom, in a healthy state of feeling, a community looks to undertake its government. They have the leisure for the task, and can give it the close attention and preparatory study which it needs. Fortune enables them to do it for the most part gratuitously so that the struggles of ambition are not defiled by the taint of sordid greed. They occupy a position of sufficient prominence among their neighbours to feel that their course is closely watched, and they belong to a class among whom a failure in honour is mercilessly dealt with. (October 1862)

Yet Cecil was aware that 'unlimited power', even with such high-minded rulers, would be 'ill bestowed' if it was left unchecked by 'an active public opinion' and 'constitutional forms'. He feared that the élite's 'rightful pre-eminence' could easily degenerate into 'the domination of a class'. Cecil believed that the chief merit of the balanced system lay in its division of power between the executive and the two Houses of Parliament. The harmonious working of that subtle arrangement could not be taken for granted. In Cecil's view it was under continual threat of collapse. He spoke of the 'incurable fitfulness of the exertions which Englishmen make to uphold the institutions which they love'. Cecil was quite sure that 'moderate Conservatism' would always be in the ascendancy in such a system, 'if victory could be secured by a mere comparison of forces'. Unfortunately the upper classes were 'naturally indolent' and 'slow to believe that political changes can possibly trouble their repose till danger was actually at the door'. Cecil wrote that 'unless Providence should in mercy send some awkward demagogue who shows the hook under the bait they will always be ready to nibble at fine sentiments about confidence in the English people until they are caught and landed beyond escape' (July 1860).

Cecil was pessimistic about human nature. He did not believe in rational progress, nor in the idea that men shared common ethical or moral ideals. 'Theories probably never inspired enthusiasm among any considerable mass of human beings. They are prized for the purpose of throwing a veil of decency over the naked passions by which political convulsions are brought about,' he wrote. 'The "rights of man" have already served as the pretext for many an orgy of bloodthirsty frenzy, at the memory of which nations now recoil.'

Moreover, despite his support for the balanced system, Cecil disliked the character of political life. He wrote of the 'pliant and malleable mind of the House of Commons', 'the world of conclaves and conspiracies, of pulse-feeling and thumb-screwing, of slippery intrigues and abortive stratagems' (18 February 1860). 'There is no blindness so unaccountable as the blindness of English statesmen to the political value of a character,' he wrote in April 1861.

> Living only in and for the House of Commons, moving in an atmosphere of constant intrigue, accustomed to look upon oratory as a mode of angling for political support and upon political professions as only baits of more or less attractiveness, they acquire a very peculiar code of ethics, and they are liable wholly to lose sight of the fact that there is a stiffer and less corrupted morality out-of-doors. They not only come to forget what is right but they forget that there is anyone who knows it.

Cecil believed that politicans were often guilty of treating their profession as if it were a game of chess 'in which mighty principles and deep-seated sentiments' were merely 'the pawns to be sacrificed or exchanged as the moment's convenience might suggest'. In his view, they were blind to 'the elementary truth, that the character of unselfish honesty' was 'the only secure passport to the confidence of the English people'.

Cecil was a firm supporter of the value of the party system. He disliked the lack of party cohesion and the aimless fluidity of mid-Victorian politics. The notion of a Commons packed with independent M.P.s was, in his opinion, ridiculous, 'an inspiration from Laputa, a mere dream of doctrinaires' (9 May 1857). On the other hand Cecil disapproved of rule through 'obscure cliques with some narrow crotchet of a policy and some paltry yelping shibboleth for a cry'. His avowed ideal of party was that of 'a union of men honestly wishing the same objects and struggling for it on that account', and not 'a mere joint-stock company for the maintenance of place and power'. Cecil believed that the lack of any clear-cut division between the parties at Westminster meant 'an unstable and capricious Commons'. In his view, this state of affairs would demoralize the electorate, who would be unable to judge on the 'general character of the leaders' of the country. Cecil argued that if the voters were not presented with a choice of genuine political alternatives at the polls, they would vote for 'selfish and sectional ends', 'for private gratitudes and grudges'. It was the paralysis of the party struggle which put 'life and vigour' into the 'cliques and crotcheteers'. Cecil sought the return to the age when politics was dominated by 'broad parties based on comprehensive ideas and guided by men who have a name to stake on the wisdom of their course'.

Cecil was an unsparing critic of his own party's faults. He was alarmed at the behaviour of the 1858–9 Derby ministry, particularly when it tried to introduce a mild measure of parliamentary reform. By July 1859 Cecil had come to the conclusion that the only issue on which he could agree with the rest of the Conservative party any longer was 'a distrust of Louis Napoleon abroad and John Bright at home'. He grumbled that while the Conservatives were founded 'to resist free trade, reform, Jewish and Roman Catholic demands', each of those aims had been 'disavowed with marvellous effrontery by the leaders and with sad but submissive weakness by the mass of the rank and file'. Cecil wanted the party to abandon what he called 'this alternation between womanish spite and Oriental cunning'. In his view, the main culprit for the rootless condition of the Conservatives was Disraeli. 'The truth is that his life, from his first appearance in the journalistic world down to the present hour, has been spent in dodging. He is bewitched by the demon of low dodging,' Cecil wrote in June 1859 of the Conservative leader. In his opinion, the Conservatives were too preoccupied with the capture of political power for its own sake. 'It is a doctrine born of mere selfishness, greed, and reeking of corruption. It strips the political contest of all that is inspiring and ennobling and reduces those who take part in it from the rank of crusaders for a principle to the level of political caterans foraying for booty,' he wrote in July 1860. He continued:

Every party, according to the conventional definition of its functions, has two tasks to perform. It has to maintain a certain set of principles and it has to obtain office for a number of its principal debaters. The one function is among the highest to which a human being can devote himself, the other is at best a matter to be extenuated and apologized for by an appeal to the known weaknesses of mankind.

Cecil feared that office was a 'matter of dread' rather than 'desire' unless the Conservatives enjoyed an overall majority in the Commons. Far better to stay in opposition maintaining 'a free and independent bearing'. It was there that the party could not merely 'preserve their own honour intact', but also restore 'in an age when it is sorely shaken, the public confidence in public men'.

Cecil soon won a reputation for the sharp and forceful style of his oratory. His maiden speech on 7 April 1854 set the tone. It was a scathing attack on Lord John Russell's measure to reform Oxford University. Cecil claimed that the bill was a threat to voluntary college endowments and it would fail to be a final settlement of the question. 'What confidence could there be that some future Ministry, with the word Conservative on its lips but destruction in its hand, would not drive home the wedge now introduced?' he questioned. Gladstone felt that Cecil's speech was 'rich with future promise'.

As an independent Conservative, Cecil often found himself at loggerheads with the party leaders. In July 1855, for instance, he seconded General Peel's resolution, which was to prevent any critical debate on the government's Crimea War policy. This was in defiance of Disraeli's tactics of alliance with the Radicals to force the issue in the Commons. Again in March 1858 Cecil differed from his colleagues in opposing a measure to enable practising Jews to become Members of Parliament on the grounds that 'a sincere Jew' would be bound to undermine the Christian foundations of the state. He also argued that the bill would make the majority of the population even more apathetic about religion and it would convince sincere Anglicans that they need take no further interest in Westminster. Cecil proved to be an effective critic, in alliance with some Liberals, of Robert Lowe's administration of the Committee on Education and in particular of the so-called Revised Code, a system of payment by results. He was also an unyielding opponent of attempts to change the form of religious instruction in the schools. In March 1855 he claimed that a bill to give local parishes the power to levy a rate for school-building would throw the schools into the hands of those who despised dogmatic instruction. 'Slowly, by degrees, the instruction given would be reduced to the colourless teaching advocated by the friends of the secular system,' Cecil warned. He turned his face against 'anything that could tend to confuse the outlines of belief, that attempted to unite the sects that were irreconcilable to each other'.

Cecil took a similarly hostile attitude to the long campaign of the Dissenters to abolish the church rate, which all parishioners were compelled to pay for the upkeep of the Church of England, whether they were Anglican or not. In his view, any attempt at abolishing the payment would be 'the first blow against the union of Church and state'. In March 1861 Cecil pointed out that the church-rate issue had been kept at bay for thirty years and the endowments wrangle for twenty years. He argued that 'at the pass to which things have come, it is better to defend the outworks at once, than let the enemy advance further'. Cecil was equally opposed to any suggestion that Dissenters might be allowed burial in Church of England graveyards. 'Dissenters might, no doubt, go through the outward ceremony of reading the Bible and singing hymns in the churchyard, but if a rain- or hail-storm came on, it would be considered the height of bigotry to prevent them entering the church and reading the service there. Until the arrival of the millennium, when the lion is willing to sit down with the lamb, the tolerance of all sorts and kinds of religionists in the same churchyard will only end in constant riots,' Cecil warned (28 June 1862).

Cecil believed that the Church of England was 'a formidable obstacle to the spirit of rash and theoretic change', 'her atmosphere was poison to revolutionary growths'. The Dissenting chapels were 'the earthworks and blockhouses for the maintenance of an untiring political guerrilla' and their ministers 'ready-made electioneering agents'. Their goal was 'a Church purged of dogma, disembarrassed of belief, embracing every error and every crotchet within its fold, but retaining its influence for the purposes of high politics, and devoting all its energies to the foundation of mechanics institutes,' he wrote (October 1861). Cecil was determined to prevent the triumph of the chapel over the Church. 'We shall either cling to our articles of faith in spite of "rationalist" and "unsectarian" teaching or we shall learn by a cruel experience, that men will not be moral without a motive and that a motive can only be furnished by religious belief,' he wrote (July 1865). He believed it was impossible for the Church of England to cut itself off from the world and degrade ministers into soliciting the means for their upkeep. He believed that

endowment was the best way of upholding the clergy without exposing them 'to the danger of despiritualizing those who profit by it'.
'Spoliation, whether public or private is, unhappily, no rare phenomenon in this evil world, but to read a man a sermon upon the sin
of covetousness at the moment you are rifling his pockets is a refine-
ment of cruelty of which there are few examples.' Cecil did not believe
that the Church could stand aside from political struggle. He urged
the formation of a strong alliance between the Conservatives and the
Anglican Church against the common enemy.

Cecil also spoke out on international affairs. He made it clear that
he had no sympathy with those who brought personal morality into
the manner in which British diplomacy ought to be conducted:

> As individuals and as nations we live in states of society utterly diff-
> erent from each other. As a collection of individuals we live under the
> highest and latest development of civilization, in which the individual is
> rigidly forbidden to defend himself, because society is always ready and
> able to defend him. As a collection of nations we live in an age of the
> merest Faustrecht, in which each one obtains his rights precisely in pro-
> portion to his ability, or that of his allies to fight for them. (April 1861)

Cecil opposed any aggressive foreign policy of national self-
aggrandisement. He disliked any interference in the internal affairs
of other countries. Lord John Russell's foreign diplomacy was the
particular object of much Cecilian invective. He described it as one
of 'fierce notes and pacific measures', which involved picking on
small, weak nations with 'an extravagant exhibition of arrogance',
while backing down in a humiliating fashion before powerful countries like Prussia over the Schleswig-Holstein crisis and Russia after
the Tsar's suppression of the Poles in 1863. 'Non-intervention in the
abstract may be good policy or bad. It is non-intervention heralded
by threats to one side and promises to the other that we condemn,'
Cecil argued. Cecil believed that the failures of the Congress of
Vienna were due to the 'practice of foreign intervention in domestic
quarrels'. He wrote in his essay on Lord Castlereagh:

> There is no practice which the experience of nations more uniformly
> condemns, and none which governments more consistently pursue. Do-
> mestic discord is bad enough: but the passions which provoke it burn
> themselves out at last: and the contending parties are eventually school-
> ed by each other into moderation which alone makes the coexistence of
> freedom and order possible. But if foreign intervention on either side be
> once threatened, much more if it be carried out, a venom is infused into
> the conflict which no reaction weakens and no revenge exhausts. The
> lesson has been taught in recent times by abundant instances, and still
> seems to have been taught in vain. The history of the last seventy years

is strewn with the wrecks of national prosperity which these well-meant interventions have caused. (January 1862)

Cecil was no enthusiast for nationalism. 'The theory of nationality is safe from refutation. The blows of argument fall harmlessly upon its insubstantial forms. Controversy is waste labour in a domain of thought where no term is defined, no principle laid down, and no question propounded for investigation,' he wrote. In his essay on Castlereagh Cecil poured scorn on nationalism:

> The idea scarcely seems to have dawned upon him [Castlereagh] that anyone had laid it down as a political dogma that no two peoples speaking different languages ought to be under the same government: and that any amount of revolutionary confusion was preferable to such an enormity. Not having mastered it he was unable to draw from it its obvious inference, that Austria in holding Venetia, Denmark in holding Schleswig-Holstein, and Prussia in holding Poland, were committing an unpardonable crime against the peoples. If he had been more instructed in what has been recently called the new European law, he might have been embarrassed at being asked to proffer to it the sanction of England, who owns, without any consent of the people whatever, more nationalities than she can comfortably count.
>
> Possibly he would have been equally impenetrable to the argument that because Dante was a citizen of Florence, or Virgil composed poetry in Rome, therefore a German ought not to reign in Venice. It never would have occurred to him as a possible theory, that governments should be overturned or treaties broken for the sake of giving a present reality to the traditional glory of some distant past.

Cecil disliked the diplomacy of bluff and confrontation. He thought that it was the task of statesmen to recognize the limitations on their capacity to influence events, and make sure that the nation's safety and honour were upheld. The success of a country's foreign policy was to be judged by the avoidance of war.

Cecil deplored the moral cant and humbug which has often been a feature of British diplomacy. During a debate on the Polish question in 1855, he suggested that it was 'a very gross piece of hypocrisy to say that England upon all occasions was to come forward in defence of oppressed nationalities when a great portion of her Empire was constituted of them'. 'There is not a quarter of the globe in which England has not increased her territory by precisely the same process of aggression,' Cecil observed. He was a powerful critic of British involvement in the 1857 Chinese Opium War, arguing that 'brute force had been employed to an extent injurious' to the country's commercial interests. 'Much has been said of the honour of England. If instead of backing up our plenipotentiaries we did not impose a check upon them, there is no saying to what extent they might not damage our interests and involve us in hostilities,' he argued. In Cecil's view 'an aggressive character is the most dangerous one this country could get'. 'A character of honour, justice and truth would do more to induce the jealous Chinese to open their ports to us than any demonstration of force and violence,' Cecil maintained.

He also refused to condone the excesses of British colonial rule. In 1857 forty-two prisoners were held captive in a room of fifteen foot square for twenty days in Hong Kong. 'It would be most disgraceful if while we were protesting against alleged atrocities at Naples, our own officers were pursuing the same or a worse course, in a distant quarter of the globe,' Cecil argued. He hated the 'nigger-despising temper' of Englishmen out in the Empire. Cecil was a forthright critic of the British treatment of the Maoris of New Zealand. He spoke of 'constant wars at distant points which bring us such large bills and such little credit and which it is afterwards their onerous task to justify'. No Little Englander, he accepted the obligations of Empire. In 1860 he opposed any attempt to withdraw defence from the colonies. While Cecil was ready to admit that 'it might be fairly questioned whether it has been wise originally to colonize' the Cape and New Zealand, he was sure that 'any proposition to abandon our colonies would be talked out' of the Commons.

None the less Cecil disliked the domination of one race or people by another. He was a zealous champion of the Confederate cause during the American Civil War, but he hated Negro slavery. Cecil said it was 'a double curse' for 'the slave debased the master: the master debased the slave'. 'The real opprobrium of the system is that its existence absolutely requires the utter degradation, moral and intellectual, of the unhappy race over whom it reigns.' Slavery, in Cecil's eyes, was 'a direct negative of the prospects of Christianity which bluster cannot shroud nor expediency wash out'. His compassion was extended to the free Negro of the Northern states, whom he likened to the pariah of India or even the 'leper among the children of Israel'. Cecil was bitter about the American system of government, which allowed such behaviour to go unchallenged. He spoke of 'persecution without the self-devoted faith which almost hallowed it, despotism untempered by the patriarchal feeling, and an aristocracy of caste, impassable, fenced off and unsoftened by the halo of chivalrous traditions'.

Cecil believed that the state should play a carefully limited role in economic life, but he was not utterly indifferent to the cause of social reform. In his first election manifesto, Cecil expressed general support

for the passage of legislation that would prove of benefit to the working classes. In the Commons, he spoke out strongly against the
adulteration of staple foods like tea and sugar by shopkeepers and
tradesmen, arguing that the state should protect the helpless from
such exploitation. He was also a persistent critic of the administration
of the Poor Law. Although he supported the principles which lay
behind the Poor Law, he disliked 'the meanness, fussiness, shabby-
genteel self-importance' of Poor Law guardians like those in St
Pancras workhouse where, Cecil claimed, 'in order to spare their
own pockets, they are defrauding those who have a right to relief'
(3 December 1859). He believed that thrift was 'the poor man's only
chance of morality or comfort', but this did not stop Cecil from
attacking the behaviour of the Charity Commissioners, whom he
alleged were 'made up of a class who make their fortunes by scraping
together petty profits and petty earnings'. In May 1863 Cecil voiced
his support for the endowed charities, when Gladstone decided that
they should be liable to pay direct taxation. Cecil protested both at
the erection of the Thames Embankment and the Victoria and
Albert Museum on the grounds that their cost would have to be met
from the revenue made from the metropolitan coal dues, which were
mainly a burden on the poor.

Yet it was not on all these issues that Cecil won his early reputation
as an abrasive *frondeur*. What made his reputation as a formidable,
uncompromising parliamentarian was his persistent denunciation of
the efforts to achieve a reform of the electoral system.

My connection with the Conservative party
has been purely one of principle –
for, as you know,
I have no feelings of attachment
to either of the leaders.
Cranborne to J.A.Shaw-Stewart,
17 April 1867

2

THE CONSERVATIVE
SURRENDER

The parliamentary reform issue dominated
British politics for most of Cecil's early years in the Commons. Between 1852 and 1867 six reform bills were introduced by ministers
alone. All proved abortive. Cecil was a strong opponent of any
measure involving a massive increase in the size of the electorate.
In his view, the balanced system was 'the highest ideal of internal
government the world has hitherto seen'. He believed that 'its self-
reliance, the habit of mutual concession, and an exclusive regard for
practical ends' were worthy of preservation. Cecil was ready to
admit that the country's electoral structure was 'a chaos without
principle' possessing 'irritating anomalies, often flagrant ones',

but all the proposed alternative reforms seemed to him highly dangerous.

In Cecil's opinion, the function of government was to preserve and broaden the limits of individual freedom without any undue intervention by the state in social and economic life. He feared that any enlargement of the franchise would threaten both life and property which governments were in existence to defend. Cecil was not opposed to all change in the electoral system, just as long as no reform placed the less-well-off sections of society in a numerical superiority among the voters. If this should ever happen, Cecil was convinced that the whole content and style of British politics would change for the worse.

It was Cecil's contention that the old political battles of the early part of the century were drawing to a close. Palmerston's consensus style of government between 1859 and 1865 could no longer disguise the harsh realities of the coming social conflict that Cecil claimed to detect beneath the surface of political life. As he argued:

> The struggle for existence among the political elements of the state is constant and severe. Our government and legislature have no independent action of their own. They are the passive tools of the victor in that struggle. The only security for the vanquished is that any oppressive action towards them is likely to involve other classes in its principle, and so to give them the opportunity of finding in new combinations the means of renewed resistance. Conflict in free states is a law of life. Under a free government there is no danger from the executive, but the necessity of self-protection against rival interests is incessant.

Cecil regarded Gladstone's decision to repeal the paper duties and place a penny on the income tax in his 1860 Budget as evidence of this new kind of politics:

> This question of the incidence of taxation is in truth a vital question. It is the field upon which the contending classes of this generation will do battle. We have no feudalism to sweep away, no privileges worth the name to contest. Till very lately there have been bitter and protracted struggles for political enfranchisement, but the spell of that chimera to excite enthusiasm has passed away. The proletariat will not now fight for a barren share in the business of legislation, unless it is to bear to each one of them a substantial and palpable fruit. The issue between the conflicting forces of society is becoming narrower and more distinct. The mists of mere political theory are clearing away, and the true character of the battleground and the real nature of the prize that is at stake are standing more and more distinctly every year. It galls the classes who barely sustain themselves by their labour that others should sit by and enjoy more than they do and yet work little or not at all. Benighted enthusiasts in other lands, or other times, may have struggled for idle theories of liberty, or impalpable phantoms of nationality, but the enlightened sel-

fishness of the modern artisan now fully understands that political power, like everything else, is to be taken in the dearest market. He cares little enough for democracy unless it will adjust inequalities of wealth. The struggle between the English constitution on the one hand and the democratic forces on the other is now in reality, when reduced to its simplest elements and stated in its most prosaic form, a struggle between those who have to keep what they have got and those who have not to get it. Across the water (in the French Second Empire) the succinct formula *'la propriété c'est le vol'* expresses in its most naked form this goal of democratic aspirations. (April 1860)

Cecil's argument was that any inclusion of the working classes within the electoral system would inevitably make them the dominant political force. Checks and balances would be powerless to stop them. As he explained:

The bestowal upon any class of a voting power disproportionate to their stake in the country must infallibly give to that class a power *pro tanto* of using taxation as an instrument of plunder and expenditure and legislation as a fountain of gain. As despots are liable to individual temptation, and aristocracies sometimes give way to class selfishness, so the pressure of want or the intoxication of passion will overpower the conscience of a democracy.

Cecil's belief in the dangers of democracy was strengthened in the spring of 1861 by the outbreak of the American Civil War. He believed it gave added proof that democracy was a weak form of government, unable to withstand internal division. Cecil called it a 'fair weather system'. As he wrote:

In a world where there are no political dangers, where discontent and discord and rebellion are unknown, where such a world is to be found, democracy may succeed. Probably no government at all would succeed better. But until we reach Utopia, opposing interests and clashing sentiments are certain from time to time to engender conflict, and a state must have a more tenacious organization and abler rulers than democracy can give it if it is to withstand the strain. (October 1862)

Cecil maintained that the American system suffered from 'a fatal combination'. It possessed 'the maximum power of arousing discontent and the minimum power of repressing it'. He wrote of the 'omnipotence of the majority, impervious as any king, greedy as any court mistress or court confessor'. The example of the United States demonstrated that a country could not enjoy democracy unless it had 'something like Caesarism to control it'. 'The feeble and pliant Executive of England is wholly unsuited to such an electoral body. A government that yields and must yield to the slightest wish of the House of Commons is only possible as long as that House of Commons is the organ of an elected minority,' Cecil argued.

He was also concerned about the despotic methods of President Lincoln's government. 'One by one all the outward signs which betray absolutism in the old world are showing themselves in the administration,' he wrote (14 September 1861). 'As soon as real danger touches her [the American government] the surface gloss of liberty fades off and the latent image of despotism develops itself with startling distinctness.' Cecil drew the conclusion that 'a body of representatives at the seat of government, although elected by the freest and largest suffrage' were no more 'guarantees for the freedom of thought and person than a Council of State'. In his opinion, 'the true guarantee of freedom' would have to be looked for 'more in the equilibrium of classes than in the equality of individuals'.

It is often suggested that Cecil hated and distrusted the working classes and it was for that reason he opposed parliamentary reform, but his fear of their potential political power was not based on any assumption about their unique capacity for selfishness. Cecil did not believe that they would behave differently from any other class in society, if they were given supreme political power. As he argued in the Commons:

> I do not understand why the nature of the poor or working men in this country should be different from that of any other Englishmen. They spring from the same race. They live under the same climate. They are brought up under the same laws. They aspire after the same historical model which we admire ourselves and I cannot understand why their nature is thought to be any better or any worse than that of other classes, but if you apply to any class of the community special temptations, you will find that class addicted to special vices. (27 April 1866)

The danger of democracy was that it would mean the formation of governments chosen 'by the class which lives on the proceeds of its daily labour'. Consequently, the political system would have to mirror the demands and aspirations of the majority at the expense of the other interests and classes in society. Governments would have to become 'obedient' to 'the slightest impulse' of the working classes, but they would still be expected to defend the rights of property and capital. Cecil predicted that such a drastic change would bring the loss of 'independent power' that was exercised by 'the educated classes, the aristocracy, the professional men, the merchants, the landowners and the manufacturers'. 'By unwearied canvassing and/ or lavish expenditure they may beg or bribe back a semblance' of power 'for a time, but even that shadow, so dearly purchased, of their former influence, they will retain on suffrance', he maintained.

The activities of the trade unions convinced Cecil that his fears were not groundless. 'The fearful sacrifice which their leaders exact and the implicit obedience of their members indicate a vigour and tenacity of which associations of the middle and upper classes are utterly destitute,' he observed. Governments could serve no other function than to attempt to satisfy the appetites of the working classes, if they were numerically dominant in the electoral system. In Salisbury's opinion, this would mean passing measures 'to fetter capital and favour labour', to restrict the freedom of the propertied classes, to levy taxes 'to be spent by men that contribute to them the least' (April 1866). Democracy would idealize mediocrity and drive honest men out of public life. Politicians would have to appeal to the baser self-interest of the working classes in order to achieve political power. This would involve corruption on the American pattern. Cecil pointed to what had already happened in the large constituencies of Marylebone, Finsbury and Tower Hamlets to indicate why this would mean a further degradation of politics. If the upper classes were deprived of influence and power, they would fail to pursue their civic duties. They would cease to be a responsible aristocracy and become a mere plutocracy of capital, 'corrupt and illegitimate'.

Cecil was not entirely opposed to the inclusion of working men on the electoral register. He was quite ready to accept their 'participation without predominance'. He was also willing to welcome, with enthusiasm, the entry of twenty to thirty working-class M.P.s into the House of Commons. In the 1880s he often complained, as Conservative leader, that local parties were unwilling to nominate working-class candidates for parliamentary seats. Cecil reckoned that working men would prove to be far more upright, honest and patriotic than those members of the middle class who claimed to speak for the labour cause. He favoured the creation of 'compensatory provisions' to reduce 'the power of mere numbers'. As Cecil wrote: 'The great object of all constitutional restrictions is to prevent any majority tyrannizing over a minority – any class dominating over another. No matter what the class, if it were able to rule another class, such is the selfishness of mankind, tyranny is almost sure to result.'

At times of economic prosperity there was no reason to suppose that the working classes would attempt to wreck a democratic political structure. The arrival of a depression, however, would threaten the new system's very foundations. Cecil explained:

The great danger is that it places supreme power into the hands of those who may be misled by hunger into acts of folly or of wrong. In the old country, no excellence of institutions can ensure that such periods of maddening want shall not occasionally occur. Where the bounty of Nature is well nigh exhausted, and multitudes exist on no other resources than the prosperity of trade, it must be that sometimes one precarious resource will fail. When such periods of distress do come, it is vain to hope that argument will restrain hungry men from relieving their own and their children's misery by any measures which the institutions of their country give them power to take. (January 1866)

Such voracious behaviour would place 'the wealth of the capitalist and the landowner, the manufacturer and the merchant, within the grasp of the poor, whose industry is in England too often keen enough to misguide the stoutest principles and clearest reason'. Cecil argued that as the needy were always 'the readiest for plunder', and the rich 'the most tempting victims', the law should ensure that the rich were especially protected from 'the inroads of the needy'.

With Lord John Russell's raising of the reform issue in 1852, it had become practical politics once again. Through the 1850s and early 1860s Cecil attempted to warn all moderate men that any further increase in the size of the franchise would push the balanced system in a dangerously democratic direction. He believed that any eventual change would come, not through popular pressure from below, but as a result of a capitulation by politicians at Westminster. As Cecil wrote:

There is no instance as yet recorded in which the multitudes who live by the daily labour of their hands have overthrown or even seriously threatened any government not absolutely centralized, unless some bitter practical grievance has inspired them. Except when fired by genuine oppression, the working classes cannot make a revolution. The middle class has often fought its way to power by their help, and on such occasions very democratic theories have found their way into very exclusive company. But as soon as the middle classes are inside the citadel instead of outside, their former allies find that democracy goes with marvellous rapidity out of fashion.

However, Cecil feared that there was 'a mysterious fatality' about parliamentary reform. While nobody wished to see it arrive, nobody dared resist it either. Cecil's concern was the influence of the Radicals over the Liberal party. Their call for universal male suffrage filled him with gloomy foreboding. He divided the Radical threat into three – the philosophical Radicals, the Dissenters and what he called the 'sentimental Radicals' who were the most pervasive of all:

They are the truest Radicals, not by accident but on principle. They are the only English Radicals who entertain a sympathy for the 'party of action' abroad. They are democratic from their admiration for a theocratic ideal. They are the only representatives of Rousseau's progeny we can show on English soil. They are great at declamation rather than argument, and impulsive rather than zealous. They have no clear and definite object to attain and only profess a vague desire to extend here and everywhere the power of the people. But their sympathies are chiefly foreign, for they like to gaze at the triumph of Republicanism abroad better than to risk the shock to their sensibilities by braving its rude touch at home. (January 1863)

Cecil believed the arrival of democracy could be successfully resisted. 'One firm will, one fixed political belief, one hearty preference of conviction before place, among the leaders of the parties' would soon have 'broken the fatal charm which is now compelling Parliament to march on to its own destruction'. Palmerston's personal ascendancy quenched the reform agitation, but this did not entirely please Cecil. He believed that Palmerston had blurred the issue. Under Palmerston's rule there was a lowering of political morality and disillusionment among public-spirited men. In Cecil's view, Palmerston presided over a ministry that was 'a cleverly tesselated mosaic of contradictory opinions' (January 1863).

He spoke of the government's 'mute impassiveness', but Cecil appreciated that the balanced constitution could work with success only if those who ruled the system retained the confidence of those who elected them. It ran effectively as long as there was 'trust in the good sense of those who exercise its powers'. 'A little blundering, a little undue self-assertion in this part or that, might at any moment bring the machine to a deadlock,' Cecil warned. 'Sovereign ministers, the House of Lords, the House of Commons, are all endowed with powers which might easily be made to clash, and if any serious collision occurred, the whole of our elaborate mechanism of government would be thrown out of gear' (July 1864).

Cecil was convinced that the optimism in progress in the mid nineteenth century was superficial. The national mood was growing more soberly realistic. He wrote in 1862:

A few years ago a delusive optimism was creeping over the minds of men. There was a tendency to push the belief in the moral victories of civilization to an excess which now seems incredible. It was esteemed heresy to distrust anybody, or to act as if any evil still remained in human nature. At home we were exhorted to show our confidence in our countrymen, by confiding the guidance of our policy to the ignorant and expenditure of our wealth to the needy. Abroad we were invited to believe that commerce had triumphed where Christianity had failed, and that exports and imports had banished war from the earth. And generally we were encouraged to congratulate ourselves that we were permanently lifted from the mire of passion and prejudice in which our forefathers had wallowed. The last fifteen years has been one long disenchantment; and the American Civil War is the culmination of the process.

B

In June 1865, Cecil's elder brother, Lord Cranborne, died and Cecil became heir to the family title. Now Cranborne, he was returned once more without a contest at Stamford in the summer general election. Elsewhere in the country, the Conservatives performed badly and they returned to Westminster with a diminished contingent. Palmerston was triumphant, but despite the appearance of smooth continuity, Cranborne sensed that 'the indefinite and shapeless' party differences of the Palmerstonian period were coming to an end. He predicted that the Whigs would compromise with the Radicals over the reform issue, just as they had done in 1852 and 1859.

Palmerston's sudden death in October 1865 transformed the political scene. Lord John Russell became Prime Minister of the new Liberal ministry, with Gladstone as leader in the Commons. Cranborne looked suspiciously at the arrival of Goschen and Forster in the Cabinet. He saw this as a move to the Left. Cranborne feared that the long-awaited assault on Church and state was about to begin. Time was running out for that party realignment which would keep reform at bay. 'A constitutional party based upon a love of freedom and a resistance to democracy as its most dangerous enemy is likely to remain the dream of sanguine bystanders rather than become an achievement within the grasp of practical politicians,' lamented Cranborne.

He indicated in his 1865 election manifesto that he was no diehard defender of the *status quo*. 'We are not in any way bound to adhere to the provisions of the Reform Act of 1832, and if any alterations in it can be made which will extend the suffrage more widely without giving undue power to any single class I shall welcome them gladly,' he wrote. 'But I should be sorry to run any risk of destroying the balance of power by which the freedom of the various classes of the community is at present maintained.' What Cranborne was willing to accept was giving the working classes a share in political power 'proportioned to the share which their labour gives them in the country's wealth'.

However, when Gladstone presented the government's Franchise Bill to the Commons on 12 March 1866, Cranborne was entirely hostile to its contents. The measure looked modest enough. It reduced the country franchise to £14 and borough franchise to £7. Compounders (those occupiers who did not pay their rates direct but through landlords) were to have the vote. There was to be a £10 lodger qualification in the boroughs and a £50 savings-bank deposit vote in the counties. Altogether, it was estimated that the bill would extend the franchise to a further 400,000 men. Cranborne lost no time in attacking the proposal. He suggested that it had been introduced at the behest of Bright and the Radicals and reflected 'a persistent, undying hatred of the rural interest'. He estimated that the bill would leave the counties under-represented at Westminster by between sixty and seventy seats and that 133 constituencies would have working-class majorities on their registers, which was nearly 40 per cent of the existing boroughs in England and Wales. Cecil also warned that a quarter of the rural constituencies would be swamped by urban interests unless there was a drastic redistribution of seats. 'The whole centre of gravity' of the electoral system would inevitably fall onto those voters who paid between £10 and £20 a year in rent.

Like Robert Lowe, Cranborne made attacks on the Liberal measure which were eloquent and forceful. He argued that it was wealth not numbers that failed to have an adequate voice in Parliament. Cranborne claimed that 'people should vote on the expenditure of taxes somewhat in proportion to the amount they contribute'. The virtue of the 1832 system was that it 'enabled trust to be placed on indirect influence on both sides, to trust to the influence of property from above and numbers of tradesmen from below'. Cranborne urged the Commons to stand firm: 'Economize your strength, keep the constitution in that condition that the decision of the more educated and calmer classes can for the time, at any rate, make head against the violent impulses of the populace, and you will possibly be able to ride over even such a tempest as that. But if you yield now, far from conquering every such danger, the only result will be that you will be weaker to confront it and the hurricane will be more terrible than if you had not yielded.'

Gladstone's attempts to push through the Bill foundered in face of combined opposition from the Conservatives and a group of Liberal rebels led by Lowe who became known as the Adullamites. On 18 June the government went down to defeat by eleven votes. Russell handed in his resignation and Lord Derby agreed to the Queen's request by forming a minority government. Cranborne was offered and agreed to take the post of Secretary of State for India with a seat in the Cabinet. The Conservative leaders made a half-hearted attempt to coax the anti-reform Adullamites into a coalition. Much to Cranborne's regret this did not succeed, but he was convinced that the Conservatives were now in a firm position to resist any further parliamentary pressure for reform. He concluded that the failure of Gladstone's bill was proof that 'the present depositories of power' in

Parliament were not going to put the working man's 'heel upon their necks'.

However, during the next few months the Conservative Cabinet began to move, at first cautiously and later with rapidity towards taking up the parliamentary reform issue as popular agitation mounted outside Westminster. In the beginning it was Lord Derby rather than Disraeli who was most keen to settle the matter. He proposed the creation of a royal commission to investigate the whole subject of reform as well as the presentation of a number of reform resolutions before Parliament in its next session. The entire cabinet, when it met on 8 November, agreed to the latter proposal. The reform resolutions were to make it clear that any future bill would ensure that the occupation franchise would be based on rating qualifications. There were to be countervailing advantages for the more prosperous voters through the creation of 'fancy franchises'. In principle it was agreed that no single class should be allowed to dominate the electoral system. The promised commission was to look at borough boundaries and obtain the necessary information on how many new voters the measure would create. This was to pave the way for 'well-considered legislation'. Cranborne was content to support this position. While the Conservatives did not turn a deaf ear to the reform compaign, they were not going to be rushed into hasty action. However, in February 1867, a week before Parliament was due to meet, Cranborne became alarmed after a conversation with Disraeli. The leader now wanted to drop the idea of an inquiry and write into the resolutions that the new franchise would involve household suffrage, pure and simple. Despite his doubts, Cranborne did not voice opposition to this when the Cabinet agreed to the changes at their meeting on 6 February. It was decided to push ahead with resolutions for rated household suffrage in the boroughs which was to be safeguarded by plural voting. This was to ensure that the voter gained more votes as his living standards improved. General Peel threatened to resign from the Cabinet if there was any specific mention of household suffrage. So it was agreed that the actual size of the franchise extension and the character of plural voting would not be divulged when the resolutions were presented to Parliament on 11 February.

But Disraeli soon realized that Parliament was not going to be satisfied with the government's reform formula. Without any prior Cabinet approval, he told the Commons that the original plan, of procedure by resolutions, was to be scrapped. Disraeli promised M.P.s that he would bring forward a fully fledged Reform Bill within a fortnight. But it was not until a week later that the Cabinet met to discuss the changed situation. A further three days lapsed before any reform scheme was put before them. By this stage Cranborne was convinced that Disraeli and Derby were bustling their colleagues into drastic action. At the 16 February Cabinet meeting it was agreed that a £5 rating franchise should form the basis of the bill, together with counterweights such as the inclusion on the register of men voting on the amount of taxation they paid, the size of their savings-bank deposits and their educational attainments. After three days Disraeli dropped the £5 rating plan, which he had agreed to with Cranborne, and reverted to the idea of household suffrage as the main basis for the bill. Disraeli hastened to reassure doubting colleagues that this change would not make the counterweights any the less effective in blunting the impact of the new electorate. He produced some calculations to prove the point at the 23 February Cabinet meeting and at the same time, much to Cranborne's anger, unfolded the government's redistribution scheme.

Over the weekend at Hatfield, Cranborne immersed himself in the electoral data. He reached the conclusion that three fifths of the smaller boroughs would come under a democratic sway through Disraeli's bill. At once he demanded another Cabinet meeting. Half an hour before Disraeli was to unveil the bill to the parliamentary party, the Cabinet backtracked under threats of resignation from Cranborne, Peel and Carnarvon. Derby hastily drew up a compromise £6 rating scheme, although neither he nor Disraeli liked the proposal. But the compromise bill met with the approval of only a few Conservatives. On 1 March Derby told Cranborne that the government intended to revert once more to the household suffrage plan. At this point Cranborne led his two dissenting colleagues, Peel and Carnarvon, out of the Cabinet.

Despite Derby's fears, the resignations did not bring about any division in the Conservative party. There was no back-bench revolt. It was glaringly clear that Cranborne, the most formidable of the resigners, was quite unable, as well as unwilling, to raise the flag of revolt. He possessed neither the skill nor inclination for political intrigue. Cranborne made no really sustained attempt to organize resistance to the bill, even when it began to undergo drastic surgery during the committee stage. Throughout the parliamentary battles of the spring and summer of 1867, he passed back and forth between Westminster and his Arlington Street home without any appearance in the clubs and smoking rooms of Pall Mall. Undoubtedly Cranborne's inaction helped ensure Disraeli's personal triumph.

Cranborne confined his opposition to speech-making in the Commons. On 18 March he warned that 'political morality and the respect in which public men are held by the people of this country is of more importance than any provisions even of a Reform Bill'. The commitment to household suffrage was in his view 'political suicide' for the Conservatives. 'I cannot help but fear that we shall reach the same end as we might if a Radical party were in power, only we shall reach it by a process which will irritate and aggravate the results when they are attained,' Cranborne argued. He put his trust in 'the moderate party – the large majority' in the Commons. Cranborne was confident that they would 'exercise sufficient control to procure a measure which shall to a considerable extent satisfy the yearnings of the skilled artisans who are conscious of political opinions and desire to see them represented in this House without submerging under a flood of numbers the capital, wealth and intelligence'.

Cranborne's resistance was by no means negative. He told the Commons that it behoved M.P.s 'to be practical men dealing with practical questions' and it was 'useless to argue on behalf of a position which both sides of the House have agreed to abandon'. Cranborne swallowed the principle that all payment of rates should be a qualification for the franchise whether they were paid personally or not, and that all householders with under £5 rental should be excluded from the rates and so have no vote. This was the compromise on which Cranborne cooperated with Gladstone and the Liberals. But no more than four other Conservatives joined him in the opposition lobby, and enough Liberal malcontents ensured that Gladstone's wrecking amendment failed by twenty-one votes.

During the Reform Bill's committee stage, Cranborne made numerous interventions. He warned that the political parties would in future expend most of their energies in attempting to strike each other's supporters off the electoral register through the registration courts. Cranborne warned: 'We are in danger of drifting into a system of nomination caucuses such as were seen in operation in America and such as would arise wherever there were large multitudes in each constituency. Wherever the multitude was so large that it swamped all local influence, that it destroyed every special local interest, what happened was the introduction of local party organization conducted by party managers, men who gave their lives to the task, not usually men of the purest motives or highest character.'

Cranborne backed Laing's amendment to assign a third M.P. to boroughs of over 150,000 population, but it was lost by eight votes. This was an attempt to preserve some form of minority representation. Cranborne considered it 'a serious danger to set against each other the squires in the counties and those who lead the large mobs in the towns, without any class between them to break the shock'. He also spoke up for the introduction of voting-papers.

Yet the cautious bill brought in by Disraeli in March was completely transformed by the time it came to its third reading in the Commons in July. All the precautions, guarantees and securities were swept away. The distinction between compounders and non-compounders was abolished. The dual vote and the taxing franchise were dropped.

Cranborne denied that it amounted to a Conservative triumph in his speech on the bill's third reading on 15 July. All the change was due not to 'government design' but to 'sheer panic'. He complained that Tories were 'men who are bold when no danger is present, but who at the first threat of battle throw their standard in the mud and seek safety in flight'. The bill was indeed 'a leap into the dark'. Except for the behaviour of freemen voters in a few boroughs and the trade union movement, the government possessed no certain knowledge of the working classes. Cranborne conceded that in quiet times the new voters would not resist the continuing return of middle-class M.P.s to Westminster. But in a crisis 'the upper and middle classes will no longer vote for the class to which they belong and that those who are elected will care more for their seats than their class'. On foreign and general policy matters Cranborne saw no reason why the new voters should differ from the old and not come to the same conclusions as 'all other sober and reasonable Englishmen'. When it came to class questions, then the 'securities' of rank, wealth and influence were 'mere feathers in the balance against the solid interest and the real genuine passions of mankind'. Cranborne warned that wherever a single class exercised supreme power they did so in their own interest and not in that of society as a whole.

His main strictures were reserved for his old party. 'Our theory of government is that on each side of the House, there should be men supporting definite opinions and that what they have supported in opposition they should adhere to in office; and that everyone should know from the fact of their being in office that those particular opinions will be supported.' Cranborne warned that if the reverse was to happen the Commons would become 'a mere scrambling-place for office', where statesmen were 'nothing but political adventurers' with 'professions of opinion' looked upon as nothing but 'so many political manoeuvres for the purpose of attaining office'. It was a fatal blow to the Conservatives and would have a serious impact on that 'mutual trust' which was so necessary in ensuring the success of party government. The Commons had 'applauded a policy of legerdemain, a political betrayal which had no parallel in our parliamentary annals'.

Cranborne accepted that the reform could not be reversed. As he wrote:

> It is the duty of every Englishman, and of every English party, to accept a political defeat cordially and to lend their best endeavours to secure the success, or to neutralize the evil, of the principles to which they had been forced to succumb. (October 1867)

This did not mean that he could forgive his party for their behaviour. Cranborne believed that Tory leaders displayed 'a strange morality'. Their activities soiled the ideals of Conservatism. As Cranborne argued:

> The tactics of parliamentary parties are often hardly to be distinguished from faction: the agencies by which they operate upon the wavering or the wayward are far from exalted: the temptation to purchase allies by concessions of principle is enormous. The one ennobling element, the palliation, if not the atonement, for all shortcomings, is that all the members of a party are enlisted in common to serve one great unselfish cause, and that it is in that service that their zeal, even when least scrupulous, is working. Take this great end away, and parties become nothing but joint-stock companies for the attainment and preservation of place.

Isolated and embittered, Cranborne did not abandon political life, but he was in no mood to forgive the Conservative leaders. Disraeli tried to get Cranborne to rejoin the Cabinet when he became Prime Minister in January 1868, but he received a dusty answer. The humiliation of 1867 was not to be so easily forgotten. It was to take another eleven years for Cranborne and Disraeli to re-establish a friendly relationship. Cranborne's dislike for the Tory leader was intense and unyielding:

> If I had a firm confidence in his principles or his honesty, or even if he were identified by birth or property with the Conservative classes in the country – I might in the absence of any definite professions work to maintain him in power. But he is an adventurer and as I have good cause to know he is without principles or honesty.

Cranborne's judgement made it clear why he could not reconcile himself to a return to the front bench. As he argued, Disraeli

> can forward Radical changes in a way that no other Minister could do – because he alone can silence and paralyze the forces of Conservatism.

And in an age of singularly reckless statesmen he is I think beyond question the one who is least restrained by fear or scruple.

In the spring of 1868 Cranborne relapsed into a characteristic gloom about the political future. 'My opinions are not such as would enable me to work heartily with the moderate Liberals – and it is only under their lead that a Conservative party in the future could be formed,' he wrote to Carnarvon. 'Pure "square" Conservatism is played out.' Cranborne feared that his political ideas belonged to the past.

The 1868 parliamentary session reinforced Cranborne's despair at the condition of his party. Gladstone was anxious to pass resolutions through the Commons proposing the disestablishment and disendowment of the Protestant Church of Ireland. When the Liberal leader called for the creation of a committee to look into the question, the Conservative front bench prevaricated. Lord Stanley moved a tepid amendment that suggested such an inquiry into the Irish Church issue might be worth having if it could provide 'considerable modifications in the temporalities' of the Church. The Conservative amendment also urged that no legislative proposal on the matter should be brought forward until the next Parliament. Such equivocation and faintheartedness aroused Cranborne's fears that Disraeli was planning yet another betrayal, intent on identifying the reform of the Irish Church with the Conservative party. He argued bitterly in the Commons that once again the Conservatives were not behaving as 'a united party contending for a great principle'. Cranborne spoke of 'the ambiguous utterances of a more than Delphic oracle'. After the experience of 1867, Cranborne was sceptical whether the party could restrain 'their erratic leader'. He suggested Disraeli had 'language of his own which he can quote in support of whatever policy he may feel disposed to adopt – for it is part of the political skill of the Right Honourable gentleman to be able to refer to phrases of his own in favour of any course he may deem advisable to take'. Cranborne remarked that he would as soon tell which way the weather-cock would point tomorrow as Disraeli's intentions. The Stanley amendment was just the latest example of that abdication of executive government which had occurred over the previous two years. It was 'too clever by half'. 'If you wish to support the Church, you must come forward and fight in the light; and not shelter yourselves behind ambiguous phrases and dilatory pleas,' Cranborne added. The object was

merely to gain time – merely to retain the cards in the hands of the executive that they may shuffle them as they like, merely to utilize great

questions of public policy and matters which excite the feelings of the
people out-of-doors to the utmost for the purposes of party and the
maintenance of the government in place.

There was one question in the 1868 session on which Cranborne
was willing to accept defeat. A bill was passed abolishing Church
rates. He questioned:

What shall we gain if we adhere to the principle of no surrender upon
the subject? That is the question, which you must answer by looking at
it in the light of the circumstances of the time. You must not only look
at the disposition of the nation out-of-doors, but at the course of events
in this House, the principles upon which parties guide their movements,
and the laws by which public men guide their movements, and the laws
by which public men regulate their conduct.

On 21 April 1868 Cranborne's father died. He automatically in-
herited the estates and became the third Marquis of Salisbury. The
prospect of going to the House of Lords did not fill Salisbury with
much enthusiasm. He once described the Upper Chamber as 'that
purgatory of orators'. 'A Quaker jollification, a French horse-race or
a Presbyterian psalm' were, in his view, more lively and exciting
than a Lords debate. When Disraeli was contemplating his own
elevation to the Lords in 1876, Salisbury warned him that he would
enter 'the dullest assembly in the world'. Yet once he left the
Commons Salisbury never bothered to visit it again to sit in the
gallery.

His change of political venue had decided advantages. For one
thing, he was no longer in close personal proximity to Disraeli. Moreover, it was a welcome escape from the pressures of the new democracy. Lady Gwendolen noted that her father departed the Commons
as its old powers were 'doomed to extinction'. The age of mass
politics was to reduce the Lower House's independence, its 'uncontrolled individual freedom, agreed conventions in conduct, elastic
order, easy social intercourse'.

To contemporaries in April 1868, Salisbury was a disgruntled,
unyielding ex-Cabinet minister with an uncertain political future.
His idealistic stand against parliamentary reform had won him his
party's respect, if not their support. Salisbury had acquired a formidable reputation as a man of high principle, faithful to Conservative
ideals and deeply concerned with the upholding of personal honour
and integrity in politics. Yet Salisbury felt he no longer had a part
to play in active political life. Lowe, however, was more perceptive
in his summary of his former ally's position. As he wrote to Lady
Salisbury:

I am inclined to think that Disraeli will have no reason to rejoice that Lord Cranborne is in the House of Lords. There was really very little for him to do in the Commons. He was isolated and for some time at any rate likely to continue so. His powers of debate only went to swell a preponderance already quite decided, while in the Lords he may, and I should think will, obtain the lead and be a most important and useful agent in rescuing them from the control of a fellow like Disraeli and bringing them more into accordance with the actual current of affairs.

The more I look at it, the less I like it;
but every alternative seems worse.
Salisbury to Carnarvon, 15 February 1874

3

THE NECESSITY
FOR
COMPROMISE
May 1868–March 1878

Salisbury took his seat in the Lords on 7 May
1868. He did not withdraw in disgust from active politics, nor did
he make any attempt to associate with the Liberals. His independent
contributions to debate were firmly on the Conservative side, although Salisbury made it perfectly clear that he neither forgot nor
forgave the way his colleagues had behaved during the Reform
Bill crisis. In his first major speech in the Upper House Salisbury
attacked Gladstone's plans to disestablish and disendow the Protestant Church in Ireland as 'an absolute and complete spoliation',
yet another 'thin end of the wedge', when the state destroyed 'the
property of a great corporation' as 'a party exigency'. Salisbury

doubted whether the Conservatives would be willing to withstand
this latest challenge to the established order. 'Personally I should
have no objection to fight *à l'outrance*, but I confess from the experience I have had, my inclination is to say, "How can you expect to
hold the fortress, it's no use holding out, for the troops won't stand
to their guns?"' he explained. Salisbury wanted the Lords to defy
the Commons on the issue. A meek surrender to the dictates of the
Lower House would, in his view, turn the Lords into the executive's
'echo and supple tool'. Salisbury urged his colleagues to agree only
to pass measures that they found unacceptable when 'the firm,
deliberate, sustained convictions' of the nation were first tested on
the matter at a general election.

Parliament was prorogued on 31 July 1868 and the country
went to the polls in November. Gladstone made the Irish Church
question the dominant theme of his campaign. He and the Liberals
were swept back into office with a majority of 110 in the new
Commons. The Conservatives suffered losses and won only 274
seats. Of 114 constituencies in Britain with populations of over
50,000 the party managed to win only twenty-five. The Conservatives did well in Lancashire – thanks to a campaign based
on anti-Catholic prejudice and the promise of social reform. There
was also some progress in suburban London. But for the most part,
the Conservatives were pushed back into their rural strongholds.
It did not look as though Disraeli's conversion to parliamentary
reform had done anything to make his party more popular with the
new electorate. Salisbury's opposition to the 1867 Act appeared to
have been vindicated.

During the early 1870s the Conservatives relapsed into lethargy
and mere obstruction, with no hope of a revival in their political
fortunes. Disraeli's grip on the leadership began to weaken. When
Malmesbury retired as Conservative leader in the Lords, some peers
actually tried to persuade Salisbury to fill the vacancy. He declined
the offer, but it illustrates the readiness of some Conservatives to
deliver a blow – albeit indirect – at Disraeli's shaken authority.
Earl Cairns held the leadership in the Lords for a year. He was
succeeded in 1870 by that amiable nonentity the Duke of Richmond.
Salisbury kept away from the sporadic intrigue among his discontented colleagues. He did not attend the famous Burghley House
meeting in February 1872 when only Northcote and Manners,
among leading Conservatives, raised any opposition to the suggestion
that Lord Derby should replace Disraeli as the head of the party.
Abstention from such activities did not mean that Salisbury was

ready for conciliation. He continued to decry the condition of the Conservatives in articles in the *Quarterly Review*.

Salisbury was not the spokesman of a reactionary brand of Toryism. On the contrary after 1867, despite his blunt speeches and apparent willingness to oppose the mildest of reforms, Salisbury believed that he was very much in the middle ground of British politics. He liked to see himself as a fusionist. Salisbury was not attracted by the prospect of a quixotic defence of the indefensible. His party ideal for the Conservatives was not a diehard combination imbued with the high-minded ideals and inflexible prejudices of a Lord Eldon or Duke of Wellington. Nor did he believe the Conservatives should become a collection of opportunists, held together by the vague, romantic notions of Disraeli. Salisbury wanted to identify the Conservative party with the political centre. He looked back to the 1790s for his inspiration, when the Portland Whigs joined with the Younger Pitt in a patriotic resistance to the foreign menace of the French Revolution. Salisbury believed the main hope for the future of the Conservatives was in a similar re-alignment of the party in the face of the common threat to the constitution. He thought that Gladstone's reform measures would help to precipitate that process of unification. Salisbury predicted a readjustment of the political balance between what he called the forces of 'movement' and those of 'consolidation' to the ultimate benefit of the Conservatives. He wrote:

Social stability is ensured, not by the cessation of the demand for change, for the needy and restless will never cease to cry for it, but by the fact that change in its progress must at last hurt some class of men who are strong enough to arrest it. The army of so-called reform in every stage of its advance necessarily converts a detachment of its force into opponents. The more rapid the advance the more formidable will the desertion become, till at last a point will be reached when the balance of the forces of conservation and destruction will be redressed and the political equilibrium will be restored. (October 1869)

Salisbury hoped that the Conservatives would not regain political power until that process reached fulfilment. Otherwise, he feared that they would again bend to pressure and rush through a radical programme. The prospect of a spell of Liberal rule did not worry him unduly. He even thought that a moderate Liberal government, backed by the Conservative opposition, was 'the only policy' by which the Conservatives could hope 'to save their country and their cause'. But despite such sentiments, Salisbury was not the man to follow the mild mannerisms of consensus politics. The imminent arrival of class conflict continued to worry him. The bloody Paris Commune of 1871 reinforced his pessimism. To Salisbury, the violence on the streets of the French capital was no mere revolt of city workers against the domination of provincial France, nor an attempt to restore long-lost municipal liberties from the clutches of an over-centralized state. It was nothing less than part of the 'death-struggle' between 'Socialism and existing civilisation', a harbinger of coming social catastrophe. As he explained in anguished sentences in the *Quarterly Review* (October 1871):

Our philosophy of politics, though old world and out of date, continues to survive the state of things in which it has life and meaning. Speakers and writers still fight battles that have been won, still repeat the watch-words that no longer represent a struggle, still urge a policy based on some shibboleths of the past, to which events have affixed a significance undreamt of when it was devised. They still talk of freedom, as though such a thing as bondage was left in the England of reform, as though we had never changed, of progress as though we had never moved. These battle-cries are a valuable property. Whose inheritance are they to become?

In Salisbury's opinion 'political progress' was 'little, if at all, dependent on intellectual discovery'. The accomplishment of 'peace and goodwill' would not come about through 'some clever contrivance which men by much debating and many experiments may hope to hit upon'. 'If they attain it at all it will be by rooting out the selfishness which good fortune nurtures and the recklessness which springs from misery.' Salisbury feared that the British political system flourished on the manufacture of discontent. Now the agitators would look to France for their ideas. He wrote:

There are rewards which can only be obtained by men who excite the public mind and devise means of persuading one set of persons that they are deeply injured by another. The production of cries is encouraged by a heavy bounty. The invention and exasperation of controversies lead those who are successful in such arts to place and honour and power. Therefore politicians will always select the most irritating cries, and will raise the most exasperating controversies that circumstances will permit. That English workmen would of themselves learn to share the fanaticism of the Parisian Socialists is exceedingly improbable, but it would be too much to expect, if their superiors in education promise them an elysium of high wages and little work, as a result of pillaging other classes of the community, that they should be keen-sighted enough to see through the delusion and refuse the tempting bait. *Ce cher peuple*, as Robespierre used to say, is no longer the object of a very enthusiastic worship: it is a saint whose legend is discredited, and whose halo has been chipped off in many a street row.

Salisbury was convinced that the franchise extension made it more, and not less, necessary that 'every party that cherished political honour' should abstain from office unless it possessed 'the full and unambiguous support of the constituencies'. The Conservatives should not trample on their principles yet again in order to win the approval of public opinion. Party integrity must not be damaged by the desire for short-term political gain. 'In a settled despotism and in an extreme democracy, in either of which organic changes are too improbable to become prominent subjects of controversy, parties are mere joint-stock companies for the acquisition of place and pay,' Salisbury argued. The Conservatives should appeal to more than self-interest. Despite his cynicism and low opinion of human nature, Salisbury wanted his own party to stand for 'the higher class of motives, to the nobler spirits'. He was optimistic enough to believe that neither party was yet 'as largely infected with the spirit which provides political principles, as market gardeners provide vegetables, to meet the tastes of the public'. Salisbury continued to warn of the dangers of blurring the differences between the parties. He wrote:

The plea of necessity, the claim of party reality, the fear of making bad worse, or the hope of mitigating the inevitable, are motives of real cogency whose proper limits are hard to define, and though after the event they are seen to afford no defence for a shifty policy, they often appear at the time sufficient, not only to justify, but to demand, the successive minute steps of concession of which that policy was made up. Such pleas may serve to excuse exceptional deviations from the consistency which the law of honour requires between the promises of opposition and the performances of office – but only so long as they are exceptional. If ever they become habitual to any party that leaders can plan them without scruple, and followers can be brought to accept them without shame or resistance, that party must renounce, unless the English character shall greatly change, all substantial share in the councils of the nation. (October 1872)

In Salisbury's view the parties reflected 'two opposite moods of the English mind' and they could expect to succeed each other in power. Salisbury continued:

Neither the love of organic change nor the dislike of it can be described as normal to a nation. In every nation they have succeeded each other at varying intervals during the whole of the period which separates its birth from its decay. Each finds in the circumstances and constitution of individuals a regular support which never deserts it. But the two camps together will not nearly include the nation, for the vast mass of every nation is non-political. From time to time as its own special requirements may urge or discourage change, or more often in pursuance of the lessons which the experience of some foreign country seems to teach, it gives its confidence to one school or the other and the rejected party must live through the winter of its discontent as best it may. It must be satisfied to use such strength as it retains to mitigate the action of its opponents or to strengthen the best element of its opponent's councils.

Salisbury still doubted that the Liberal alliance between the Whigs, the moderates and the Radicals could remain intact for much longer, particularly with the rise of the more militant radicalism of Joseph Chamberlain and the Education League. In the past, the middle classes used to warn that a working-class revolution would break out, if the middle classes did not get their own way. After the reform triumphs of the past forty years, Salisbury now believed the middle classes shared far more in common with the upper than with the lower orders. He argued therefore that their obstinate attachment to moderate Liberalism no longer made political sense. In his opinion, the future of British politics lay with those moderate men of property who once provided the main support for Palmerstonian government. 'It is to their uncertain policy and their unnatural alliances that much of our embarrassment is due, and upon them depends whether political conflict shall be restored to the dignity of a war of principles or shall sink, as in America, to a reckless struggle for personal advancement,' Salisbury argued. Previously, Liberals sought to remedy specific abuses to bring an end to controversy and establish political repose. Now Salisbury insisted their emphasis was on a 'vista of perpetual subversion':

> To uproot institutions, to sow bitter resentments, to give to class or sect the spoliation of a rival by the brute force of a legislative majority may possibly in some cases of extreme emergency be a task from which governments cannot escape, but it is a field of duty to be entered with sorrow, and to be quitted with the utmost speed. In the improvement of the local government, of salutary arrangements, in the alleviation, so far as statutes can procure it, of the sufferings of the poor – matters which can give triumph to no class and no denomination – there is much material for the labour of Parliament, little for the manufacture of cries and the excitement of politicians. It is not for those that wire-pullers work, or party bonds are formed, or close divisions taken. They will never be more than the obligatory tarnish of the programme of the Radicals. (October 1873)

Salisbury acknowledged that party ties were hard to break, that 'personal attachments' could not be 'laid aside like a suit of clothes'. None the less he was convinced that the proper use of the party system was to 'sacrifice small objects in order that by union greater objects' might be achieved. In Salisbury's opinion 'to lend your name and aid to revolutionary projects' which a man hated in order to stay true to the party was 'to elevate means above the end, to degrade reasonable usage into pernicious superstition'. He warned that the triumph of Radicalism would bring suffering to 'the well-to-do triflers with Revolution, the allies whose hesitating patronage they can fain to use, but whom in using they openly despise'.

Salisbury was a forthright and prominent critic of Gladstone's 'heroic measures' between 1868 and 1874. He accepted the nation's verdict over Irish Church disestablishment and so did not oppose the Liberal bill. On the other hand, the government's attempt to placate Irish agitation with the 1870 Land Bill drew his withering scorn. In Salisbury's view Ireland, suffering under the terrorism of the Fenians, needed firm government not land reform. 'You are dealing with a population of a lower civilisation,' he explained to the Lords (29 March 1870). 'While liberty and representative government are a healthy aliment to the English they are a dangerous stimulant to the social condition of the Irish nation.' 'In this country you are content only to guide; in Ireland it is essential that you should govern,' Salisbury argued. 'Until you have learned that – until you have established it – you will not get them to listen to your views and arguments, nor will you gain the full result of these remedial measures, which as far as they are just, I heartily approve of.' Salisbury supported the so-called Bright clauses of the 1870 act which were designed to encourage peasant proprietorship. He was convinced, from the French example, that any widening in the ownership of property would bring political stability and social cohesion. This was later to become a major plank in the Unionist policy for Ireland. At heart, however, Salisbury doubted whether there was any panacea at all for the Irish problem. As he wrote:

The optimist view of politics assures that there must be some remedy for every political ill, and rather than not find it, it will make two hardships to cure one. Is it not just conceivable that there is no remedy that we can apply for the Irish hatred of ourselves? That other loves or hates may possibly elbow it out of the Irish peasant's mind, but nothing we can do by any contrivance will hasten the advent of that period. May it not, on the contrary, be our incessant doctoring and meddling, awakening the passions of this party or of that, raising at every step a fresh crop of resentments by the side of the old growth, that puts off the day when these feelings will decay quietly away and be forgotten? There is no precedent, either in our history or in any other, to teach us that political measures can conjure away hereditary antipathies which are fed by constant agitation. The free institutions which sustain the life of a free and united people sustain also the hatreds of a divided people. If it were in the genius of our government to be stable in its purposes for a single generation – still more if we could acquire with the world a credit for the firmness which we have utterly lost – the hope of separation might in time fade away from the Irish mind, and agitators's promises might at last be disbelieved, even by the Irish peasant. Ireland must be kept, like India, at all hazards, by persuasion if possible, if not by force. (October 1872)

Other Gladstonian legislation also met with Salisbury's implacable hostility. He opposed the abolition of the university tests, a move to open up higher education to 'orthodox Dissenters' excluded by the need to accept the Thirty-nine Articles as a necessary qualification for university entry. Salisbury did not want to keep Dissenters out of universities on principle, but because he believed that they would eventually undermine religious instruction. While he admitted that the old battle between church and chapel had lost much of its 'intense earnestness', Salisbury was sure that the removal of the tests would encourage the 'violent movement to utter unbelief' which he feared was so widespread among educated circles through the influence of Eastern ideas and the progress of the physical sciences. He was convinced that if colleges elected tutors on the basis of their 'intellectual superiority' alone, this would transform them into 'citadels of infidelity'. Salisbury maintained that religion should hold 'a primary and indispensable element in any education' regulated by the state (16 March 1871).

He was opposed to Cardwell's army reforms, which abolished the purchase of commissions, on the grounds that the old recruitment methods were far better 'in power, value and efficiency' than 'those mere paper institutions which may be devised upon the soundest possible principles'. Salisbury also criticized the establishment of school boards. He claimed that it would excite religious antagonism between the Anglicans and Dissenters. He was a resolute opponent of the introduction of the secret ballot in parliamentary elections. In his view, this would encourage 'the dangerous vice' of 'political abstentionism'. Yet he was unable to convince his colleagues of the need to reject the measure. The Conservative front bench preferred to abstain. The House of Lords was still reluctant to confront the measures of a Liberal government. The meekness of the Lords filled Salisbury with gloom. He was anxious to see the assembly exerting its constitutional authority and independence. This is partly why he spoke up for Russell's bill for the creation of life peers. Salisbury believed that the inclusion of men from the world of industry and commerce would provide the House of Lords with an expertise in the 'health and moral conditions of the people'. He was also a supporter of a proposal that bills should not automatically lapse if they failed to reach the statute book during one session. Salisbury disliked the tradition of cramming all the important debates in the Lords to the summer months. He felt that this 'involuntary pressure' made all the parties delay the passage of legislation, so that secondary, worthy but non-controversial measures failed to become law. In his view, this was 'a perfect disgrace and scandal' because it made people 'doubt the adequacy, vigour and rapidity of parliamentary government'.

Salisbury also spoke out on foreign affairs in the early 1870s. He was critical of Bismarck's annexation of Alsace-Lorraine after Prussia's victory over the French Second Empire. Salisbury called it 'an outrage upon the feelings and conscience of modern Europe' to subjugate a population against its will. He predicted that such an action would leave behind 'a bitter and enduring disaffection'. 'The time will come when their [the Germans] ambitious dreams will cross the path of some power strong enough to resent them: and that day will be to France the day of restitution and revenge,' Salisbury wrote (October 1870). In his opinion, the collapse of the Second Empire was due to the 'feebleness of the very principle of government caused by chronic revolution'. This held lessons for England. Salisbury began to worry over the lack of military preparedness, which he saw as a fault of the British system of government. He was convinced that no prime minister could hope to win the solid backing of Parliament in order to embark on a massive armaments programme, unless there was a serious national emergency. Salisbury argued that a government Whip was compelled to garner in the vote 'from the extreme men in politics, the religious brigades, who subordinate political questions entirely to their ecclesiastical views, the disciples of small Utopian schools, the neglected men who are yet open to overtures, the superseded men whose wrath is past appeasing'. Consequently, Salisbury reasoned, governments like Napoleon's had to live a hand-to-mouth existence. 'The Prime Minister is content to let alone what he can and only touch what is forced upon him, as far as possible to break up no established routine, to frighten no vested interests, to spend nothing this year that can be deferred to another,' Salisbury argued. The new post-reform system already displayed the vice of 'drifting'. The Commons was disintegrating into the incoherence of rival splinter groups. Parliament was paralyzing the executive's ability to make decisions. Yet the war between France and Germany demonstrated that armed conflict was no longer unthinkable. Salisbury warned that the bloody carnage of 1870–71 dealt a blow to the assumptions of the believers in universal peace: 'The new

gospel – a compound of commerce and philosophy – is being extensively taught and believed, to the effect that the "peace on earth" which Christianity has been unable to bring about has been secured by the locomotive and the spinning-jenny.'
'We live in an age of blood and iron,' wrote Salisbury.

If we mean to escape misery and dishonour, we must trust to no consciousness of a righteous cause, to no moral influence, to no fancied restraints of civilization. Those bulwarks may be of use when the millennium draws near; they are empty verbiage now. We must trust to our power of self-defence, and to no earthly aid. (October 1871)

Not all Salisbury's time during the Opposition years of the early 1870s was spent in active politics. In 1869, on the death of Lord Derby, he agreed, with some reluctance, to become Chancellor of Oxford University. 'I not only did not seek the post, but sought to decline it: feeling, with you, that the holder of it should be less of a politician and more of a scholar,' he wrote to his academic friend Sir Henry Wentworth Acland. Salisbury felt that he was an unsuitable person to preside over the University. 'An Ethiopian cannot change his spots – nor can I put off my Toryism – my deep distrust of the changes that are succeeding each other so rapidly,' he explained to Acland. 'Numbers of men support them who are not of the spirit that bred them: but that spirit is essentially a Pagan spirit, discarding the supernatural, and worshipping man not God. It is creeping over Europe rapidly and I cannot put off the conviction that it is disturbing every cement that holds society together.'

Salisbury's close acquaintances tended to come from the world of academia and the Anglican Church and not politics. Men like Bishop Wilberforce, Dr Liddon, Froude and Dean Stanley were frequent guests at Hatfield dinner-parties during the 1870s. These were also the years when Salisbury built up his substantial collection of books and pamphlets on the French Revolution. He read a great deal, notably the novels of Jane Austen and Scott's historical romances. Salisbury also enjoyed the poetry of Pope and Byron, but his favourite authors remained Virgil, Euripides, Tacitus and Shakespeare. He used to carry pocket editions of their work around with him, so that he could dip into them during the day when the opportunity came. Salisbury left the upkeep of his widespread estates to his wife's able management. In the early 1870s he had a holiday home built for the family at Puys near Dieppe. It was christened Chalet Cecil.

Salisbury found the time to act as temporary chairman of the Great Eastern Railway for four years after 1867. He nursed the company through its financial troubles and back into solvency.

Salisbury also became chairman of the Quarter Sessions for Hertford-shire. He spent his leisure hours either with his growing family of five sons and two daughters at Hatfield, or pursuing his hobbies of botany, photography and physics. This was also the time when he began his experiments with electricity.

Gladstone dissolved Parliament on 24 January 1874 and went to the country in search of a fresh mandate. He made the abolition of income tax the main issue of his election campaign. But the Liberals fought under disadvantages. Over the past five years the government had upset many of its moderate supporters, who believed that its legislation had been too drastic. On the other hand, the Radicals argued that the government had not gone far enough to meet their demands. In the event, the Conservatives won a convincing victory. With a net gain of sixty seats, they returned to Westminster with their first overall Commons majority since 1841.

Disraeli became undisputed Prime Minister. All but one of his twelve-man Cabinet had served in the 1866–8 ministry. His most important move was to persuade Salisbury to return to his old post at the India Office with a place in the Cabinet. It was not until the very last moment that Salisbury agreed to join the government. He doubted the wisdom of accepting a job from a man whom he was still unable to trust. On 7 February Salisbury returned alone from a family holiday in Italy to make his decision. His stepmother Lady Derby acted as go-between. She urged him to swallow his scruples and doubts and accept Disraeli's offer. Close friends, notably Carnarvon and Heathcote, pressed him to join the government. He spent three days at Hatfield wrestling with his conscience. Salisbury believed that if he decided to accept office again under Disraeli, it would amount practically to 'a submission'. 'I never knew what perplexity was before,' he wrote to his wife. 'On the one hand, humiliation and every kind of discomfort; on the other, isolation, with the suspicion of cowardice and the consciousness of having shrunk from an important post at a moment of danger.' Salisbury's 'intense dislike' of Disraeli made him hesitate. On 17 February the two men met to discover whether they could reach agreement. Disraeli gave Salisbury a reassurance that he had no intention of moving against ritualism in the Church of England. It was after this that Salisbury agreed to join the Cabinet. His decision rescued him from the political wilderness, but it was still to be some time before Salisbury was prepared to revise his hostile judgement of the Prime Minister. Within a few months of taking office the two men found themselves in bitter dispute. Salisbury disliked the government's proposed Endowed Schools Bill, but he felt that it was too small an issue on which to resign. Nor could he disguise his hostility to the Public Worship Regulation Bill. It was Salisbury's acid comment on that measure which provoked the Prime Minister's celebrated retort that Salisbury was 'a great master of gibes and flouts and jeers'. Disraeli hastened to reassure his colleague that the remark was only meant to be 'a playful reply' to Salisbury's criticism. Although the incident was soon closed, Disraeli's tactics still rankled. Salisbury confessed in a letter to Carnarvon that the Prime Minister could not throw off his old habits and that he showed far more consideration 'to one trimmer who wants humouring than to the ninety and nine staunch men who needed no persuasion'. 'He is in no sense a sensitive man,' Salisbury wrote of Disraeli.

But he is far from imperturbable. On the contrary, when he is beaten, or in danger of being beaten, his temper gives way entirely. D. evidently thinks he has made a great blunder, and dreads lest it should create trouble. But to the outside world I think he has generally given the impression that he wishes to get rid of me. (14 August 1874)

Salisbury served in only two departments of state during his life. His work at the India Office has gone virtually without recognition. Yet during his second period as Secretary of State, from February 1874 to February 1878, Salisbury was, in the words of his Under-Secretary, Lord George Hamilton, 'at the zenith of his vigour'. 'Only those who served under him and whom he liked can have any idea of his charm as a chief, or the delight of working in subordination to him,' Hamilton wrote. 'His extraordinary quickness of appreciation spoiled one, for you rarely had to finish a sentence before he intervened with a remark anticipating your conclusion.' Lady Gwendolen passed rapidly over her father's record at the India Office in her biography. In her opinion, it was of no real, lasting value because accepted constitutional tradition left 'the initiative' in Indian affairs almost wholly to the administration in Calcutta. She believed that Salisbury's interventions were 'mainly consequential and advisory'.

This is less than a fair description of Salisbury's years at the India Office. It is true that, during his few months as Secretary of State in the 1866–7 ministry, he was willing to allow the experienced Indian Viceroy, Sir John Lawrence, a free hand in the administration of the subcontinent with the minimum of interference from London. Salisbury accepted the imperial mission without question. He believed that the British task was to 'reduce to order, to civilize and develop native governments'. In the aftermath of the 1857 Indian mutiny there was general agreement on the need for internal consolidation and economic development. Salisbury was publicly optimistic about the condition of India. 'I believe that we were never safer in India than at the present time. There never was a time – whether we have to rely on our swords, or whether, which I hope is now the case, we may rely on the sense which the natives entertain of the justice they may expect from us, or the security which our government confers upon them – when we have a better right to calculate on the stability of our power in that country,' he told the Commons (22 February 1867). 'India is now in a quiet, pacific condition and it is our happiness not to have to produce a policy. To keep the peace and to push on the public works – that is in brief the policy we have to follow,' Salisbury proclaimed (19 July 1866). He sympathized with Lawrence's reluctance to try and extend British influence into the Indian buffer state of Afghanistan. Like the Viceroy, he refused to believe that Russian advances in Central Asia justified a more active policy on the North-West Frontier. 'Indian resources are wanted for other work besides the extension of territory just now,' he agreed with Lawrence. 'I cannot bring myself to look on the alarms of Russia's advance even seriously. When there is so much room for her to the eastward of Bokhara it would be sheer wantonness on her part to provoke a powerful antagonist by turning to the south.' However, unlike the Viceroy, Salisbury was anxious to ensure that Upper Burma was eventually brought firmly within the British sphere of influence. This was not to happen until the close of his first ministry in the winter of 1885.

Despite an outward appearance of contentment, Salisbury soon grew restive at his lack of powers. A Secretary of State for India faced a thankless task. Although he was ultimately responsible to Parliament for the administration of the Indian Empire, he was unable to exercise sufficient authority. This was partly due to the 'conclusive and absolute veto' which the nominated worthies on the Indian Council in London were always ready to wield against the minister. The distance of over a thousand miles that separated the Viceroy's administration from the civil servants in Whitehall also posed a moral problem. By the spring of 1867, just before his resignation, Salisbury was consulting the Attorney General, Sir Hugh Cairns, in the hope that some hidden legal rights might be discovered which could give him some powers which might enable him to become a more active minister.

Out of office, Salisbury became a powerful critic of what he called 'the evil of over-regulation' in the Indian civil service. 'Its tendency to routine; its listless, heavy headlessness, sometimes the result of its elaborate organization; a fear of responsibility; an extreme centralization – produce an amount of inefficiency which, when reinforced by natural causes and circumstances create a terrible amount of misery,' Salisbury told the Lords (24 May 1867). He refused to believe that British rule in India could in any sense prove to be popular. 'One thing at least is clear – that no one believes in our good intentions. We are often told to secure ourselves by their affections, not by force. Our great-grandchildren may be privileged to do it, but not we,' he wrote to Northbrook, the Viceroy (28 May 1874). Such an opinion was not meant to suggest that the British government should not work to safeguard the prosperity of their Indian subjects. Salisbury believed that the people's welfare was 'the one justification' for Britain's presence on the Indian subcontinent. On the other hand, he saw no sense in trying to rule India in a European way. 'No greater mistake has been made of recent years, in regard to Indian matters, than that of thinking we could produce a copy of the English constitution in India,' he argued (11 March 1869). He suggested that there was a need 'to govern Asiatically'. Government methods were becoming 'refined but cumbrous and tardy'. Salisbury called for 'a more despotic ideal of government' which would provide 'a more rapid, though perhaps ruder, justice' for the native population.

On his return to the India Office in February 1874, Salisbury was determined to take a more positive role in policy-making. He went back to his old department with a reputation for being 'somewhat wild and impulsive'. And it was not long before he found himself wrangling with the Viceroy, Lord Northbrook, and his policy of 'steady government'. Salisbury wanted to break through the stuffy, complex bureaucratic procedures and establish a close working personal relationship with the Viceroy. He could see no reason why the Viceroy's Executive Council should enjoy 'too independent an existence'. Salisbury explained to Northbrook:

I am afraid of your council, if ever it should happen to have a weak Governor General at its head, finding out its power of moving the machine at home, by manipulating the organs of opinion in India; and it will do so all the sooner if it is encouraged to have a high idea of its own corporate individuality and independence. The danger of such a practice would be very great, for it would in the end mean appealing to native opinion against the English government and then we should have before long an Independence cry fostered by white leaders. (30 July 1874)

The Whig Viceroy disagreed with Salisbury's arguments. North-brook believed that he should work through the Executive Council. Otherwise, he reasoned, there would be inevitable friction between Calcutta and London and a resulting deterioration in the efficiency of the government's performance. None the less, Salisbury began to insist on a much tighter control over the administration. He demanded to see any proposed draft of a bill before it was placed before the Indian Legislative Council, with a full explanation of why the measure was needed. Only proposals of 'slight importance' or those 'urgently requiring speedy enactment' were to be exempt from the ruling. Although Northbrook was able to dilute that particular instruction in practice, it showed that Salisbury was determined to keep a much closer eye on the running of India than his predecessors had done. The Secretary of State also annoyed Northbrook with his decision to appoint a public works member to the Executive Council, without giving the Viceroy prior notice.

Differences between Salisbury and Northbrook grew wider over the months. The Secretary of State insisted that the Viceroy should take action against the 'unmixed nuisance' of the Indian newspapers with their 'habitual sedition', but Northbrook was unwilling to do so. A more serious difference of opinion arose over the Indian cotton import duties. The powerful Lancashire cotton lobby were pressing the home government to abolish the import duties on fine-quality cloth and yarn entering India. Salisbury agreed with this demand and he instructed Northbrook to phase out the duties, when the state of Indian finances was able to allow this. The Viceroy and his Council failed to appreciate the pressures for abolition. They wanted to keep the duties in order to benefit from the substantial customs that they brought into the Indian exchequer. Northbrook decided to reduce the import duties on various items in his Budget, but keep a small *ad valorem* duty on Lancashire cotton goods. Salisbury refused to accept this and he countermanded the Viceroy's proposal. His Under-Secretary, Sir Louis Mallet, was even sent out to India to remonstrate with Northbrook about the urgency of abolishing the duties altogether. Salisbury was insistent that the tariff was 'an imperial question' and not just one for India to settle alone. In the event, the depreciation of silver required a postpone-ment of the repeal of the duties. It was not until 1879 that all the import duties, except for those on fine cottons, were eventually abolished.

Salisbury was also insistent that he should have a direct hand in recruitment to the Indian civil service. He questioned the wisdom of employing native Indians in positions of 'real trust'. What he wanted was some control over permanent appointments, even if it was only a veto power. In this way he hoped to stop 'the danger of a Viceroy being bitten with the mania which occasionally attacks our Residents, and putting natives into all the chief posts of confidence' (19 February 1875).

The most serious division of opinion between Salisbury and North-brook broke out over Indian frontier policy. The Secretary of State continued to believe that a Russian attack on India was 'a chimera'. None the less he had reached the conclusion that British agents should be stationed in the buffer state of Afghanistan so that they could keep a close eye on Russian activity in Central Asia. In con-trast, Northbrook was content merely to follow the non-interven-tionist policies of his predecessors, Lawrence and Mayo. In January 1875 Salisbury insisted that the Amir of Afghanistan should be com-pelled to agree to the establishment of British agents in his state at Herat and Kabul. He warned Northbrook that the British position had become 'both dangerous and humiliating' because of the Amir's hostile attitude. Salisbury urged the Viceroy not to be 'seduced into solving a difficult question by the attractive alternative of doing nothing'. 'We cannot leave the keys of the gate [into India] in the hands of a warder of more than doubtful integrity, who insists, as an indispensable condition of his service, that his movements shall not be observed.' The lack of any British presence in Afghanistan had 'the effect of placing upon our frontier a thick covert, behind which any amount of hostile intrigue and conspiracy' might be 'masked'. Salisbury was not suggesting any military expedition against the Amir. 'We cannot conquer her – we cannot leave it alone. We can only give it our utmost vigilance,' he explained to North-brook (5 March 1875). There was a need to trust to self-restraint in making sure there was no forward movement. 'We cannot shape our national policy by an ascetic rule, and shun temptation on the side where we believe our moral nature is weak,' he wrote to Northbrook (14 January 1876). 'We must do what is politic, trusting that our successors will have the sense not to draw from it a motive for doing what is impolitic. I have little fear on that head. We have never shown any great aptitude at unprofitable conquests. I have no fear of our being tempted to move troops into Afghanistan unless further onward steps from Russia should one day drive people here into a panic. But the more inactive we are now the more we increase the danger of that panic.'

Both Salisbury and Disraeli were relieved when Northbrook, using the excuse of a private problem, cut short his Viceroyalty and resigned in September 1875. Salisbury appreciated Northbrook's efforts during the 1873–4 famine. He urged a reluctant Disraeli to give the Viceroy an earldom, pointing out that Northbrook had at least 'not added territory to the Empire – for the policy of the day is adverse to war or annexation'. Lytton, the British consul in Lisbon, was Salisbury's choice as next Indian Viceroy. He wanted to see an energetic but cooperative figure at the head of the Indian administration. Salisbury was troubled by the difficulties of his position as Secretary of State. As he explained to the retiring Northbrook: 'It is of no use to ignore the enormous difficulty under which we work in having to rule such an Empire as in India in subordination to such a parliamentary institution as that of England. I am intensely impressed by the untrustworthy character of the House of Commons as to all matters which it has not been compelled to study carefully. It is not that they wish consciously to take the Government of India into their own hands but on Indian subjects they have so little genuine knowledge or conviction that they vote like women, on the impression or whim of the moment. A clever appeal to sentiment – the invocation of some English commonplace or claptrap – will swing round into the wrong lobby a sufficient number to make a decrease by which the whole Government of India might be thrown into confusion. You must bear in mind that it is only in consequence of this claim of the House of Commons to govern India that the Secretary of State exists at all' (10 December 1875).

Salisbury underlined the problem to Lytton on his arrival in India: 'They [the councillors] are too apt to imagine that the India Office is their only difficulty and that if it were out of the way, they would be uncontrolled. In truth when we differ with them, we are generally only acting on a danger signal of an impending collision with Parliament. If ever it should happen that this danger signal ceased to work, and that their first warning of danger was a division in which a government was beaten they would have to reverse the policy with a speed not entirely safe and far from desired. The power of the House of Commons over India is so uncontrolled and so free from any restraint except a sense of ignorance – but it is wise to move out of the way with all convenient dispatch, every controversy on which it will feel itself at home, and on which therefore it will be disposed to act' (24 March 1876).

Salisbury was willing to support Lytton's romantic notions of how India should be governed, although questioning their value. He thought the passage of the Royal Titles Act, which made Queen

Victoria Empress of India, hardly worth the while because of the resulting political controversy. 'The bill is a curious specimen of the difficulty of governing under the impulsive sway of a democracy. If we could have at all foreseen the storm that would arise, we should certainly have abstained from exposing the Queen to so much discussion,' he explained to Lytton (24 March 1876). Nevertheless Salisbury gave his blessing to the Viceroy's plan for a Proclamation Durbar on 1 January 1877, an extension of honours in the Indian Empire and the creation of an Indian Privy Council composed of loyal princes. 'It is worth making an effort to secure their loyalty,' he agreed about the Indian princes. 'The only thing to remember is English ridicule and abuse is able to destroy the value of any expression of goodwill, which appeals to sentiment and not self-interest.' Salisbury accepted that nothing could be expected from any attempts to work through either the mass of the population or the Indian intelligentsia. He wrote to Lytton:

No fact comes out more sharply in the history of this century all over Christendom than the political lifelessness of the 'masses' and that under the strongest stimulants democratic arrangements can supply. They wake up for a moment from time to time when you least look for it – aroused by some panic or kindred sentiment, or some sharp suffering which they lay at the door of the wrong person and the wrong law. But for the most part they are politically asleep and must never be counted upon to resist their real enemies or sustain their real friends at the right moment. If this is true in the West, how much more so in India?

To expect political support at a pinch from the natives of India, as a consequence and recognition of good government, is an optimist's dream. Good government avoids one of the causes of hate; but it does not inspire love. The literary class – a deadly legacy from Metcalf and Macaulay – are politically alive enough; but under the most favourable circumstances they never give any political strength to a state, whatever benefits they confer, they seldom go far in the affirmative direction than to tolerate the existing order of things. In India they cannot be anything else than opposition in quiet times, rebels in times of trouble. (9 June 1876)

Salisbury advised Lytton to behave 'circumspectly' in his wish to confer military titles and commands on the princes so that he should prevent either an outburst of 'official prejudice' in Britain or the rise of 'any wild hopes' among the native population. The Secretary of State appeared to believe that the most serious threat to the success of Lytton's internal policy lay not in resistance by the Indian people, but from resentment from the Anglo-Indian community. He explained to the Viceroy: 'In the distant future, the Empire if it is to endure must stand not on one leg but on two. The Anglo-

Indian community, following the precedent of the St Domingo planters, the Jamaican planters, the Confederate slave-owners, is getting to imagine that it is strong enough to defy at once the distant government and the native millions by its side. The feeling is but in germ now – but according to all example it will strengthen with their strength. If England is to remain supreme she must be able to appeal to the coloured against the white, as well as the white against the coloured. It is therefore not merely a matter of sentiment and justice, but as a matter of safety that we ought to try and lay the foundations of some feeling on the part of the coloured races towards the Crown other than the recollection of defeat and the vexation of subjection' (7 July 1876).

Salisbury doubted whether Parliament would understand or agree with Lytton's plans. He advised caution in the powers that the Viceroy intended to confer on his Indian Privy Council: 'Co-operation for the common prosperity and security is a pleasanter idea, a more grateful subject of contemplation, than consultation for the better ordering of mutual chastisement. Eton schoolboys might like to place constitutional checks on the headmaster, yet a meeting for deciding the best means of beating Harrow at cricket would be more popular than a meeting for drawing up a code of regulations under which boys should be flogged. Caution in conferring real authority will not be misplaced. As Stephen says, never leave go of the thin rope of power.'

'The Legislative Council must keep in mind the sensibilities of these great subject communities,' Salisbury warned the Viceroy. 'They must wear the chain, but it must not be allowed to gall them. They must not be allowed to feel that in matters which purely concern them their voice is treated as of no account and the remonstrances of their foremost dignitaries are disregarded. If such a feeling were to gather strength the unity of the Empire would be much endangered' (27 October 1876).

Resistance to Lytton's plan did not take long to develop both among the Indian Office civil servants and the Executive Council in London. Salisbury blamed 'mercantile dislike of display in any form, and all the circumstances of power' as well as the 'jealousy of the liberal grant of honours'. But Salisbury's legal advisers warned him that the Privy Council scheme was *ultra vires*. It would require parliamentary legislation to come into practice. Salisbury comforted Lytton with the suggestion that the cultivation of closer personal relations with the princes at the Durbar might prove to be just as effective as any Council.

Salisbury did not sympathize with Lytton's more radical ideas for admitting Indians into the government service. He disliked the extension of large-scale recruitment among the educated Indian class. 'I can imagine no more terrible future for India than that of being governed by competition Baboos,' he argued with Lytton (13 April 1877). 'A very little dose of that dangerous remedy ceases to satisfy and only whets the appetite. There is a little danger that the Indian mind may get into the state of things of always expecting some new benefit and threatening to revolt if not granted.'

At first, Lytton enjoyed warm relations with Salisbury. 'It is impossible to do business with him and not love him. I can't conceive how he ever acquired the reputation of being overbearing,' the Viceroy wrote to John Morley (9 September 1876). 'I find him singularly considerate, most sympathetic, and most loyal in supporting me through my difficulties.' However there was soon a growing friction between the two men. Within a few months of his arrival in India Lytton became a powerful and militant advocate of the forward-policy school in Central Asia, even if this brought a confrontation with Russia. He spoke scornfully of government diplomacy as 'dictated by the heart of a hen to the head of a pin'. The Viceroy had gone out with full instructions to ensure the Amir of Afghanistan agreed to resident British agents in his country. But the Afghan government refused to agree to such a request. This convinced Lytton that the Amir was in close collaboration with Russia. Salisbury advised caution. He was opposed to any military step against the buffer state. What he sought was influence and not conquest. Salisbury advised Lytton to follow 'a middle holding ground' between war and ambition. The outbreak of the Russo-Turkish war in the summer of 1876 strengthened Salisbury in his conviction that Russia would not attempt any advance towards Afghanistan at such a time. 'The feeling of Parliament and government must govern,' Salisbury warned the Viceroy (10 August 1877): 'If they could once be persuaded that we are merely employed in making our own frontier strong and have no thought of going beyond it, we should meet with little opposition. The vision of a Central Asian expedition makes it quite unmanageable. My wish is to hold a temperate mean between the two extremes, to advocate the policy of "defence not defiance".'

However, Salisbury was soon convinced that Lytton lacked stable judgement with his fiery anti-Russian dispatches. He came to the conclusion that the Viceroy's 'leading passion' was a 'gaudy and theatrical ambition'. For the rest of his period at the India Office

Salisbury found himself attempting to calm his impetuous, fire-eating colleague, who had been entirely convinced of the need for a military advance against the Amir by his Calcutta advisers. Salisbury dismissed the immediate danger of any Russian intrusion into India. 'I cannot help thinking that, in discussions of this kind, a great deal of apprehension arises from the popular use of maps on a small scale,' he explained to the Lords (11 June 1877). 'As with such maps you are able to put a thumb on India and a finger on Russia, some persons think that the political situation is alarming and that India must be looked to . . . The distance between Russia and British India is not to be measured by the finger and thumb but by a rule.'

It was not until after Salisbury had left the India Office that Lytton ventured on a military expedition into Afghanistan. This resulted in three border wars that helped to tarnish Disraeli's foreign policy record in the eyes of the British electorate.

C

A lath painted to look like iron.
Bismarck on Salisbury
at the Congress of Berlin, June 1878

4

THE

INDISPENSABLE MAN

November 1876–April 1881

Salisbury's appointment as the government's plenipotentiary at the Constantinople conference in November 1876 brought his first direct involvement in international politics. There was a wide welcome for Disraeli's decision to send him out to Turkey to carry out the task. Gladstone believed that Salisbury shared 'no Disraelite prejudices', kept a conscience and possessed 'plenty of manhood and character'. Even John Bright spoke favourably of Salisbury's 'liberality, justice and strong intellect' which, the old Radical was convinced, would ensure 'fair play' at the conference.

In the autumn of 1876 Salisbury's sympathies lay with Russia and not Turkey. Carnarvon was later to recall that Salisbury believed that the plight of the Christians living within the Ottoman Empire was 'of absolute, essential, vital importance – in which morals as well as politics were involved – and on which real sacrifice could be accepted without a personal sacrifice of honour and right from our point of view'. Bosnia and Herzegovina revolted against Turkish rule in the summer of 1875. In the following year, there was a rising against the Sultan in Bulgaria, which was bloodily suppressed. Salisbury believed that the despotic but fragile Turkish Empire was on the brink of collapse. He disliked the traditional British policy of supporting Constantinople in order to keep Russia out of the Eastern Mediterranean and safeguard the British sea-route to India. In a letter to Carnarvon in September 1876, Salisbury actually suggested that the Sultan's friendship was 'a reproach' to the British government. In his opinion, the 'Turk's teeth would have to be pulled out', even if he was 'allowed to live'. Although Salisbury failed to sympathize with Gladstone's moral crusade against Turkish atrocities in Bulgaria, he agreed with the Liberal leader that 'some kind of reliable machinery' would have to be devised to make sure that Christians in the Ottoman Empire enjoyed protection in the future. In his view, 'mere promises of better government' by the Porte could no longer satisfy international opinion. The main difficulty was that it was unclear how such internal control could be established without undermining Turkish rule. 'A government of some kind or other must be found for all these wretchedly oppressed multitudes,' Salisbury explained to Carnarvon. 'It cannot be left as a no-man's land. But the division of that kind of jetsam is peculiarly difficult. If the powers quarrel over it, the calamities of a gigantic war must be undergone. If they agree, people will call it partition and denounce it as immoral.'

Salisbury would have liked the British government to abandon its old Crimea policy of propping up Turkey and seek a close understanding with Russia, who claimed to be the chief defender of the Slavs under the Sultan's domination. Such a change of strategy would have probably gone down well with public opinion, now mainly hostile to the Turks. Moreover Salisbury was convinced that Russia was no longer either an immediate or a serious threat to the British presence in India. He had come to the conclusion that the government could no longer defend the indefensible at Constantinople.

Salisbury did not look forward to the long journey out to Turkey to attend a conference of the European powers with the aim of constructing a reform programme to impress upon the Sultan. He

feared that it would prove to be 'an awful nuisance . . . involving
sea-sickness, much French and failure'. The Prime Minister offered
encouragement. 'This is a momentous period in your life and career.
If all goes well you will have achieved a European reputation and
position which will immensely assist and strengthen your future
course,' he wrote to Salisbury. From the beginning, Salisbury doubted
whether the conference could reconcile Russia and Turkey. He was
instructed by the Cabinet to demand administrative autonomy for
the rebellious regions of the Turkish Empire with effective guarantees.
However no coercion or occupation of any Turkish territory was to
be tolerated.

Salisbury left England on 20 November for Constantinople, complete with a large retinue of family and civil servants. *En route*, he
stopped at the main European capitals to discuss the situation. In
Berlin Salisbury met Bismarck and he was received by Emperor
William I. The German Chancellor left the impression that he believed war was inevitable between Russia and Turkey. Salisbury also
visited Paris, Vienna and Rome. He reached the Turkish capital on
5 December. It did not take him long to realize that his worst fears
about the conference were well founded but he was agreeably
surprised to discover that Ignatiev, the Russian delegate, was
enthusiastically in favour of a settlement. The powers soon ham-
mered out a programme of reforms to present to the Sultan. They
agreed that an international commission should be set up to super-
vise the internal changes, supported by a gendarmerie officered by
Europeans.

But the Sultan refused to swallow the proposals. Salisbury concluded that the main reason for this obstinacy was the conviction
that the British government would not desert him in the last resort.
The intrigues of the British ambassador, Sir Henry Elliot, upset
Salisbury. He tried to persuade Beaconsfield to withdraw the
diplomat but without success. In fact, the Prime Minister disliked
Salisbury's opinions. He believed that his envoy was 'more Russian
than Ignatiev, *plus Arabe que l'Arabie*'. Beaconsfield, without his
Cabinet's knowledge, reassured Elliot that he would support him.
On 20 January the Sultan formally turned down the reform proposals. The Constantinople conference broke up three days later.
Salisbury returned to England, a bitter man. He used to say that he
was sent out to Turkey 'without a purse to buy with or a sword
to threaten with'. Salisbury's suspicions of the Prime Minister
revived. Carnarvon recalled that his colleague retained 'one feeling
– a rooted belief in Disraeli's untrustworthiness and a dread of the

policy which he thought Disraeli intended to pursue'. He also came back from Constantinople with the added conviction that it was no longer possible to sustain the Sultan. 'The patient may linger on for some time – but the disease seems to me past cure,' he explained to Lytton (9 February 1877). 'Sustaining the Sultan – unless he will listen to some advice – is, I fear, out of the question. The people here won't do it and I doubt whether it is materially possible. It was very convenient while it lasted – but we have not the political force to sustain it, even if we desired to do so. However we shall do what we can to keep Russia's hands off but I am not sanguine.' Salisbury feared British foreign policy was 'to float lazily downstream, occasionally putting out a diplomatic boat-hook to avoid collisions'.

During March 1877 he did his best to persuade the divided Cabinet that it should support the other great powers in standing up to Turkish obdurance. It was mainly due to Salisbury's efforts that his colleagues agreed to join in the London Protocol that was submitted to the Sultan. This called on the Porte to reduce his army and agree to the adoption of the reform proposals made by the Constantinople conference. However, Salisbury was unable to make any headway with his suggestion that the government should renounce its old policy towards Turkey and accept the country's partition. Beaconsfield denounced the idea as immoral and unacceptable. 'I trust we shall never hear any more Bathism, Lyddonism, really Gladstonism within these walls,' he remarked. The joint Protocol was signed on 31 March in London. Predictably, the Sultan lost no time in rejecting it. Russia declared war on Turkey on 24 April. The Cabinet was undecided on how it should react to the conflict. Eventually, the government took a middle course with a declaration of partial neutrality. Unless British interests were threatened at the Straits, Istanbul, Suez or in the Persian Gulf, Britain would stay aloof. This formula was uninspiring and makeshift, and it displeased Salisbury, but at least it kept the Cabinet together for the moment. Certainly, it stopped Beaconsfield from pursuing any uncritical pro-Turkish policy.

At the outset of the Russo-Turkish war Salisbury doubted whether Russia intended to annex new territory. He tried to calm the anti-Russian feelings of Lord Lytton out in India. But he also made it clear that if his opinions were proved wrong by events, the government should end its neutrality. 'We shall have probably to defend Constantinople, if attacked, for reasons of prestige which those who govern Oriental nations cannot afford to overlook,' he explained to the Viceroy (27 April). But Salisbury was convinced that if Austria-Hungary firmly supported the British position, Russia would not threaten Constantinople. Yet he was reconciled to taking action alone, if Russia could not be stopped through diplomatic pressure. From the start, therefore, Salisbury's attitude differed from that of both Carnarvon and Derby, who were passionately pro-Russian. All the same, he was convinced that Turkey would soon sue for peace with Russia. In April and May 1877 Salisbury opposed the proposal to send the navy to the Dardanelles as a contingency measure. He continued to believe that the most sensible place to defend the route to India was no longer at Constantinople but in either Crete or Egypt.

Through the summer of 1877, Salisbury did not change his opinion that while the Turks would suffer defeat, Russia would not be able to deliver a knockout blow. The resulting bloody stalemate would provide an opportunity for the great powers to intervene diplomatically. 'Russia will be enormously weakened in men and money by this war – even if she gains a few strategic positions and the effect of modern changes is constantly to diminish the value of strategic positions and to increase the value of pecuniary resources,' he explained to a doubting Lytton (8 June 1877). 'There is nothing in the events of the present campaign to give me an overweening idea of Russian strength.' But by the early autumn the Russian forces had penetrated deep into the Turkish Empire. They crossed the river Danube in late June and reached southern Bulgaria by the end of July. Russia lay siege to Kars, and to Plevna in the Balkans. At a Cabinet meeting on 5 October Beaconsfield called for British intervention on Turkey's side but Salisbury opposed him. Plevna fell to the Russians on 9 December. The road to Constantinople lay open. The Sultan appealed to the great powers for mediation. Beaconsfield proposed to recall Parliament for an emergency session at a Cabinet meeting on 14 December. The Prime Minister also wanted a vote of credit to increase the armed forces and a declaration that Britain would act as a mediator. Salisbury joined Derby in opposing such a step. He still refused to accept that the Russians would not abide by their own assurances that Constantinople and the Straits were not to be occupied. Salisbury feared that Beaconsfield's proposed course of action might well encourage the Turks to abandon any idea of negotiation and carry on fighting. But he was no longer prepared to go all the way with the pro-Russian contingent in the Cabinet. On 18 December Salisbury made it plain to Northcote, the Chancellor of the Exchequer, that if mediation broke down the government would have to demand war credits, send a fleet to the Bosphorus and occupy the Gallipoli peninsula as a precautionary move.

By early January the Cabinet was in danger of breaking up. Both Derby and Carnarvon threatened resignation if the government took a vigorous pro-Turkish course. Salisbury made an effort to calm the divisions. 'Providence has put in our hands the trust of keeping the country from entering on a wrongful war. Do not renounce such a task on account of a rude phrase by a man whose insolence is proverbial,' he wrote to Carnarvon (8 January 1878) who had been admonished by Beaconsfield for his attitude in Cabinet. But the onward march of the Russian armies and their refusal to accept Turkey's call for mediation began to toughen Salisbury's response to the crisis, particularly as it had become obvious that Austria-Hungary did not intend to support the British position. On 12 January the Cabinet demanded an assurance from the Tsar that Russia would not occupy the Dardanelles. When this was not forthcoming Salisbury led the call in Cabinet for the fleet to be sent to Gallipoli on 15 January. The order was rescinded a few hours later on receipt of a belated Russian assurance. At Cabinet meetings on 21, 22 and 23 January Disraeli was able to persuade most of his colleagues that negotiations should be opened immediately with Austria-Hungary, that public notice should be given of a request for £6 million of defence credits, and that Admiral Hornby should be dispatched to the Dardanelles. Carnarvon and Derby resigned. On the 24th, however, news reached London that the Russians had agreed with the Sultan on terms for an armistice. Under pressure, Beaconsfield reversed the order to send out the navy and Derby decided to stay on at the Foreign Office. Yet within a fortnight the Russian armies were moving forward again and by 5 February reached the outskirts of Constantinople. It looked as though Russia was ignoring the armistice.

Salisbury called for urgent action on 6 February. Even the dithering Derby accepted its necessity and orders were sent off to Besika Bay for a squadron to enter Turkish waters. When the Grand Duke Nicholas warned that if the British fleet appeared in the Bosphorus the Russians would enter Constantinople, the Sultan appealed to the British government to countermand the order. This time the Cabinet refused to budge. Salisbury was now the firm advocate of a tough stance. 'As a matter of ultimate policy and in view of the immediate moral effect, our fleet ought to force its way in without delay,' he urged Beaconsfield (10 February). On 15 February the British ironclads were anchored off the Golden Horn. 'One hour of frankness on

Russia's part would have avoided the whole imbroglio,' Salisbury assured the sceptical Marquis of Bath (31 January).

Beaconsfield and Salisbury had discovered common ground in the Balkan crisis. The Indian Secretary found many of the Prime Minister's qualities suddenly to his liking. In return, Beaconsfield came to acknowledge that Salisbury was 'the only man of real courage' whom he had worked with. Although Derby continued to sit in the Foreign Office, the country's foreign policy was increasingly in the hands of an inner junta composed of Beaconsfield, Salisbury and Cairns. Matters came to a head in March. The Turks were compelled to sign a peace treaty with the Tsar at San Stefano. This amounted to a total surrender to Russian demands. A huge, autonomous Bulgaria was to be carved out of the Turkish Empire from the Danube to the shores of the Aegean, from the Black Sea to the Albanian frontier. With a Russian commission to draw up its constitution and 50,000 Russian troops to stay there for two years, the new state was going to be a satellite of Russia. This was a triumph for the Pan-Slavists in St Petersburg. A circular was sent to the great powers calling for an international conference to approve the treaty's contents. The British government made it plain that it would attend no such gathering unless all the San Stefano terms were included on the agenda for discussion. The other European powers were not insisting on such a condition. Russia refused to accept the British position. There was a dangerous deadlock. On 27 March the Cabinet decided to show its firmness by calling out the reserves and transporting troops from India into the Mediterranean. This was too much for Derby to stomach and he resigned immediately. No effort was made to keep him in the Cabinet. Salisbury took his place at the Foreign Office. It was to be the start of a long and happy tenure, which was to last intermittently for the rest of his public life.

His arrival at his new post brought swift action. Uncertainty and vacillation at the Foreign Office were swept away. As the Hungarian diplomat Andrassy put it, Salisbury's presence was like 'a gleam of light' shining through the darkness. Salisbury was later to comment that his early work was 'only picking up the china Derby had broken'. His famous diplomatic circular of 1 April made an immediate and effective impact on the chancelleries of Europe. He wrote it in the early hours at Hatfield after a dinner-party. It still rates as a great state document. Salisbury's aim in April 1878 was clear enough. He was determined to reduce Russia's influence in the Balkans with, if possible, the help of Austria-Hungary. In return, he was willing to compensate Russia for any loss of diplomatic face that might ensue with an acceptance of the bulk of her Asian conquests in the recent war with Turkey.

Salisbury was not prepared to accept the Russian terms for the proposed Congress. He believed such a gathering would do more harm than good, unless it was clear beforehand that Russia was willing to accept substantial changes in the treaty of San Stefano. Salisbury disliked big international gatherings because they often intensified enmities and drew public attention to differences of opinion, so making 'retreat on either side a loss of honour'. He wanted to neutralize the conflict from the beginning. Bismarck was asked by Salisbury to act as mediator between Britain and Russia, to initiate a mutual withdrawal of forces from the Constantinople area. At this stage, the Foreign Secretary wanted to preserve Turkish independence in the southern part of the proposed Greater Bulgaria and 'push Slav power behind the Balkans'. The German Chancellor agreed to act as a go-between. A cautious diplomatic dialogue was opened up between London and St Petersburg. Salisbury was making a simultaneous effort to reach an understanding with Andrassy in Vienna. Salisbury wanted the Austrian Foreign Minister to support his demands to Russia, but Andrassy proved evasive. He wanted the inclusion of Bosnia and Herzegovina within the Hapsburg Empire and Salisbury agreed to the proposal. But it was with Russia that Salisbury made a break-through. The waning of pan-Slavic zealotry at the Tsar's court helped him. Salisbury was determined to 'show no flinching' of resolution, nor at the same time 'inflict any gratuitous humiliation upon Russia'. To the surprise of Bismarck and jingoes in Britain, Salisbury was ready to accept the Russian annexation of Batoum and Kars in Central Asia and Bessarabia on the Black Sea coast in return for Russia's acceptance that Bulgaria could not become a large Russian satellite, but would have to be partitioned with the southern half of Eastern Roumelia remaining under Turkish suzerainty. When the Anglo-Russian memorandum was signed on 30 May, the only outstanding matter left to resolve was whether the Sultan should keep the right to garrison troops south of the Balkans. Salisbury was not entirely satisfied with the agreement. The document was not intended for public eyes, but within a day of its signing the contents were splashed in the *Daily Globe* to the indignation of the jingo lobby.

At the same time, Salisbury was negotiating successfully with the Turks. He had reached the conclusion from his own bitter experience that the Sultan could not hope to retain power unless he was backed up forcibly by another power such as Britain. 'You have hitherto laboured to prevent Russian preponderance by sustaining the Turkish breakwater,' Salisbury pointed out to the British ambassador in Constantinople, Sir Henry Layard. 'But the breakwater is now shattered, I fear, beyond repair, and the flood is pouring over it.' The Foreign Secretary felt that 'another dyke' could only be put in Russia's way if Britain acquired a territorial 'counter-poise' in the Eastern Mediterranean. The Sultan was therefore asked to cede territory to the British government. In return, Britain would guarantee Turkey's Asiatic possessions. Salisbury was actually thinking of the possibility of 'a defensive alliance with the Porte' to defend her Asian Empire from Russian attack. The Cabinet agreed to this proposal on 16 May. While Salisbury was reconciled to the decay of Turkish power in Europe, he wanted to underpin the rest of the rickety Empire with British protection from Syria to Mesapotamia and the Persian Gulf. This could only succeed, however, if the Sultan gave 'specific assurances' that he would rule justly and effectively over the Asiatic Christians, and secondly that he would accept the British occupation of Cyprus. That tiny island off the Turkish coast was regarded as a more sensible location to provide support for the Porte than other possible points of arms such as Lemnos, Crete or Alexandretta on the Syrian coast. On 24 May Layard was instructed to present the British demands to the Sultan and told to force an assent within two days. If the Porte refused the terms, then Turkey was to be left to her fate at Russia's hands. This was no idle threat. The Sultan agreed to what Salisbury proposed.

The diplomatic road to Berlin was now unblocked. On 2 June Salisbury announced that Britain would attend the proposed Congress. It began eleven days later. Bismarck and Beaconsfield seized the limelight at Berlin, but Salisbury can be justifiably acknowledged as its unprepossessing architect. He did most of the British negotiating behind closed doors. The Russians proved to be tough customers over the military occupation of Southern Bulgaria. 'Some time may be required in order to persuade them to be skinned quietly,' Salisbury remarked to his wife (20 June). 'Our meetings in Congress are perfectly futile. Everything in reality depends on our private fights over Bulgaria.' The jingo pressures back in England over the leaked Anglo-Russian memorandum interfered with his careful diplomacy. There was a sharp division of opinion between Britain and Russia on the exact status of Batoum. The Russians were able to bamboozle Beaconsfield into an acceptance that it should be *'essentiellement'* a free port and not *'exclusivement'* one. As a way of outflanking party criticisms, Salisbury sought agreement on a freedom of passage for England through the Dardanelles. Under the 1871 revision of the Peace of Paris it had been agreed that the Sultan had the power to decide who should and should not use the straits. What Salisbury proposed was to turn the waters into an open sea for international shipping. But the rest of the Cabinet reported opposition and the matter was dropped. On 7 July Salisbury informed the French Foreign Minister, Waddington, about the secret Anglo-Turkish convention and he promised that Britain would not stand in the way of any French activity in Tunis.

Four days later a British man-of-war reached Cyprus to haul up the Union Jack. With Bismarck determined to take his usual convalescence at Kissingen, the Congress of Berlin came to an end on 13 July. Rapturous crowds welcomed Beaconsfield and Salisbury on their return to London. The Prime Minister assured them that he returned with 'peace with honour'. Salisbury was not convinced by the popular emotions. He believed that his policy was not well supported in the country. It was his opinion that the wire-pullers would make a great blunder if they thought that Berlin was going to prove a triumph with the electorate. Salisbury agreed, with much reluctance, to receive the honour of a knighthood of the Garter for his work. He only did so on Beaconsfield's insistence, because the Prime Minister was receiving the same decoration.

Although the Anglo-Turkish Convention aroused partisan tempers at Westminster, it was the linchpin of Salisbury's Near East policy. For the remaining eighteen months of his first spell at the Foreign Office, he struggled to ensure that it did not fall to pieces. Salisbury was only too well aware of the shortcomings of the Sultan. The task of trying to cleanse his government of corruption was a daunting one. Salisbury's old doubts about the future of the Turkish Empire had not disappeared. He explained to Layard on 24 July 1878 that the ambassador's job promised to be one of 'constant struggle'. 'Battle there must be – for there are rival interests to satisfy and we had to choose between an immediate appeal to arms – or to postponing, with the chance of avoiding, that arbitrament, by substituting for it a protracted diplomatic struggle,' Salisbury argued. Layard must insist on 'far-reaching' reforms from the Sultan to satisfy his Asiatic subjects as well as British public opinion. At the same time, the ambassador had to be careful that he did not usurp any 'of the semblance of power from the Sultan, nor too much of the reality'. Salisbury was not 'very sanguine' that the Eastern

Roumelian experiment would last. He informed Layard that he must do what he could to see the province was furnished with 'workable institutions'.

The Foreign Secretary wanted the Sultan to agree to the appointment of European officers in his administration who could enjoy 'a tolerably secure tenure for a short term of years' in which to ensure 'a pure administration of justice'. Salisbury spelt out what he wanted to see in Turkey in a dispatch to Layard on 8 August 1878. The regions of Asiatic Turkey were to have governors appointed for a fixed number of years, with virtual control of the police, judiciary and tax-collection in European hands. The main trouble was that Salisbury was in no position to rescue the Sultan from his financial plight. Generous British subsidies might have made the Turkish regime more willing to carry out the necessary internal reforms. However, the Treasury was in no mood to display such generosity. It refused to contemplate Salisbury's suggestion of a public loan which would have helped the building of a railway from Alexandretta on the Mediterranean coast of Syria to Baghdad. Despite his special pleading, Salisbury found no support in the Cabinet for the Sultan's repeated calls for financial help. The diplomatic events of 1878 had increased British power and influence in Constantinople, but Salisbury could do nothing to ensure this renewed position of strength was built on a permanent basis. Resistance at home to the idea of providing British taxpayers' money for Turkey proved too strong. Salisbury made no impression on his colleagues with his demand for multi-million-pound help for the Sultan in return for British control of the entire administration of finances in the Turkish Empire. Such a degree of intervention found no backers. There was fear that it could damage the government's majority in the Commons. Parliament was recalled for an emergency session in November 1878, but this was in order to provide credits for dealing with the war in Afghanistan. Salisbury was even unable to persuade the Cabinet to agree in the sanction of a small grant with which to help Moslem refugees who had fled from Russian-occupied areas of the Empire.

Another obstacle to reform was the very character of the Sultan's regime itself. Reports were soon pouring in from British observers in Asiatic Turkey which predicted both Arabs and Christians were about to revolt. Salisbury and Layard continued with their efforts to make the Turkish authorities mend their ways. 'The Sultan has not the faintest conception of the slenderness of the thread by which his dynasty holds onto its existence,' Salisbury lamented to his ambassador (2 October 1879). 'Will the English people – little inclined as they are for any exertion that will increase their burdens – go to war to maintain the Turkish Empire, if they have once acquired the conviction that the Porte is absolutely insincere in promising reform?' 'The reluctance of England to enter on a full policy of partition will not bear more than a certain amount of strain and that reluctance is the solitary support on which the Sultan's Empire now rests.'

Salisbury realized that there was nothing to be done with the Turkish regime but go on 'pegging away'. In November 1879 the Sultan finally agreed to accept Baker Pasha as Inspector-General of Reforms in Asia Minor. Yet this led to no increase in the tempo of Turkish interest in achieving a more efficient and just system of government. 'The time seems to be passed when the old policy of governing the Porte by diplomatic thunderstorms can be relied upon,' argued Salisbury (3 January 1880). He began to contemplate the creation of a Council of State in Constantinople, which would curb the Sultan's authority. However, three months later the Conservatives lost office. Gladstone's new government lost no time in withdrawing the military consuls from Turkey. With their departure, British influence declined rapidly at Constantinople. Yet by that time Salisbury was beginning to accept that his strenuous diplomatic efforts had been futile. He wrote to Layard on 22 April 1880: 'My impression is that the Sultan's day of grace is past and that in every government in Europe his Empire is looked upon as doomed. For the sake of the Turks I regret this little – but the bloodshed which will probably accompany this fall is not pleasant to contemplate.'

Salisbury was more successful in making sure Russia abided by the terms of the Congress of Berlin, but even this was an uphill task, which was made no easier by the Sultan's readiness to ignore his treaty obligations. Russian troops were supposed to be withdrawn from the Balkans by 3 May 1879, but the Tsar appeared to be prevaricating. His army was reinforced and the Russians fought a rearguard action on the boundary commission, which had been set up to draw the frontier line between Eastern Roumelia and Bulgaria. 'Every trick which it is possible for imagination to conceive, every subtle misconstruction of the treaty, is being used for the purpose of hindering the proper execution of the treaty,' Salisbury complained (16 October 1878). He gave Turkey a firm guarantee of British support to implement the treaty if the Russian withdrawal had not taken place by the following May. But the main reason for Salisbury's success lay in firm Austrian support for Russian withdrawal. By 3 August Russia had withdrawn its troops from the Balkans.

Relations were strained between Germany and Russia in the aftermath of the Congress of Berlin. There was a rumour in the early autumn of 1879 that Russia, France and Italy were planning to attack Germany and Austria. The old alliance between the three eastern empires appeared to have no hope of revival. Bismarck was now seeking an alliance with both Austria and Britain and he found Beaconsfield favourable to such an idea. Salisbury was more sceptical. He believed that for Russia to seek a quarrel with Germany was 'madness'. Salisbury questioned the value of any alliance if it led to the possibility of a future clash between Britain and France. At the same time, the Foreign Secretary made it clear that it would be difficult for Britain not to go to war if Russia attacked Austria. The British government was kept fully informed of the negotiations leading to the alliance between Germany and Austria. Salisbury suggested that the news of such an arrangement was 'glad tidings of great joy'. 'Of course we have to pick our steps so as not to seem to err from the straight path in France's eyes for France is capable of giving us a great deal of trouble,' Salisbury explained to Britain's ambassador in Berlin, Lord Odo Russell (14 January 1880). 'But on the sound rule that you love those most whom you compete with least, Germany is clearly cut out to be our ally.' A good deal of Salisbury's time at the Foreign Office was devoted to the problem of the Khedive Ismail's regime in Egypt, where Britain and France were supervising his finances. In September 1879 the Western powers managed to have Ismail deposed and he was replaced by Tewfik, who was no more than a puppet. Salisbury accepted parity of influence in Egypt, but he recognized the possibility that Britain might have to step in and take direct control, if the new regime proved incapable of putting its financial house in order. But in 1879 Salisbury was preoccupied with the Afghan campaign and the outbreak of a war in South Africa with the Zulus, which resulted in a disastrous British military defeat at Isandhlwana. In the closing months of the Conservative government its foreign policy came under bitter attack from Gladstone and the rejuvenated Liberals. Beaconsfield was accused of following a bombastic policy, which led the country into humiliating debacles.

Yet Salisbury's handling of the Foreign Office enhanced his reputation enormously. Before the spring of 1878 he had not yet managed to live down the opinion that he was a political extremist, who lacked the necessary finesse to make a successful Foreign

Secretary. His firm control and decisiveness during those early months in the department helped to transform Britain's diplomatic position after a period of indecision and weakness. Lord Rosebery was later to maintain that Salisbury's 'great moment' was in the weeks before the Congress of Berlin, when he placed a vigorous hand on the direction of the country's policy and won a European reputation. Without any of the resources that Bismarck could call upon, he had safeguarded British interests in the Balkans and inflicted a humiliation on Russia after San Stefano, which he achieved almost single-handed.

In early 1880 Salisbury suffered an attack of severe internal congestion, which he caught after taking a cold bath. This brought internal complications and the onset of a serious illness, which was made no better by Salisbury's stubborn insistence that he should keep a close eye on his official work, even from his sick-bed. However, when Beaconsfield decided to dissolve Parliament and call a general election at the 6 March Cabinet meeting, Salisbury escaped from his government duties to convalesce at Biarritz. He was already in a despondent mood. 'What fearful weather you seem to have had!' he had written to Lady Manners from the French Riviera in January. 'It is the sort of weather that precedes great revolutions, like the celebrated winter of 1788. Here the weather may be described as simply radical, not revolutionary.' Gladstone's great victory at the polls came as an unexpected blow to Beaconsfield and the Queen. The Liberals returned to the Commons with an overall majority of 137. Salisbury's old pessimism about the future was rapidly revived. Although he was personally glad to be rid of the strains of office, he feared inevitable social conflict. 'The hurricane that has swept us away is so strange and new a phenomenon that we shall not for some time understand its real meaning,' he confessed to his nephew Balfour (10 April 1880). 'It seems to me to be inspired by some definite desire for change and means business. It may disappear as rapidly as it came – or it may be the beginning of a vexatious war of classes. Gladstone is doing all he can to give it the latter meaning.'

Salisbury predicted that 'the country gentlemen' would have as much to do with the government of their country before the end of the new Parliament as 'the rich people in America' had in the running of their system. He feared that Gladstone would take revolutionary action. 'He still cherishes his belief in an early hermitic retreat from this wicked world, and he is feverishly anxious to annihilate his enemies before he takes it,' Salisbury wrote of the Liberal leader to Balfour (16 June 1880).

Salisbury was convinced that the 1880 defeat was a 'perfect catastrophe' for the Conservatives. He feared it would break up the party. Nor did the events of the 1880 parliamentary session do anything to reassure him. 'I have ceased to be able to understand much about English politics – only I have a dim apprehension that we shall none of us have any rents, rabbits or religion when the session is over,' he wrote to Lady Manners from Homburg in July. Salisbury came back to the Lords to condemn the Irish Compensation for Disturbance Bill as confiscatory and a direct assault on property rights. He wanted to see the Upper House flex its muscles and throw out any contentious legislation which it disapproved of. 'I decline in deciding how I shall give my vote, to ask, what will be thought of the action of the House of Lords out-of-doors,' Salisbury asserted. 'We have a higher responsibility to keep in view. The motto for the House of Lords should be, "Be just and fear not" and be sure that if you fear you will not long be just.' Their Lordships threw out the measure by a huge majority.

In the autumn Salisbury added his voice to the platform oratory of the Conservative opposition. At Hackney on 19 November he defended the House of Lords which he asserted had the function of representing 'the permanent as opposed to the passing feelings of the English nation'. Salisbury detected the steady movement of middle-class support in the south-east away from Liberalism. 'Conservatism is the normal condition under which healthy societies must live,' he claimed. 'Excitement and sensation of perpetual change bring results which are disastrous to all classes alike.' He gave his blessing to the ginger-group activities of the young Lord Randolph Churchill and his so-called 'fourth party' by speaking on the same platform with the party rebels at Woodstock. It was there that he called for the repression of the land agitation in Ireland 'with a strong hand'. 'If you permit the disorder to continue in the hope that you will have time to produce your remedial measures, you run the danger of persuading the people that your offers are only due to the horrors they have inspired,' Salisbury argued.

Although Salisbury appeared to sympathize with Churchill's *à l'outrance* strategy of opposition, he agreed with the consensus style of the hapless Conservative leader in the Commons, Sir Stafford Northcote. 'He may hope by adopting a moderate attitude to lure over the Whig rank and file to become Tories and this, if Gladstone is violent, is not an unlikely concurrence,' Salisbury confessed to Balfour (5 October). 'I think his tactics so far wise. The leader, even of a diminished party, must behave as arbitrator between its various sections and if he has fair ground for hoping to attract a new section, they must come within the scope of the arbitration.' But Salisbury was not optimistic about the party's ability to regain its strength in the Commons. 'I am afraid that the efficiency of our party will decay and that we shall not recover the confidence of the country,' he admitted to Balfour (2 September). 'For it is the central figure of a party in the Commons to which constituencies are wont to look if their confidence is asked for that party. We must have patience and make up our minds to wait for some time.'

Salisbury was anxious to ensure that the Commons under a Liberal majority did not turn Parliament into a legislative rubber stamp. The suggestion of the *clôture* to stop the obstructive tactics of the Irish Nationalists, which were paralyzing government business, filled him with horror. During the 1880 session Gladstone was able to achieve little constructive change because of the antics of Parnell and his party. This did not upset Salisbury. He explained to Balfour (15 January 1881): 'It is the old story – Gladstone is master of the country but cannot manage the House of Commons. His great quality is eloquent indistinctness of expression. It deceives the electoral gull easily, but of course it breaks down where the draughts-man has to translate it into clauses. I hope that we shall not go too far in accepting the *clôture*. In my view there ought to be a strong distinction drawn between those parliamentary functions, performance of which is absolutely necessary to secure the working of the executive machine, and those which having no other object but to change laws under which we are living quite tolerably, can be suspended certainly without serious injury, and often with great advantage.'

While Salisbury was ready to concede the necessity for the executive to have the power to stop filibustering in the Commons, he was convinced that governments should not be allowed to enjoy restrictions which would allow them to bulldoze through legislation. 'It is not our interest to grease the wheels of legislation – on the contrary it may do all the Conservative classes of the country in-finite harm,' he concluded.

Despite his contributions to debate Salisbury did not accept Beaconsfield's entreaties that he should attend debates regularly and give the old leader close support on the front bench. 'I am afraid D. has rather an unagreeable team to drive – but I doubt if I should be any help,' Salisbury confided to Balfour (31 January 1881). 'I confess that with all inclination, natural to man, to magnify my own importance, I do not see what use I can be at present.' On

19 April 1881 Beaconsfield died. During his last year of opposition he drifted along in despair, wracked by ill health. Salisbury had grown to respect his former adversary. He wrote to Balfour that Beaconsfield was 'as a politician . . . exceedingly short-sighted, though very clear-sighted. He neither could, nor would, look far ahead, or attempt to balance remote possibilities; though he rapidly detected the difficulties of the immediate situation, and found the easiest, if not the best, solution for them.'

But Salisbury's complaints of Beaconsfield as 'head of a Cabinet' are less than fair. Indeed, they match up very closely to the remarks which were later to be passed on his own methods as Prime Minister by Lord George Hamilton:

His fault was want of firmness. The chiefs of departments got their way too much. The Cabinet as a whole got it too little, and this necessarily followed from having at the head of affairs a statesman whose only final political principle was that the party must on no account be broken up, and who shrank therefore from exercising coercion on any of his subordinates.

*It will be interesting
to be the last of the Conservatives.
I foresee that will be our fate.*
Salisbury to Lady Manners,
10 December 1882

5

WHAT IS IT
THAT LIES BEFORE US?

1881–5

Beaconsfield's death plunged the Conservatives into further despair. Salisbury concluded that the party would hardly believe 'in its own existence' without him. He believed that the loss of Beaconsfield meant 'the passing away of an epoch'. Despite some party doubts, there was no overt opposition to the choice of Salisbury as Conservative leader in the Lords. He was nominated for the post by the Duke of Richmond and the Earl of Cairns. At a meeting of Conservative peers in the Marquis of Abergavenny's home in Dover Street, London on 10 May, Salisbury won their unanimous endorsement. Despite the active lobbying of supporters on the council of the National Union and Alfred Austin's backing in *Standard* editorials, Salisbury did not become leader of the Conservative party as a whole. It was agreed to shelve the delicate question of the eventual succession. Northcote was to remain Conservative leader of the troublesome parliamentary party in the Commons. The two men were to share joint responsibility for the management of the opposition. In practice, such an arrangement proved unwieldy and ineffective. Salisbury was convinced, after four years of experience, that the dual leadership of a political party was a grave mistake. He later warned Lord George Hamilton that it was 'contrary to the spirit and conception of responsible government, and would bring any party thus conducted to real political disaster'.

The formation of a Conservative duumvirate was mainly the result of Salisbury's own insecure political position. While some leading Conservatives confidently predicted that he would inherit Elijah's mantle, Salisbury's intemperate, impulsive past could not easily be forgotten. In the eyes of many contemporaries, he was still an irresponsible diehard. *The Times* likened him to 'a French noble of the Legitimist type'. It spoke of Salisbury as 'a menace to the constitution', 'a reckless and defiant spirit' to head 'a great, mute, inarticulate party'. Even Queen Victoria questioned whether Salisbury could really be looked upon as a future Conservative prime minister. She hastened to reassure Northcote that she regarded him as 'the real leader and should let it be known that she did so'. On the other hand, the Liberal diarist Sir Edward Hamilton proved more foresighted when he suggested that Salisbury would eventually 'absorb' Northcote. Nobody doubted his strength and intellectual ability, but there were still question-marks over Salisbury's political judgement. Lytton provided a succinct portrait of his old colleague on becoming Conservative leader in the Lords in a letter to his wife:

> Salisbury is amazingly clever; his knowledge of men and things is far more varied than that of Cairns. He represents a great name and social position. He has been prominently engaged in great affairs and he has no lack of audacity. Nor is he without flashes of insight. But he wants consistency and the sincerity of his character suffers in reputation from the inconsequence of his action. He has many of the most necessary qualities of a leader – great powers of work and a charm of manner very attractive to those who are immediately about him. But he makes bitter personal enemies and the country at large mistrusts him.

As a party leader, Salisbury was no autocrat. In Lady Gwendolen's words, 'his conception of loyalty was fidelity to a trust, not submission to authority'. Salisbury recognized the Conservative party was a coalition, and that a successful leader must behave as 'an arbitrator between its various sections'. He sought to win the support of the party, not through appeals to loyalty or tradition, but through the intellectual strength of his own arguments.

Salisbury was not a 'popular' man. There was never any 'bond of personal sympathy' between himself and his party. As Lady Gwendolen admitted, her father lacked 'that elemental power over the wills and imagination of others'. Even during the early 1880s when he was consolidating his leadership, Salisbury remained a virtual recluse. He spent most of his time when outside the Lords either with his devoted family at Hatfield or on holiday at the Chalet Cecil. These were the years when Salisbury returned to his experiments with electricity, and also developed a more active interest in the financial management of his vast estates. Salisbury did not appreciate the fluctuating moods of his party or the public at large. His own mordant common sense and intuition often proved canny, but he was first to admit that his decisions were reached without any clear idea of what other people thought. 'My engagements – and to some extent my idiosyncrasies – make it difficult for me to know as much as I ought to know of what people in the party are thinking on pressing questions,' he admitted to his private secretary Henry Manners in 1882.

Salisbury did not confide very closely in any of his immediate colleagues, even in the Lords. Nor did he take much active interest in helping out Northcote with his rebellious back-benchers. Between 1881 and 1884 Salisbury was out of sympathy with the calls for prudent restraint from the less adventurous leading Conservatives like Cairns and Richmond. He sought an early showdown with Gladstone's government. Salisbury believed this could only be done if the House of Lords flexed its muscles and used its veto power to destroy radical bills that came up from the Commons for approval. Salisbury was quite ready to provoke a constitutional crisis. His aim was plain enough – to make Gladstone call an early general election, before the Liberals brought in their long-promised Franchise Bill for the counties which would give the vote to most rural householders. During the summer of 1881 party feeling ran high over the Irish Land Bill, which gave freeholders fixity of tenure, fair rents and free sale. Salisbury condemned the measure as 'confiscation', because he believed it would leave the landlord as 'a sort of mortgagee on his estate, with an uncertain and precarious hold on his income'. His 'passion for individual liberty reinforced his judgement in its conviction that the Bill would prove as ineffectual as it was provocative'. Despite misgivings, the Conservatives decided not to destroy the bill.

In 1882 a serious internal crisis broke out among the Conservative leaders over what to do about Gladstone's Arrears Bill. This measure was designed to wipe out an Irish tenant's debts to his landlord if he could prove that he was in default on his rent payments because of stricken circumstances. The state and the landlord were to jointly meet the losses. Most Conservatives detested the proposal. It looked to them like another gesture of appeasement to rural agitation. Party managers reported back to Salisbury and Northcote that the Conservatives would win an early general election. There was virtual unanimity when the two leaders discussed the situation with their colleagues at Arlington Street on 21 July. It was agreed that Salisbury should move two toughly worded amendments to wreck the Arrears Bill when it reached the Lords. These were carried by large majorities on 31 July. The measure was sent back to the Commons in a mutilated condition. Doubts then began to spread in the Conservative ranks. Gladstone's resort to coercion in Ireland and the government's decision to quash Arabi Pasha's nationalist regime in Egypt belied Conservative criticism of government softness and boosted, if only temporarily, the government's popularity. On 8 August the Commons removed the Lords amendments from the Arrears Bill. Gladstone made it clear that he did not intend to bow to pressure from the Upper House. By this stage Cairns and Richmond were both calling for a retreat. Salisbury wanted to stand firm. He was more than ever convinced that once the Irish and Egyptian troubles were under control, Gladstone would hatch a reform measure that would 'efface' the Conservative party for a generation. Salisbury's colleagues did not share his belligerence. At a meeting of Conservative peers on 10 August he found few supporters in his call for resistance. He was left, in Northcote's words, 'like Uriah in the front of battle'. Salisbury withdrew his amendments in a bitter speech in the Lords. He did not disguise his view that the Conservatives had lost 'a golden opportunity for breaking Gladstone's dictatorship'. 'When shall we have another?' he lamented to Cross. The Arrears Bill crisis temporarily weakened Salisbury's authority. It was even rumoured that he might resign from the leadership in disgust at the way he had been treated. Bitterness and division grew in the party, which appeared to drift along rudderless, without cohesion or ideas.

Salisbury did not restrict his political activities to sharp diatribes in the rarefied atmosphere of the House of Lords. During his first four years as Conservative leader in that assembly he made an increasing use of the public platform 'out-of-doors' to spread his astringent brand of Conservatism. More than most of his contemporaries, Salisbury recognized that what happened in Parliament no longer enjoyed the same degree of importance in the country as it had done during Palmerston's time. It is estimated that Salisbury delivered over seventy speeches outside Westminster between 1881 and 1885. These performances, fully reported in the national press, were not made to tiny crowds of party faithful in rural backwaters, but mostly to thousands in the industrial cities of the Midlands, North and Scotland. It was Salisbury, and not Gladstone or Chamberlain, who became the first major politician to fully exploit the techniques of the new democratic politics. 'A long time ago all was done at Westminster. Now all is done, or much more is done in assemblies of electors such as these,' he told an audience in Reading in October 1883. 'It is from you that the direct impulse of political power proceeds.'

In his more cynical moments, Salisbury doubted the value of stump oratory. He once called it a 'refined luxury' which soon 'palled' on those who listened to it. 'As a rule I observe that the places where we win seats are the places where no Tory leader has spoken,' he confessed to Balfour in September 1881. Salisbury retained both a 'fundamental and incurable' disbelief in his own power to influence other people, and an intense 'dislike of manifestations of popular applause'. None the less his services as an orator were always in demand among the party faithful, and despite his natural reticence, Salisbury did make the effort to accept as many invitations as possible to speak. Party bosses in the provinces like Arthur Forwood of Liverpool, Sir William Houldsworth of Manchester and Satchell Hopkins of Birmingham were highly appreciative of Salisbury's active interest in the welfare of growing urban middle-class Conservatism. Unlike Disraeli, Salisbury neither ignored nor neglected the big cities. His visits to local party associations put fresh zeal into the unpaid party workers. Salisbury was quick to appreciate the value of local organization, although this often involved much tiresome activity. 'I assure you I am not living in perpetual strain. It is rather a perpetual little tiny pull. When I die of it my epitaph must be, "Died of writing inane letters to empty-headed Conservative associations,"' he wrote to Lady Manners (9 March 1884). Salisbury was careful to draw a clear-cut distinction between the kind of electoral machine of use to the Conservative cause and that hated Birmingham-style caucus perfected by Joseph Chamberlain. There was never any suggestion from Salisbury that local parties should actually have any direct say in the making of Conservative policy. He explained that the purpose of the caucus was 'to dictate to the men whom they had got into Parliament'. In contrast, Conservative associations should remain firmly involved in the provision of assistance to candidates at election time, keeping the register in order and spreading party principles among the voters. Salisbury told the Birmingham Conservatives: 'When I praise organization do not let me be supposed to have given any kind of backhanded approval to that special production and manufacture which is called the caucus. The difference between them is this, that while you organize to rally the strength of your party to bring yourselves together and induce everyone to put forward his utmost exertions on behalf of the cause, they organize for the purpose of dominating their member when they have selected him and of making him the mere slave and creature of the organization by which he was elected' (30 March 1883).

In the winter of 1883–4 a long and bitter conflict broke out with the young, ambitious Churchill and the National Union against the party organizers at Central Office. During this period, Salisbury refused to modify his firm conviction that the party organization should not be allowed to usurp or challenge the prerogatives of the leadership, something that Churchill and his National Union allies were threatening to do. He did not favour any self-governing centralized body to represent rank-and-file opinion, if this meant a neglect of the value of the local nature of constituency associations. This does not mean that Salisbury was content to see the party merely run, as in the past, by a small aristocratic clique with no interest in what party members felt and believed. Salisbury's aim was to reconcile the traditional structure of party decision-making with the political demands of a society with a broader electoral base. He wanted to graft the new methods of politics onto the traditional concept of centralized constitutional authority. In Salisbury's eyes the biggest danger to representative government lay in attempts to usurp its functions through the spread of the caucus with its idea that Members of Parliament were not elected by the voters, to make decisions in the interests of the whole community as their representative, but were mandated delegates from the party association. Salisbury worried over 'the growth of the power of the wire-puller, centred in the caucus, acting under the direction of a Prime Minister'.

At the same time he recognized that the Conservative party could expect no future if it failed to make electoral inroads into urban England. Salisbury went out of his way in the early 1880s to win the support of the urban middle classes for Conservatism. His task was indirectly helped by the seemingly leftward drift of the Liberal party under the virulence of Chamberlain's radical demands and the Irish land legislation which many staid Liberal moderates regarded as an attack on the rights of property. Unlike Northcote, Salisbury did not worry over the formation of the Primrose League in 1883. In his view such an internal party pressure-group to champion Disraeli's rather romantic ideas of Tory democracy could help to organize 'villa Toryism' through its quixotic flummery and patriotic appeal. While Salisbury gave local Conservative chairmen social prestige and a sense of their own self-importance, his political ideas began to make a favourable impression on many moderate Liberals.

Salisbury knew quite well that mass demonstrations were no substitute for elections in discovering the people's will. The lesson of Gladstone's Midlothian campaign was never lost on that pessimistic observer of the fickle moods of public opinion. Salisbury believed that the Liberals had 'gulled' the voters in 1880 with moral platitudes. 'The logic of elections is merciful and suffers the hollowest claptrap to figure as solid statesmanship. The logic of events is pitiless, and pierces the prettiest windbags without remorse,' he reflected. It was the arrival of the secret ballot which produced 'a regime of surprises'.

Elections were matters of 'mere accident'. Their outcome depended on 'random impulses', that happened to dominate public attention 'at the critical moment'. Salisbury did not draw the conclusion that politics was now merely a question of manipulation or opportunism, of an appeal to a voter's self-interest, but he appreciated that the reasons for political change were often no longer due to politicians themselves. Later, as Foreign Secretary, Salisbury often recalled the moral revulsion against the more sensational examples of Beaconsfield's foreign policy, but he believed that the Liberal triumph of 1880 arose from the harsh facts of the economic depression. It was mainly a vote of no confidence in the Conservative handling of the economy. As Salisbury wrote:

To those who have found breakfast with difficulty, do not know where to find a dinner, intricate questions of politics are a matter of comparatively secondary interest. They were ready to subscribe to any system of politics or ethics of which they were assured that increased wages and steady employment would be the practical result. (April 1881)

Salisbury sought a return to what he called 'the earlier spirit' of British politics that 'modern theory and crotchets' had driven out. The Conservatives should seek to bring the nation together and concentrate its 'united force on objects of national importance' instead of 'splitting it into a bundle of unfriendly and distrustful fragments'. To Salisbury, society's worst evil was 'disintegration'. The country's 'defective political machinery' and 'the public temper of the times' was pushing the party conflict in a destructive direction. Salisbury believed this was manifest, not just in the threats to the integrity of the Empire, but also in the growing class divisions at home. His fears about class war were as strong as ever in the early 1880s. Salisbury was filled with gloom at what he saw as the collapse of 'the common sentiment and mutual sympathies which combine classes in a patriotic state'. He was quite convinced that industrial change itself was undermining the traditional political system. In a passage in his important October 1883 article in the *Quarterly Review* he wrote of the rise of class conflict:

> Freedom greatly tends to the increase of industry and commerce; and as they increase, wealth is accumulated, and inequalities of fortune necessarily become more and more marked. For some not very evident reason, they are borne more impatiently than the inequalities of an aristocratic type, which have almost always originated in conquest. After some time the contest becomes very intense. Vast multitudes have not had the chance of accumulating or have neglected it, and whenever the stream of prosperity slackens for a time, privation overtakes the large crowds who have no reserve, and produces widespread suffering. At such times the comfort or luxury of a comparatively small number becomes irritating and even maddening to look upon; and its sting is sharpened by modern discoveries which have brought home to the knowledge of every class the doings of its neighbour. The organizer of decay, the Radical agitator, soon makes his appearance under these conditions. He easily persuades those who are too wretched, and have thought too carelessly to see through his sophistry, that political arrangements are the causes of differences of wealth, and that by trusting him with political power they will be redressed. He does not tell his dupes how it is possible they should live if industry languishes, or how industry and enterprise can flourish if men conceive their fear, that the harvest of wealth which they and theirs have sown and reaped and stored may perchance be wrested from them by the politician. Then arises that long conflict between possession and non-possession which was the fatal disease of free communities in ancient times, and which threatens so many nations of the present day.

Salisbury wanted the Conservatives to struggle against this trend, even if it meant an uphill battle against inevitable social forces. This did not mean that the Conservatives should set their faces against all change. 'The object of our party is not and ought not to be simply to keep things as they are,' Salisbury argued. The Conservative party must become the guardian of the constitutional state with a broad appeal to what Salisbury described as the 'large intermediate body of many shades' which lay in the political centre and who kept 'the equilibrium of the constitution'.

But it was not just the unpredictable, menacing social impact of industrialism which worried Salisbury in the early 1880s. The flimsy structure of the political system also aroused his gloom. Control of the executive, in his view, was no longer in the hands of either Crown or aristocracy. It lay with 'the democracy'. Parliament was powerless to withstand the 'sudden result of panic' or 'mere impulse' among M.P.s. Unlike the United States, England lacked any checks and balances to thwart the sovereign will of the people. There was an urgent need to bring about a realignment of political forces to combat such disintegration.

Salisbury believed that the rising menace of Radicalism had to force the industrial and landed interest to join forces. The Liberal experience between 1880 and 1885 re-emphasized the impossibility of any permanent political alliance built between aristocratic Whigs, moderate Gladstonians and Chamberlainite Radicals. Surely, as Gladstone was forced by his left wing into the unknown terrain of class politics, Salisbury reasoned, the Whigs would at last realize that they could no longer defend their rights and privileges within the Liberal party? Salisbury believed the Whigs were 'a mere survival, kept alive by tradition' when their real function and significance had passed away. Their stubborn attachment to Gladstone made them nothing but 'the superintendents and distributors of political Danegeld'. Whig concessions to Radical appetites further undermined the social order. Now the Whigs were 'condemned . . . for their many sins in past generations . . . to the political torment of constantly voting against their principles, which they detest, in order to support a ministry they distrust'. The time was not going to be long postponed, Salisbury argued, when the Whig and 'the violent and advanced Radical' could no longer be 'induced to move in the same line by honeyed words and empty platitudes'. Both Lansdowne and the Duke of Argyll resigned from Gladstone's Cabinet in protest at his Irish land policy in the early 1880s, but other Whigs stayed within the Liberal alliance. The predicted split was not going to come about so easily, whatever the tensions and differences in Liberal ranks.

Salisbury maintained that the Conservatives should keep their moral integrity and do nothing that would harm the steady drift of Liberal moderates away from their party. He devoted much of his oratorical skill to demonstrating that it was the Conservatives who stood for moderation and common sense and were the real inheritors of the Palmerstonian tradition. He attacked over-centralization and the bureaucratic state, which he claimed had grown stronger under both parties. This became a common theme of his speeches in the early 1880s. Salisbury poured scorn on 'the great dictator, the inspector – an image made of wood and clothed with red tape, set up by this generation in a temple'. He disliked civil servants, not just because their activities often threatened individual freedom, but because they denied the right of the citizen to practise self-government. Salisbury liked to argue that it was now the Conservatives and not the Liberal party who were the champions of liberty. As he explained in a speech to Liverpool Conservatives: 'In respect to personal freedom the issues of politics are shifting. The Liberal party is less every day the party that supports liberty. Abroad the phenomenon is known very well. The tendency of thought which thinks only of equality and has allowed liberty to slip entirely out of sight has become one of the recognized phenomena of politics, and what is called "authoritative democracy" appears to be the cause which commands the greatest amount of assent from the party of progress. There is more and more a tendency to concentrate authority in a central power, to disregard the claims of individuals, to bring everybody to school under the state, to make all mankind pass their life in one long period of inspection' (14 April 1882).

At Glasgow, Salisbury warned of the dangers to political liberty from the Liberals: 'If you will study history you will find that freedom, when it has been destroyed, has always been destroyed by those who shelter themselves under the cover of its forms and who speak its language with eloquence and vigour. If you have any danger to fear to the free working of our institutions, it is from the growth of power of the wire-puller, centred under the direction of the Prime Minister, master of the Commons, master of the Lords, yielding but apparent and simulated obedience to the orders of the Sovereign' (1 October 1884).

Salisbury condemned the efforts of the Radicals to inflame feeling between the classes. 'If our system of party government works so that it shall be necessary for one party, whenever it is in difficulty, to appeal to any discontent that may exist among any class or in any section of so highly artificial and multifarious an Empire as ours, it is not difficult to see that the Empire will be put to a terrible strain for its very existence.' And he concluded in a speech at Newcastle: 'This lends weakness to our councils, this destroys our national cohesion, this will reduce us from the position of a united nation to a mere bundle of conflicting classes and nationalities, bound together only by the slender tie of a decaying tradition' (11 October 1881).

It was Salisbury's contention that divisive measures harmed the very people they were supposed to help. Radical attacks on property would produce a slump. 'When commerce stagnates, when industry is paralyzed, undoubtedly the rich man will suffer in the long run, but the first to suffer is the working man. Conservatives of all classes know that the whole community from top to bottom thrives on an honest and intelligent application of the laws of property,' Salisbury argued in a speech at Kingston (13 June 1883).

Although Salisbury did not believe in the necessity of a party 'legislative programme', he was not unsympathetic to social reform. 'What we need is legislation which shall be beneficial to the people, which shall be directed to meeting the evils under which they suffer,' he told a meeting in Bermondsey (30 May 1883). Its aim should be to 'reduce to as small a degree as possible that dangerous antagonism of classes, the desire of which constitutes the modern Radical'. Salisbury did not even raise doctrinal objections to legislation, which appeared to infringe property rights, if it was proved to be necessary. He criticised the dogmatic Earl of Wemyss over the 1883 Agricultural Holdings (England) Bill: 'No doubt, it would be a very fine thing if we could always legislate on principle, but if we refuse to pass this Bill, the farmers of England, never having had the advantage of experiencing what its powers are like, will think it to have some extreme merit, and that we are the persons who have taken its benefits from them. On the other hand, if we pass the Bill, they will have such experience of the results of interference with freedom of contract that they will not be apt to come to this House to ask for further measures of the same kind. That is the mode of action we shall have to adopt in much of our legislation: if people ask for an undesirable thing, if it is very bad and very dangerous, refuse it: but if not, give it them, in order that they might learn by experience not to ask for the same thing again' (7 August 1883).

Salisbury's main interest in social questions lay with working-class housing. He spoke out eloquently over the human squalor of the cities. Unlike the moralistic temperance fanatics, Salisbury did not believe the evil of drink stemmed from individual human failure, but from the social conditions in which people were expected to live. 'Constant efforts are made by our legislators to deal with the great plague of intemperance which is the moral scourge of the present generation,' he maintained. 'But how are we to hope that men will be kept out of the public house, when the home presents such horrible, loathsome features?' Poor housing, in Salisbury's opinion, also lay at the roots of the education problem. 'We pay great

attention to the education of the people; but how are we to hope
that popular education will flourish, when children after the education is over are dismissed to their homes where they cannot undertake
any study and where anything like literary interest is impossible,
owing to the great mental and physical depression of mind and body
under which they exist?'

Salisbury did not believe that the state should shirk its responsibilities to alleviate social evil. 'Freedom of contract is not on a level
with the Ten Commandments. One of the most elementary principles
of English law is that the law will not sanction contracts contrary to
morality or the interests of trade,' he argued (7 August 1883). In a
debate on the Water Company Bill in March 1885 Salisbury even
expressed the opinion that Parliament must not tolerate any sanitation system which was 'injurious to the health of the population',
because of any bargain struck by a previous Parliament with the
private water companies. He suggested that there were 'no absolute
rules or principles in politics'. In his opinion 'material and moral
laws ought to prevent the state from being indifferent to the social
condition of the people'.

The shrill *laissez-faire* extremism of the Liberty and Property
Defence League made no appeal to Salisbury. It was obvious to him
that the plight of London's poor did not stem from any personal or
moral failure, but from the massive redevelopment of the capital's
centre. The homes of thousands of people had been swept away to
build viaducts and law courts as well as railways. The dispossessed
were compelled to find new homes in a tight property market.
Salisbury explained the problem in a *National Review* article in
November 1883:

As competition becomes closer, the sufferings of the poor from bad
housing become very severe. Thousands of families have only a single
room to dwell in, where they sleep and eat, multiply and die. For this
miserable lodging they pay a price ranging from 2s. to 5s. a week – a
larger rent, on the whole, than the agricultural labourer pays for a cottage
and a garden in the country. It is difficult to exaggerate the misery which
such conditions of life must cause, or the impulse which they must give
to vice. The depression of body and mind which they create is an almost
insuperable obstacle to the action of any elevating and refining agencies.

In Salisbury's opinion there were two alternative ways of tackling
the evil. High flat blocks could be built and let out in the city at
modest rents, which the poor tenant could manage to pay; or the
poor must be encouraged to move out and live in the suburbs with
the establishment of a cheap subsidized public transport system.

Salisbury blamed the low wages paid by employers for the condition of the poor. He advocated that public enterprises such as the Post Office, the Police and the Customs and Excise Board might build homes for their workers at a fair rent and set an example. In February 1884 Salisbury called for the creation of a royal commission to investigate working-class housing. He made a powerful plea in the Lords: 'We must never forget that there is a moral as well as a material contagion which exists by virtue of the moral and material laws under which we live and which forbid us to be indifferent, even as a matter of interest, to the well-being in every respect of all classes who form a part of the community. Whatever the political constitution of the state may be, the foundation of all its prosperity and welfare must be that the mass of the people shall be honest and manly and shall have common sense. How are we to expect that these conditions will exist among people subjected to the frightful influences which the present overcrowding of our poor produce?'

In the event, a royal commission was established to look at the problem under the chairmanship of the radical, Charles Dilke. Salisbury agreed to become a member. When the commission eventually presented its findings in April 1885, he added a short note of personal reservation on London's particular difficulties. It was Salisbury's belief that the law should provide the local authorities with the necessary power, if a landlord failed to enforce sanitary laws. While the economic laws of supply and demand could be expected to solve overcrowding outside London, this was just not possible in the capital because of the excessive cost of land for building. The Peabody Trust were able to build flats for the working classes, because they managed to purchase sites from the Metropolitan Board of Works at an artificially cheap price, but even so the Trust could not meet the wants of most of London's poor. Although Salisbury disapproved of the interference of the state in the provision of housing, he suggested that derelict prison sites in London should be used for building homes for the poor.

During the early 1880s there was a groundswell of support among the Conservative rank and file for some steps to combat the economic depression. This usually took the form of a vague questioning of the truths of Free Trade. Some Conservatives called for a return of protectionism to help hard-pressed agriculture and vulnerable industries like Sheffield steel and Lancashire cotton. They called their cause 'Fair Trade'. Salisbury gave such opinions little encouragement. He did not believe that it was practical politics to advocate a return to the practices of the early nineteenth century. On the other hand,

D

Salisbury disliked Free Trade fanaticism. He believed that it was obvious that the original hopes of the Manchester School were no longer being fulfilled. 'When free trade was adopted, we hoped that free trade would spread through the world, but we are almost the only converts after nearly half-a-century has passed,' Salisbury pointed out (21 October 1884 at Dumfries). 'Employment is becoming scarcer, wages are becoming smaller and the distress of the population is becoming larger and the blessings of free trade, which ought to have been enormous, have been robbed of half their value owing to the precipitate and improvident manner in which the position of this country as regards other countries was sacrificed.' Conservatives were divided on the Fair Trade issue, but party leaders found common ground in calling for a royal commission to investigate the causes of the economic depression. Salisbury was self-defensive. He reassured sceptics that he sought no action 'inconsistent with sound Free Trade'. The sugar export bounties enjoyed by Austrian and French manufacturers aroused considerable annoyance, but Salisbury realized that any hasty action towards even reciprocity could threaten Britain's cheap-food policy. His main answer to the depression was to call for the return of a government which could win the confidence of capital and labour. He argued that:

Industry cannot flow unless capital is confident, and capital will not be confident as long as it fears that Parliament may meddle with it and walk off with its profits. There is no question of this, that of recent years, Parliament has been singularly meddlesome. I do not say that it is from a bad motive – on the contrary, usually the motive has been philanthropy.

Until the summer of 1884 Salisbury held an uneasy sway as one of the party leaders. It was the Reform Bill crisis which enabled him to establish an unquestioned authority. Salisbury had not retained his old antagonism to the principle of franchise extension. The prospect of two million more voters coming onto the electoral register no longer filled him with alarm. He thought the agricultural labourers were 'dull, unenlightened, slow to receive new impressions, conservative in the sense of not being disposed to change their habitual habits and customs'. A further dose of reform might be the prelude to the long-promised Radical assault on the Church of England and the landed classes, but to Salisbury the question was no longer fundamental. The difference of opinion with the Liberals was now over the manner in which political power could be 'distributed so that all classes might be respected, that a true mirror of the actual numerical condition of opinions in the country might be produced

within the walls of the House of Commons'. Gladstone introduced his
bill in the Commons on 28 February 1884. It was simply an enfran-
chisement measure. A redistribution of constituencies was promised
for the next session. From the start, Salisbury declared his total
opposition to the Franchise Bill. He believed it meant rural opinion
would be swamped by the urban interests. The measure failed to give
'adequate representation' to the middle classes.

Salisbury demanded an immediate general election. The Liberal
Cabinet's decision to separate the franchise from the redistribution
issue provided an astute common cause on which the divided Conservatives could fight. While Salisbury argued that Conservative
resistance to the bill was due to 'parliamentary tactics' and not to
'great conscientious scruples' or 'splendid principles', the government refused to believe him. Gladstone was convinced that no more
than a handful of urban Conservatives supported an extension of the
franchise. On 9 July the Lords threw out the bill, but by a majority
of only fifty-nine. Cross-bench peers and the bishops supported the
government. Once more, moderate Conservative leaders sought a
compromise. But Salisbury refused to bow to the backroom pressures
that built up over the summer. Rumours of a threat to his leadership
did not worry him. He confessed to Canon MacColl: 'To be leader
of a great party – still more to be leader of anything resembling a
coalition – requires a large measure of the gifts of pliancy and optimism and I, unfortunately, am very poorly endowed in either respect.
English politics keep hold of those who are in them because its
framework of modern life is so tight that men find it hard to change
their pursuits. But to those who know English politics well they are
not attractive. Their highest rewards confer no real power. And they
fill up life with incessant labour.'

A Liberal agitation against the House of Lords failed to alarm him.
'Such stuff as frightens peers and nothing more,' he jibed. Neither
diligent members of the Queen's Household like Sir Henry Ponsonby,
nor moderate Liberals like Hartington could make Salisbury change
his mind about compromise. He continued to insist that the increased
franchise proposal and seat redistribution should reach the statute
book at the same time. The Conservative leader was still trying to
goad Gladstone into dissolving Parliament. In his view, if the Lords
decided to surrender to street demonstrations, this would encourage
the Radicals to apply the same methods in the future over other
controversial issues. Salisbury did not let the case of the Upper
House fail by default. He defended the peers, arguing that it was
their business 'to prevent irregular advance and too rapid advance'.

At the same time, Salisbury did his best to counter the widespread but wrong assumption that he was opposed in principle to any increase in the size of the electorate. In an article in the *National Review* he reckoned that of the 266 M.P.s in seats representing under 5,000 voters, no fewer than 183 of them were Liberal and only eighty-three Conservative. Salisbury claimed that he was ready to reduce the number of rural constituencies and increase the representation of the big cities.

Through the summer Salisbury kept clear of 'attempts at compromises, bridges, open doors and the rest'. 'I think the government are in a hole. This is not our business to pull them out,' he argued. Salisbury feared the appearance of 'some cunning half measure' which surrendered 'everything', but might appear 'to the obtuser lords to save their dignity'. When Parliament reassembled for a special session in October 1884, his intransigent attitude was unchanged. By the autumn it was no longer just a reform crisis. Salisbury believed that the future independent rights of the Lords were at stake. He wrote to Ponsonby:

Our constitutional law is built up of precedents. If the House of Lords abandons a resolution, under threats, because a majority of the government object, it will by that very act become constitutional law that the House of Lords is bound to submit to a vote of the House of Commons. From that moment the Lords will be absolutely powerless and unchecked power will have passed away to the Commons. (28 October)

However by mid-November many Conservatives were no longer willing to follow Salisbury into the last ditch. The ice began to crack beneath his feet. Salisbury finally accepted Gladstone's offer of a cross-bench conference to settle the reform issue. On 19 November Northcote joined Salisbury for a first session at Downing Street. By that stage, it was quite clear who counted in the Conservative leadership. Salisbury 'took the whole matter out of the hands of Northcote, who sat by him on the sofa like a chicken protected by the wings of the mother hen', Gladstone noted in his diary.

Salisbury was the main unacknowledged architect of the 1884 reform settlement. To Radical astonishment, it brought a sweeping change in the British electoral system. Chamberlain described it as 'a revolution more important and more far-reaching than any previously accomplished in English history'. Many Conservatives feared that Salisbury had taken a far more perilous leap into the dark than Disraeli's in 1867. Chaplin complained that the secret talks put a rope round the party's neck which was being 'pulled and tugged' by Salisbury. Lord George Hamilton warned Salisbury that there

was 'a state of great discontent and apprehension' among the rank
and file at the settlement.

Gladstone was amazed at Salisbury's lack of respect for tradition.
'It is my singular fate to love the antiquities of our constitution
much more even than the average Tory of the present day,' he
confessed to Granville. Salisbury's willingness to sacrifice all boroughs
of up to 20,000 population raised Liberal eyebrows. It was also
agreed not to reduce the Irish representation from one hundred.
Neither the grouping of seats nor minority representation found
favour. Salisbury was a champion of the single-member constituency.
Those would provide 'the only hope' for minorities. The social
divisions, reflected in housing patterns in the cities, provided a chance
for the Conservatives to win seats in middle-class suburbia.

Salisbury made no real effort to conciliate his colleagues. Their
faintheartedness had stopped him from forcing a general election,
so he was quite ready to ignore their later protests. Not that Salisbury's behaviour was dictated by party pique. He did not want to
preside over the decimation of the Conservatives at the next polls.
The settlement might upset the Party's right wing, but Salisbury's
calculations were a far shrewder appreciation of the political future
than the Radicals' or many Conservatives'. The virtual end of the
two-member constituency drove a wedge between the Whig and the
Radical in the Liberal camp. Local Liberal associations could no
longer present a balanced ticket to the electorate. The separation of
town and country by Lambert's boundary commission preserved a
rural domination for the Tory squires. But in the winter of 1884–5
there was a considerable body of opinion which predicted the demise
of the Conservatives. 'They may periodically return to office, but
they will have place not power. If I was a Tory I would poison
Salisbury's rum and water,' Chamberlain enthused. 'If he had been
in the pay of the caucus what more could he have done to destroy
his party and give up everything for which it has hitherto existed?'
Whatever his doubts, Salisbury harboured no regrets at what he had
done. He explained to Lord George Hamilton, 'I am sorry for the
feelings of the Irish landowners and other Conservatives. I have very
little comfort to offer them. If I had been allowed to make a crisis of
the Arrears Bill we might have put off this trouble for several years.
But given the Franchise Bill there was nothing to do for them.'

The Conservatives returned to Westminster in a restless mood in
February 1885, but the fall of Khartoum to the Mahdi and the
murder of General Gordon shook the government and rallied the
Opposition. The Russian seizure of Penjdeh in Afghanistan brought

Britain into confrontation with Russia in Central Asia. There was also tension with France and Germany. Salisbury doubted whether the government could carry on for much longer, but he disliked the idea of taking office with such a legacy to inherit. However Churchill and other party rebels in the Commons were determined to force a showdown with the Liberals. The Cabinet was bitterly divided on every major issue. On 8 May the government suffered an unexpected defeat on the increase in the beer tax in the Budget by a majority of twelve. Gladstone decided to resign at once. Much to his annoyance, Salisbury was asked by the Queen to try to form a minority government. By the spring of 1885 his succession to the overall party leadership was unquestioned. During the Reform Bill crisis and the wrangle over the National Union, Salisbury had established a solid authority over the party rank and file. But the very worst had now happened. Salisbury deplored governments which ruled with a minority support in the Commons, because they were vulnerable to pressure. His bitter memories of 1867 had not yet died away.

I never admired the political
transformation scenes of 1829, 1846, 1867;
and I certainly do not wish
to be the chief agent in adding a fourth
to the history of the Tory party.
Salisbury to Lord Bath, 27 December 1885

6

BATTLE
FOR THE UNION
June 1885–January 1887

Salisbury had no wish to become Prime Minister in June 1885. On his arrival in Balmoral, after the overnight train journey from London in a third-class compartment to avoid attention, he urged the Queen to make Gladstone stay on in office. It was only when the Liberal leader telegraphed back refusing to do so that Salisbury realized he faced no other alternative but to try to form a government. The Queen's entreaties to the Conservative leader were powerful and persuasive. The Liberal legacy of unfinished business was guaranteed to test the will of any new government. Abroad, England stood in isolation. Danger of war between Russia and England had not yet died away. The arbitration talks over the Afghan border dispute were at a sensitive stage. England's influence at Constantinople had become almost non-existent. Relations had been strained with France ever since the British occupation of Egypt in 1882. Bismarck appeared to be supporting the French and Austria-Hungary had reached an understanding with Russia in the Balkans. There appeared to be a real danger that the 'Concert of Europe' had indeed emerged, but as a hostile coalition against England. As Lady Gwendolen commented, 'Salisbury found himself the inheritor of a *tabula rasa* in continental friendships.'

At the same time, the Mahdi stood triumphant in the Sudan. There were fears in Cairo that he might march down the Nile valley and attack Egypt. At home, Ireland continued to smoulder. Yet the Conservatives would have enormous difficulty in using coercive means to root out Irish rural terrorism any longer. The Budget and the service estimates still required Parliament's approval. But Salisbury's obvious reluctance to become Prime Minister derived not merely from the mammoth problems on the Cabinet agenda. Nor was it due to a natural diffidence and regret that Northcote had been passed over for the post. His hesitation was due to the unique political position which faced the Conservatives in the summer of 1885. Without any majority in the Commons, the government could not dissolve Parliament before the autumn. This was because the passing of the Seats Bill had scrapped the old constituency boundaries and the new electoral system would not be finished until November at the earliest. The party leaders wrangled for a fortnight before Gladstone gave an assurance that the Liberals would not try to impede the Executive's vital work. Salisbury and his Cabinet took their seals of office on 24 June.

Salisbury always disliked the task of picking his Cabinet and handing out the patronage. Those necessary chores used to leave him 'sore all over'. His task in June 1885 was particularly odious. Cranbrook noted in his diary that Salisbury was 'weary of self-seekers, beggars, impracticables'. Lord Randolph Churchill's refusal to accept the Secretaryship for India, unless Northcote ceased to be head of the parliamentary party, annoyed Salisbury. It was, however, on the advice of moderate Conservatives like Smith, Manners and Gibson that Salisbury decided to give Northcote an earldom and a sinecure post in the Cabinet as First Lord of the Treasury. Hicks Beach became Chancellor of the Exchequer and Leader of the House, while Churchill entered the Cabinet as Secretary for India. Salisbury sent his old political associate, Carnarvon, out to Ireland as Viceroy. He knew that Carnarvon took a conciliatory attitude to the Irish problem and enjoyed a reputation as an imperial federationist.

The Cabinet realized that it was impossible to renew the Irish Crimes Act, if the government hoped to survive the summer. Salisbury was advised by his Irish experts that the government could drop coercion without any adverse effects. The new policy of conciliation towards Ireland was most apparent in Carnarvon's activities as Viceroy. Salisbury declared that it was possible to combine 'good feeling to England' and 'good government to Ireland'. The Liberals, not unnaturally, suspected that Salisbury had reached some kind of understanding with Parnell and his party. This was not entirely true. The Cabinet was seriously divided over its attitude to Parnell's call for an inquiry into the capital sentences passed during the previous administration on the murderers of a family at Maamtrasna. Salisbury was irritated by the behaviour of Hicks Beach, Churchill and Gorst, who publicly repudiated Earl Spencer's regime and sympathized with the Irish leader's demand. 'If we hold together till the prorogation, it is as much as we can do,' Salisbury confessed to the Queen (19 July). Salisbury was compelled to disassociate himself from the opinions of his colleagues in the Commons. To the Queen's relief he spoke in defence of the administration of justice in Ireland under Liberal rule. The Cabinet was also divided on whether to support Carnarvon's effort in saving the Munster Bank from financial collapse. 'The hopelessness of managing England and Ireland together was never brought into such startling relief. The old crucial question is still there,' Salisbury wrote to the Irish Viceroy (22 July). 'How is England to be made to swallow measures that Irish authorities consider necessary for Ireland?'

Salisbury's government tried to prove their good faith through legislation. A valuable Irish land-purchase measure was introduced by Ashbourne in the Lords. This provided a £5 million Treasury grant so that tenants could borrow the full purchase price of their holdings, to be repaid over forty-nine years. The Act was a modest start for future Unionist land policy. Salisbury warned that the measure should not be seen as 'final and complete' or as a 'panacea', but 'a further experiment on the path which many have travelled'. An Irish Labourer's Bill was also rushed through in the short session, despite the protests of Ulster members. And Churchill piloted an Irish Educational Endowments Bill through Parliament to please the Roman Catholic community. Carnarvon even managed to persuade the Treasury to provide financial support for Irish technical education.

But at no stage during the summer of 1885 did Salisbury give the impression that he was willing to settle the Irish question on Parnell's terms. It is true that the Prime Minister sanctioned Carnarvon's own suggestion that, as Viceroy, he should meet the Irish leader secretly and find out what Parnell really wanted and what he was ready to settle for. Yet Salisbury's blessing for this encounter was mainly due to his understanding that Ashbourne, the Irish Lord Chancellor, would also attend as a third party. However, it was Carnarvon alone who met Parnell on 1 August in the empty house in Mayfair. Salisbury had warned Carnarvon to make no commitments of any kind, and the Viceroy agreed not to do so. Nevertheless, Parnell came away with the misguided impression that the Conservatives would be willing to go a long way to meet his demand for Irish Home Rule. Carnarvon reported back to Salisbury at Hatfield immediately after the Mayfair meeting. The Prime Minister decided not to inform either the Queen or the Cabinet about the matter. He was alarmed to discover that Ashbourne had not attended the meeting with Parnell. During the bitter debate in 1886 over Home Rule, Salisbury was accused of deception. He never made much effort to defend himself from the charges, which became common coinage in Irish Nationalist and Radical circles. Yet as Lady Gwendolen noted, 'his curt denial of disloyalty, backed up by no argument or explanation or disclosure of corroborative circumstance, had indeed more the quality of a challenge than a defence. But it was accepted by his party without question or hesitation, and, so far as has ever appeared, with unanimity.' It was Churchill and Carnarvon, not Salisbury, who aroused suspicions among many Conservatives as the main figures in the party, who were ready to 'ditch' the Liberals by contemplating a measure of internal self-government for Ireland that would satisfy Parnell.

During the remaining weeks of the 1885 Parliament Salisbury and his Cabinet piloted a number of measures, left outstanding, onto the statute book. In doing so, the Conservatives revealed that they were willing to legislate in a moderate and responsible way. The Prime Minister did not relish all the bills which his government passed. He expressed deep reservations in the Lords on the measure ending the disenfranchisement of voters who had received medical relief. Salisbury doubted whether it was 'a fit subject for a moribund Parliament' to determine. Although the immediate effects of the bill would 'not be injurious', he confessed that ultimately it might give cause for 'some little anxiety'. Nevertheless Salisbury did not stop its passage.

In contrast, he raised no objection to the Housing of the Working Classes Bill. Salisbury spoke up in the Lords in its defence. This measure strengthened the powers of local authorities in dealing with bad sanitation and overcrowding. It also allowed old London prisons to be sold to the Metropolitan Board of Works at below market prices. These sites were to be let for the purpose of building working-class houses on them. *The Times* suggested that this was 'an appreciable step in the direction of State Socialism' (17 July).

Salisbury's government won a quick reputation for moderate reform. The Conservatives showed that they could govern, but during the summer of 1885 there was a sense of drift in government counsels. The main trouble was that Salisbury was unable to give his full attention to internal problems. He was Foreign Secretary as well as Prime Minister. During the five months in the period before the general election he was immersed in the complexities of international diplomacy. Salisbury wanted to escape from dangerous isolation with an overture to Germany. On 2 July he wrote to Bismarck in friendly terms, asking for the Chancellor's cooperation in the raising of an Egyptian loan. The Chancellor replied in courteous terms and he agreed to help promote the loan. On a visit to Germany Sir Philip Currie from the Foreign Office met Bismarck at Friedrichsruhe as Salisbury's emissary. It was there that the Chancellor was asked to mediate with Russia over the issue of the Zulifcar pass in return for 'laying the foundations of a closer and more intimate alliance between the two countries'. Bismarck was unforthcoming. Nevertheless, Salisbury proceeded to demonstrate that his goodwill towards Germany was not just rhetorical and he mediated on Bismarck's behalf in Germany's dispute with Spain over the Caroline Islands. The Prime Minister also worked for a settlement of the Zanzibar question, that would placate Bismarck. He was convinced that his conciliatory attitude would help to persuade the German Chancellor to sympathize with the British attitude to Russia, Turkey and Egypt. 'He is rather a Jew,' Salisbury confessed to Iddesleigh (24 August 1885) of Bismarck. 'On the whole I have as yet got my money's worth.'

At the end of August, the Russians, after weeks of futile wrangling, accepted the English position over Zulifcar and on 7 September the Anglo-Russian protocol was signed. This brought an end to the Afghan border dispute. In Egypt, Salisbury performed a holding operation. He did not share the opinion of the jingoists that the government should announce its permanent stay at the mouth of the Nile. On the other hand, Salisbury could not conceive evacuation from Egypt unless that country was not only solvent, but enjoying a settled government as well. In August 1885 he was even envisaging an eventual reconquest of the Sudan from the Mahdi, which he admitted was 'wholly out of the reach' because of 'present penury'. Salisbury sent Sir Henry Drummond Wolff out to Constantinople with the aim of winning the Sultan's active collaboration in a defence of the Egyptian frontier against Dervish attacks. Salisbury's aim was to leave Egypt, provided that any treaty which brought this about acknowledged England's right of reoccupation if the country lapsed into chaos. Wolff's mission came to nothing, but it demonstrated to the other European powers that England was not attempting to override Turkey's treaty rights. Salisbury praised his emissary for turning the Egyptian issue 'from an international one into an Anglo-Turkish one'.

Salisbury's shrewd handling of foreign affairs was put to a severe test during the autumn of 1885, with the outbreak of a revolt in Eastern Roumelia. A group of army officers deposed the Turkish governor of the province and invited Prince Alexander of Battenburg, the Bulgarian monarch, to join their cause. On 20 September the Prince proclaimed the union of the two Bulgarias. Salisbury was on holiday in his villa at Puys when the crisis broke in the Balkans. He immediately called on the Austrian, German and Italian governments to join him in a protest against this clear breach of the Congress of Berlin. Both Germany and Austria-Hungary made it clear that they had no wish to do any such thing. Bismarck feared that the Bulgarian crisis might wreck the Three Emperors alliance, which had been formed in 1881. The German Chancellor tried to make the Tsar disavow Prince Alexander's action. He even suggested that England should give the Sultan moral support with a naval demonstration. Salisbury decided that the only sensible outcome was an acceptance of a 'personal union' between Bulgaria and Eastern Roumelia which left the systems of government intact in both countries. This was agreed to by Germany and Austria-Hungary. In his Newport speech on 7 October Salisbury claimed that his attitude to the crisis was shaped by a desire 'to cherish and foster strong self-sustaining nationalities'. Privately, Salisbury regretted the disruption of the Berlin settlement. 'I have not much hope myself that a big Bulgaria will be avoided. It is an evil, and a danger to Turkey. But there seems nowhere the will to stop it,' he wrote to the English ambassador in Constantinople, Sir William White (24 September).

The revolt in Eastern Roumelia, however, could not be so easily contained. Serbia and Greece now claimed compensation at Turkey's expense in Macedonia. Salisbury made it clear that England would not support any Turkish or Russian attempt to crush Prince Alexander's action. He realized that the 'big' Bulgaria was unlikely to be a Russian satellite. 'I do not imagine that we should dare to assist or even encourage the Turk to recover his province on the eve of a general election,' he wrote to Churchill (21 September). 'And yet if we leave him in the lurch what worthless allies we shall appear to him.' All the same, Salisbury's new policy was an attempt to meet an old objective. Prince Alexander's Bulgaria was to be a protective buffer for Turkey against Russian intrigue, a way of keeping Russia out of Constantinople.

When the big powers met in conference on 7 November at Constantinople to discuss the Eastern Roumelian situation, Salisbury was alone in supporting the idea of 'a personal union'. Russia with the support of the Triple Alliance powers demanded a return to the *status quo*. The Prime Minister was adamant in his opposition to 'sanctioning a policy of armed repression', despite White's demand for compromise. Salisbury told his ambassador to play for time and 'oppose any hasty action or tendency to hurry on matters' (6 November). The conference broke up in deadlock on 25 November. Nine days earlier Serbia had declared war on Bulgaria and marched across her frontier. Within a week Prince Alexander won a stunning victory at Slivnitza. This victory brought a change of mind among the European powers. Salisbury's firmness had been vindicated. In the space of six months he had transformed England's diplomatic position in Europe.

While Salisbury was attempting to break out of 'dangerous isolation' and keep his worried Cabinet together over Ireland, the election campaign began to gather pace through the summer. The main conflict that appeared to be developing was not between the two main parties, but within the divided ranks of Gladstonian Liberalism. Chamberlain was intent on pushing the party further to the left, while Hartington fought a rearguard action to prevent it. Gladstone stood in the middle, trying to hold his disgruntled supporters together around a common policy. Many Conservatives were quite content to sit back on the sidelines and enjoy the spectacle of a damaging public quarrel in the Liberal party. Moreover the Tory cause was helped by Chamberlain's threatening attacks on the landed interest, which were alarming stolid middle-class voters. As long as the Conservatives proved to be moderate and united in government, the disaffected moderate ex-Liberals could be expected to flock into the government camp. However, not all Conservatives were willing to accept do-nothing tactics. Salisbury was reluctant to make a major policy declaration, but the pressure on him to do so became too strong.

With the Cabinet's unanimous approval, he seized the opportunity of his speech to the National Union conference at Newport on 7 October to unveil the Conservative proposals for the future. This 'programme' was to become the main point of reference for Conservative domestic policy over the next seven years. Newport helped to destroy the myth that the Conservatives under Salisbury were a reactionary political force out of touch with the times. 'Clever, comprehensive, and free from Tory prejudices and apprehension,' Edward Hamilton summarized Salisbury's 'counter-blast'. 'He picks out of Mr Gladstone's political pudding the best plums.'

Local government reform was the main plank in Salisbury's platform. He argued that popularly elected county authorities were quite consistent with the Conservative aim of reducing the over-centralized power of the state. Salisbury expressed a willingness to provide the new bodies with substantial powers, which were to be devolved from the Local Government Board. Even a highly contentious issue like the Sunday closing of public houses was to be left to the discretion of the proposed councils, as well as the thorny matter of the licensing of the pubs. Salisbury believed that the need to pay out 'fair compensation' would deter extremist temperance fanatics from confiscating the livelihood of publicans. The Conservative leader also called for the reform of the rating system so that people could 'pay according to their ability' for the upkeep of their local government. He advocated a reform of the land laws to make land cheaper and more easily available for sale. Salisbury supported the right of the Church of England to sell off property 'to the class of agricultural labourers desiring to become small farmers'.

Although he shrank from support for the right of all children to receive a free state education, he expressed the hope that children would be educated in the Christian faith and not in that 'lifeless, boiled down, mechanical, unreal religious teaching prevalent in Board Schools'. On Ireland, Salisbury trod a diplomatic path. He warned that one of the weaknesses of local government was that councils were 'more exposed to the temptation' and enjoyed 'more of the facility, for enabling a majority to be unjust to the minority'. Salisbury maintained that the Conservatives regarded the integrity of the Empire 'as a matter more important than almost any other political consideration'. He added that the party 'could not regard with favour any proposal which directly or indirectly menaced that which is the condition of England's position among the nations of the world'. Salisbury ruled out any prospect that the idea of an Imperial Federation might provide 'a satisfactory solution' for the Irish problem. His references to Ireland in the Newport speech were studiously vague. They did not add to Carnarvon's difficulties, nor did they deflect Parnell from his campaign against the Liberals. Yet Salisbury had no intention of accepting Home Rule. He revealed his thoughts in a letter to the Manchester Conservative, H.H.Howorth, on 10 September: 'The mere extension to Ireland, in a more or less modified form, of such arrangements for local self-government as are proposed for England, would not I fancy satisfy the demands of those who seem to have the allegiance of Irishmen in their pockets and would not therefore staunch the steady flow of discontent which is reducing the strength of Ireland and of England also. Whatever happens, I do not believe that the mass of the Tory party will ever consent to any measures savouring of separation.'

Salisbury delivered a number of speeches in the election campaign which re-emphasized the proposals sketched out at Newport. He was sceptical of the effects of a complete freedom in the land market. 'If you take up the baulks of your sea walls that confine your beach, the sea beach flies to the side towards which the prevalent current of the channel drives it. The same is true of land,' he told a meeting in Brighton (15 October). 'Remove every obstacle, destroy every restriction, make land transfer cheap, forbid any deeds that will prevent free transfers of land, the only result will be that the land will flow with greater and greater volume towards that direction to which it naturally tends.' Chamberlain's land plans would bring 'a want of confidence', Salisbury claimed. 'What is the great interest of the working man?' he questioned. 'Wages. Nothing you can offer him is equal in his mind to wages sufficient in amount and work constantly furnished. But that provision of work, and that flow of wages will only exist when confidence exists, where the capitalist is sure of being repaid.' Salisbury made the 'Church in danger' cry one of the major themes of the Conservative campaign, when it was discovered that the Liberation Society had pledged two thirds of Liberal candidates in England and Wales and four fifths in Scotland to Disestablishment. 'A wave of infidelity sweeping over the land' was to Salisbury 'the great issue of modern civilization'.

In a speech in South London, Salisbury expressed his faith in 'real Free Trade' but he made it clear that he did not worship the doctrine as 'a sacred dogma'. 'Legitimate acts of self-defence' were necessary to encourage other countries not to hinder British trade. Salisbury went on to speak of the differing attitudes to industry displayed by the Tory and the Radical: 'The Conservative desire is to manage affairs, so to remove all restrictions, so to give the necessary stimulus to industry, that you shall advance forward and conquer new realms of industry yet uninvaded – that you shall obtain the entry to markets which are now closed to you giving the opportunity of finding in the wealth which that industry will create ample satisfaction of all our wants. The Conservative points the workman forward to obtain wealth which is yet uncreated. The Radical turns his eye backward, does not help him and does not tell him to create new sources of wealth but says that the wealth which has been already obtained is badly divided, that some have got something and many have got nothing at all, and that the real remedy is to turn back and fight among yourselves for the wealth which has been already obtained.'

The Whig refusal to break with the Liberal party brought a typical Salisburian rebuke. 'I am afraid that the predatory Radical, who is the dominant animal in the Liberal menagerie, owes it entirely to the Whigs if he is able to provide some fragments of sheep's clothing to hide the familiar lineaments of his species.'

Ireland did not come to the foreground in the election but Salisbury did not entirely ignore it. As he explained at the Lord Mayor's Banquet (9 November): 'The traditions of our party are known. The integrity of the Empire is more precious to us than any possession that we can have. We are bound by motives not only of expediency, not only of legal principle, but by motives of honour, to protect the minority, if such exist, who have fallen into unpopularity and danger because they have followed or been the instruments of the policy England has deliberately elected to pursue. Within these lines any English government is bound to do all that it possibly can to give prosperity, contentment and happiness to the Irish people.'

Salisbury believed that British politics was on the edge of a great convulsion. He wanted to revive his old aim of a concentration of the established parties in the defence of order against the dangers of English radicalism and Irish nationalism. Salisbury concluded his Mansion House address: 'Compared with the other nations of the globe we have a very small territory with a weak military force – we have a great Empire with means of maintaining it apparently far inferior to the means of its neighbours, for they have armed forces at their disposal and in those countries all power is placed at the disposal of the central authority and the only way you can meet these nations is by this talisman – the unity of the whole people by whom these islands are inhabited. It is because you are a united people, because apart from all the questions which have divided us into parties and have constituted our party divisions – there has been a deep unity which has over-borne and overridden every trial, that you have been able to meet these nations. If our divisions shall ever separate us so that the malignity of classes shall put each with the other in such conflict that they will prefer party to their country, then the era of your preponderance and power in the world will have passed away never to return.'

On 21 November Parnell issued a manifesto in which he called on the Irish voters in Britain not to vote Liberal. In the election the cities of England moved against Gladstone and the Conservatives recorded impressive gains there. The Liberal party was saved from defeat by victory in the counties where many agricultural labourers showed their support for Chamberlain's programme of 'three acres and a cow'. The Liberals returned to Westminster with a Commons majority of eighty-four seats over the Conservative party, with 334 M.P.s to 250. The Conservative share of the vote totalled 47·3 per cent. The balance of power was held by the Irish Nationalists, who returned with eighty-six M.P.s.

Lord Randolph Churchill wanted Salisbury to make an immediate overture to the moderate Liberals. He urged the Prime Minister to draw up a bold legislative package that would appeal to them. Salisbury did not think the moment was ripe for such a departure. 'The Whigs hate me as much as they hate you. The time for a coalition has not come yet – nor will, so long as the Grand Old Man is to the fore,' he wrote to Churchill on 30 November. While he was willing to accept 'the extra tinge of Liberalism' to the government's policy that would be essential in any future political bargaining, Salisbury remained cautious. 'If we are too free with our cash now, we shall have no money to go to market with, when the market is open,' he warned Churchill.

On 16 December an anonymous communiqué in some national newspapers transformed the political situation. It was disclosed that Gladstone was proposing to repeal the Act of Union with Ireland. The Liberal leader kept silent, although it was his son Herbert who was responsible for the leak. Gladstone wanted Salisbury to grasp the Home Rule nettle and settle the Irish problem through bipartisan agreement on the lines of the 1884 Reform accord. On 21 December Gladstone met Balfour at a weekend party at Eaton Hall and suggested that if Salisbury was willing to grasp the issue, he could count on Liberal support for doing so. The Prime Minister was 'sickened' by what he regarded as Gladstone's 'hypocrisy'. Salisbury wanted to escape from office as soon as possible and force Gladstone to reveal his plans for Ireland. 'All my relations who have got seats look like men who have just finished a term of six month's imprisonment on bread and water with very hard labour,' he confessed to Lady Manners (25 December). Internal division in the Cabinet with the impetuous, impossible Churchill strengthened his wish to resign. Moreover, Carnarvon's conversion to Home Rule proved a deep embarrassment, although the Viceroy found no support for his views in the Cabinet. His resignation in early January had been agreed to when he originally took the Dublin post, but it increased Salisbury's troubles. 'Oh, for a good adverse division!' Salisbury wrote to Lady Manners (24 January). 'What with Cabinets, opening of Parliaments, and journeys to Osborne, and many other things, I am more chevied than ever.'

Salisbury sought the approval of the Cabinet for the suppression of the National League in Ireland, which had been organizing the tenantry in the boycott of their landlords. At the pre-Parliamentary Cabinet meeting on 16 January, both Churchill and Hicks Beach expressed their opposition to a return to coercion. The Prime Minister persevered with his arguments. 'Do not let us take any line which will brand us in the eyes of our countrymen – or will enable our opponents to do so – as the timid party, who let things float because they dare not act,' he explained to Churchill. Within a few days his two recalcitrant colleagues stepped into line. On 26 January Hicks Beach gave notice that he intended to suspend normal Commons business to enable the government to hurry through a measure to make the National League illegal. The Tory–Irish Nationalist *entente* was at an end. Salisbury deplored the signs of vacillation in the Cabinet. Yet his government had been able to show its resolve before the passing of Jesse Collings's amendment on the Address placed the Conservatives in a minority in the Commons. To the Queen's distress, Salisbury resigned at once. He travelled down to Osborne House on the Isle of Wight, with the rest of the Cabinet, to hand over the seals of office. Salisbury assured the Queen that he would do everything that he could to help her. In return, the Queen presented him with an enamelled photograph of herself as a gift.

The Conservatives went into opposition in 'a sore and irritable mood'. Salisbury soon made it quite clear that his party had no intention of supporting any measure which gave Ireland internal self-government. His aim was to make the new Liberal ministry 'speak out at once' on its Irish policy. Sir Henry James noted that Salisbury was now favouring a 'put-your-foot-down policy' towards the Irish. 'No doubt the blow will have to be struck, and if so the sooner it is struck the better,' the Conservative leader argued. 'We must not desert the loyal people of Ulster. No doubt much has been done we may all regret, but it is not too late yet to save the battle.' Churchill provoked criticism by his inflammatory speeches in Belfast in February, but Salisbury was well pleased. 'You avoided all the shoals and said nothing to which any Catholic would object and yet contrived to arouse great enthusiasm among the Protestants,' he wrote to his colleague. In a speech at the Crystal Palace on 2 March Salisbury indignantly denied that his government had been in collusion with the Parnellites during its months in office. He spoke of the laws and institutions of the country becoming 'a shifting quicksand'.

Although neither Hartington nor Goschen were willing to join Gladstone's new Cabinet, the Whigs retained a deep suspicion of Conservative intentions during the spring of 1886. Hartington still preferred to trust 'the caucus rather than the Carlton'. On 4 March Salisbury met the Whig leader at Arlington Street. The two men tried to discover how to establish a 'definite common action' in wrecking Gladstone's Irish scheme. At that stage, Hartington was content merely 'to express the hope that they might act together in defeating any proposition for a separate Parliament'. This did not mean that they would stay together after that was achieved. The next day Salisbury left England to take a holiday on the French Riviera. It was during his short stay there that Lord Rowton introduced him to La Bastide, at Beaulieu. This was to become Salisbury's holiday home. Absence from the political crisis at home aroused disquiet in the Conservative ranks, but Salisbury was kept fully in touch with the intrigue of high politics, particularly by Churchill, who was orchestrating relations with discontented anti-Home Rule Liberals in the Commons. Salisbury was annoyed at Hartington's caution, and the Whig leader's public attacks on the Irish policy of the previous Conservative government. 'It was said of the Peelites of 1850 that they were always putting themselves up to auction, and always buying themselves in. That seems to be the Whig idea at the moment,' Salisbury wrote to Churchill (16 March). 'I do not think it is necessary to make any new advances to them – the next steps must come from them.' Salisbury still hoped for the eventual fusion of the Conservatives and anti-Home Rule Liberals on some common basis, which should 'represent the average opinion of the whole mass'.

He returned to England on 3 April, confident that in whatever shape the Home Rule Bill might be it would be defeated in the

Commons. Leading Conservatives like Churchill and Hicks Beach were ready to accept a purely Whig government in power backed up by the Conservatives. But Salisbury was seeking something far better – a dissolution of Parliament and another general election. This time it was to be fought solely on the Home Rule issue. On 8 April Gladstone unfolded his plan for Irish self-government. It was designed 'to reconcile imperial unity with a diversity of legislation', 'a way not to sap or impair but the way to strengthen and consolidate unity'.

Salisbury took little part in the public debate. It was left mainly to Hartington and Chamberlain to lead the struggle against Home Rule in the Commons. The Conservative leader was anxious to establish friendly relations with the Liberal malcontents. On Churchill's insistence, he even agreed to meet Chamberlain for a talk at the Turf Club. However, the anti-Home Rule Liberals were reluctant to be seen consorting too openly with the Conservatives. A joint meeting was held on 14 April at the Opera House in London under the chairmanship of Lord Cowper. It aroused widespread misgivings and the exercise was not repeated. 'The tendency of grouping – caused by the existence of various cliques of supporters – is becoming irresistible,' complained Salisbury.

None the less, he did his best to pacify Liberal sensitivities. Salisbury was concerned that the Conservatives should do nothing that might push the Liberal rebels back into their party's fold. He advised against the holding of any purely Conservative demonstrations against Home Rule until after the bill's second-reading debate. 'I am very anxious not to spoil the division and above all things to do anything behind the back of the Whigs which would give them cause to doubt our good faith,' he explained to T.W.Freston, the leader of the Manchester Conservatives. 'Their view seems to be that in allying themselves with us they are contracting a *mésalliance* – and though they are very affectionate in private they don't like showing us to their friends till they have had time to prepare them for the shock.'

Salisbury did not keep a completely self-imposed silence during the Home Rule crisis. On 16 May in a speech to the National Union in St James's Hall in London, he provoked a good deal of ill-feeling with some typically 'blazing indiscretions'. Salisbury argued that there were 'two nations' in Ireland 'deeply divided and bitterly antagonistic'. He suggested that 'free representative institutions' could not be conferred on Hottentots, nor on the Oriental peoples of India, 'although finer specimens of human character you will hardly find than some of those who belong to these nations'. In Salisbury's view, neither the Greeks nor the Russians were capable of self-government either. Only the Teutonic races could apparently enjoy it. Such an outburst detracted from Salisbury's sensible analysis of the Irish question, which is delivered in the same speech: 'Confidence where it carries with it the grant of representative institutions is only fitly bestowed upon a homogeneous people. It is only a people who in the main are agreed – who upon deep questions that concern a community think with each other, who have sympathy with each other, and have common interests, and look back on common traditions and are proud of common memories – it is only people who have these conditions of united action who can be, with any prospect of prosperity and success, entrusted with the tremendous powers which have been granted in the past and – let us thank God for it – granted safely and with great and prosperous results to the British people.'

Salisbury called for twenty years of 'honest, consistent, resolute' government for the Irish. He spoke of the need to encourage mass emigration from Ireland to the underdeveloped regions of the Empire. This would create a labour shortage in Ireland and thus bring a rise in real wages and a fall in rent levels. Such a suggestion did not mean that Salisbury envisaged a future Conservative government trying to enforce dispersal. He believed that market forces would encourage the free movement of labour. But he was realistic enough to accept that firm government and emigration (his critics called it 'manacles and Manitoba') could provide no instant solution to the Irish problem. Ireland is suffering from 'a chronic disease', he told a Merchant Taylors Company dinner (10 May), but he refused to accept that it was within 'the power of Irish disaffection to mar the career of a great nation'. At a rally at Hatfield on 13 June Salisbury described Home Rule for Ireland as government by the National League. This meant the desertion 'of more than a million men of our own race and of deep sympathies with our own nationality'. Home Rule spelt doom for 'all the minority, all the loyalists, all the industrious, commercial and progressive part of the community'. In a speech at Leeds on 18 June Salisbury drew loud applause for his attack on Irish labour migration into Britain: 'It is not good for them; it is not good for us [*cheers*]. There is not that excess of employment here that we want to bring in new competitors to seek for it. All they will do will be to demoralize the labour market and lower the cost of wages, and bring more British workmen down to the terrible level which is known in economics by the name of the starvation point. But if they cease to have the means of living in Ireland, to England they will infallibly come unless they are assisted to go abroad. They will come to England and every workman in every labour market in Britain will feel the fatal results of our Irish.'

Earlier in the month the long political crisis over Home Rule had reached its climax on the evening of 8 June when the Commons voted on whether to give Gladstone's Bill a second reading. Last-minute efforts by the government to reassure the Liberal rebels failed. The measure went down to defeat by 341 votes to 311. Ninety-three Liberals joined the Conservatives in the opposition lobby. The news of Gladstone's defeat was telegraphed to a post office near to Hatfield. Lord Hugh Cecil raced up the hill with the news early in the morning. Lady Frances Balfour recalled that night:

> It was past two o'clock when through the open window outside, while a heat-mist was making the summer night dark, we heard a loud shout coming nearer the house. The voice in the dead silence was recognizable, it was Hugh Cecil who had waited at the Post Office. It was a note which had victory in its tones, and we looked at her Ladyship. Then, we heard many voices and in a second or two Hugh burst breathless into the room. Majority thirty. We were on the ground floor, gathered in the summer parlour though we had strayed to the north front to be nearer the mes-senger. As we stood scarcely believing the size of the majority, the door at the further end opened, and framed in the light behind him stood his Lordship's massive figure. He seemed quite unconscious that on his shoulder in majestic calm sat a grey Persian cat, Bul-bul, which I had given to Hugh as a kitten. 'It is too good, Gladstone will resign and not dissolve,' was his comment.

Salisbury's immediate reaction was wrong. Gladstone decided to appeal to the country in what virtually amounted to a personal referendum on his Home Rule Bill. The end of the struggle at Westminster was now to demonstrate the importance of Salisbury's contribution to the Liberal defeat. With his immense prestige as party leader, Salisbury managed to get all but six of the ninety-three Liberals, who voted against the Home Rule Bill, free runs in their constituencies at the election. This was no easy task. It required all Salisbury's authority and persuasion to convince many sceptical local Conservative associations that they should not oppose anti-Home Rule Liberals with their own candidates. Such self-sacrifice strained the patience of many of the Conservative rank and file, but this was not pure altruism nor in Lady Gwendolen's words 'a substantial achievement in patriotic self-suppression'. It was based on hard-headed political calculation as well. As Salisbury wrote to Lord Lothian:

The reason why it will pay us as Conservatives to bring Liberal Unionists into Parliament is that by so doing we are driving home the wedge which is rifting the Liberal party into two. But this motive cannot be avowed in a public letter. Yet this is the only party motive. There is besides the patriotic motive – that the Irish question is more important than any other and all others should be made to yield to it.

Salisbury questioned whether the anti-Home Rule appeal was really an election winner. 'I doubt any popular stirring on this question,' he confessed to Churchill. 'The instinctive feeling of an Englishman is to wish to get rid of an Irishman. We may gain as many votes as Parnell takes from us; I doubt more. Where we shall gain is in splitting our opponents.'

Salisbury decided that his particular job was finished when the polls began on 1 July. He spent the rest of the month at Royat in the Auvergne, taking the waters. The Unionist cause triumphed. A total of 394 M.P.s went back to the Commons pledged to the Union (316 Conservative and seventy-eight Liberal Unionist). The Gladstonian Liberals numbered 191 and there were eighty-five Parnellites in the new Parliament. However the popular vote proved to be less decisive. The Conservatives actually polled 180,000 fewer votes than the Gladstonians. What really mattered was the large number of unopposed returns of Unionist candidates. In England 105 seats were not fought by the Gladstonians.

Gladstone and his Cabinet resigned on 21 July. Queen Victoria telegraphed Salisbury at Royat to come home and form a government. 'I wish the old sinner had put off his resignation for another fortnight,' he grumbled. Salisbury agreed to try and form a ministry which would be as 'strong a one' as possible to 'prevent' what the Queen described as 'the recurrence of frequent changes which are so bad for the country'. He doubted the sense of establishing a purely Conservative administration. Once again Salisbury hankered after coalition with the Whigs. He was even ready to give up the premiership to Hartington, though this would undoubtedly have aroused much Conservative criticism, after the lack of consideration displayed by the Liberal Unionists to their allies during the election campaign. Balfour disliked any idea of self-sacrifice. He believed that the anti-Home Rule Liberals were 'more usefully employed as nominal Liberals in embarrassing Liberal tactics, than they ever would be if they called themselves Tories', and brought the party 'nothing but their eloquence and the reputation of turn-coats'. In Balfour's opinion, Gladstone was the most powerful 'solvent' to Liberal unity. As long as he stayed at the head of his party, there would be no

Liberal reunification. Conservative alarm was premature. Salisbury's sincere attempt at persuading Hartington to become Prime Minister in a coalition government failed. He could not even get the Whig leader to join forces with him. The Liberal Unionists were only willing to give the Conservatives in the Commons support on 'the most general measures'. Chamberlain believed that Salisbury's 'best security' lay in the anti-Home Ruler's 'evident instinct to keep him in power' until Gladstone's retirement broke up party allegiances. Salisbury's refusal to countenance Chamberlain in his Cabinet gave Hartington a suitable excuse to reject the coalition idea, but none of his Whig friends, notably Northbrook, Derby nor Sir Henry James, approved either. The Liberal Unionists were intent on keeping their separate identity and sitting on the opposition benches in the Commons. Salisbury was only promised their 'independent but friendly support'.

To his obvious distress, Salisbury was therefore forced to form a Cabinet out of the Conservative ranks alone. This meant a major promotion for the mercurial Churchill. He became Leader of the House of Commons and Chancellor of the Exchequer, much to the chagrin of staider colleagues. Hicks Beach went to the Irish Office. The rest of the Cabinet were mainly the familiar greybeards. Half of the fourteen members sat in the Lords. Cross was made a Viscount and given the India Office. W. H. Smith took charge of the War Office, while Lord George Hamilton went to the Admiralty. Salisbury decided not to take on the burdens of the Foreign Office again. When both Lytton and Lord Lyons, the British ambassador in Paris, turned down the post, Iddesleigh became Foreign Secretary.

From the beginning of his second ministry, Salisbury went out of his way to keep the Liberal Unionists fully informed of his government's intentions. He showed a willingness to listen to their constructive suggestions on Ireland. Salisbury welcomed Chamberlain's idea of setting up investigatory commissions for Ireland to examine the rent question, public works and transport. But he believed the first priority must be the restoration of law and order. Sir Redwers Buller was dispatched to Dublin to take charge of the police force there. Salisbury displayed an unyielding face to the Irish Nationalists in Parliament. Parnell demanded a downward revision of the judicial rents fixed by the land courts to take account of falling prices. The Prime Minister declared that such a step would 'destroy all hopes of finality in agricultural questions'.

Except on Ireland, Salisbury's government held an uncertain mandate and no comfortable Commons majority. Churchill's erratic behaviour added to Salisbury's troubles. Lord Randolph was now at the height of his power. He had won high praise for his tactful handling of Parliament during the brief post-election summer session. Yet it was not long before he was once more at loggerheads with the rest of the Cabinet. On a visit to Windsor in September 1886 Churchill alarmed the Queen with his prediction that the government would suffer an early collapse. Salisbury rushed to reassure her that such an opinion reflected Churchill's 'temporary physical exhaustion'. Lord Randolph bombarded the Prime Minister with hysterical notes, mainly attacking Iddesleigh's running of the Foreign Office. Churchill had become an arch-isolationist with marked pro-Russian sympathies. In early September he joined the two service ministers, Smith and Hamilton, in demanding that the government should stay clear of the Balkans. Their apparent willingness to sacrifice Constantinople to the Russians horrified Salisbury. 'A pacific and economical policy is up to a certain point very wise,' he wrote to Churchill. 'But it is evident that there is a point beyond which it is not wise to go, either in a patriotic or party sense, and the question is where we shall draw the line. I draw it at Constantinople. My belief is that the main strength of the Tory party both in the richer and poorer classes lies in its association with the honour of the country.' Churchill's intrigues with the German ambassador, Hatzfeldt, also worried Salisbury. It looked as though the government was drifting along without any coherent foreign policy.

Churchill also appeared to have eclipsed Salisbury at the head of the Cabinet. It is often overlooked that the Prime Minister expressed prior approval for Churchill's celebrated Dartford speech which appeared to commit the government to a wide-ranging domestic programme. Indeed, the actual proposals which Lord Randolph made did not run counter to Cabinet opinion. Nevertheless there were growing fears that Churchillian opportunism was beginning to detach the Conservatives from their traditions and principles. By early November Churchill's domineering and maverick performance was beginning to weary Salisbury and his colleagues. When Chaplin voiced opposition to Churchill's suggestion of a closure of parliamentary debate by a simple majority, Churchill complained to Salisbury that the Dartford 'programme' was 'falling to pieces' and that the Conservatives were incapable of reform. The Prime Minister once more tried to explain the art of the possible to his truculent lieutenant. He pointed out that Conservative bills, by their very nature, must evolve with more caution than Liberal measures. The party could not hit at the classes who gave them support through

'drastic and symmetrical' legislation. Salisbury advised Churchill
to behave like a diplomat 'trying to bring opposing sections of the
party together and not that of a Whip trying to keep the slugs up
the collar'.

His words did nothing to calm Churchill, who continued to demand drastic change. His call for a democratic local-government
system, with the extension of the elective principle into the administration of the Poor Law, alarmed most Conservatives. So did his
support for the principle of compulsion in a measure to provide
allotments for agricultural labourers. Salisbury was compelled to
compose a critical memorandum, which opposed the compulsory
suggestion. Yet the Prime Minister's reticence in Cabinet began to
alarm its more moderate members. Cranbrook, Manners and Smith
urged him to take a firmer grip on proceedings. 'You have too much
self-renunciation for a Prime Minister,' Cranbrook complained to
Salisbury (23 November). 'You have rights which you forego in
guiding our deliberations.' 'My self-renunciation is only an attempt
– a vain attempt – to pour oil upon the creaking and groaning
machine,' Salisbury replied. The Prime Minister attempted to patch
up a *modus vivendi* between Churchill and the rest of the Cabinet.
On local government and the allotments issue a compromise was
reached. And in a speech to an audience of City of London Conservatives on 8 December, Salisbury was reassuring that the 'Conservatives were quite as Conservative as ever'. He argued that there
were no threats to property rights in any proposed domestic reform.

Within a few weeks, however, Churchill was once more at odds
with his colleagues. He was busy preparing a highly radical budget.
This would undoubtedly have provoked another Cabinet crisis.
Fortunately, Churchill took objection to the size of the proposed
War Office estimates. On that question, he was unlikely to win much
sympathy from the party rank and file. Churchill threw down an
ultimatum – either Smith cut his army expenditure or he resigned.
Salisbury did not hesitate to support his Secretary of State for
War. On 20 December Churchill dispatched his resignation in a
letter from Windsor Castle. Two days later Salisbury sent him a
sympathetic but unyielding reply. This brought a bitter riposte from
Churchill. In the following morning's *Times* came the news of his
resignation. The Prime Minister had been reluctant to see Churchill's
departure, because of its likely adverse effect on the government's
ability to withstand Liberal opposition and defend the Union from
attack. But his turbulent colleague left him no alternative. Churchill's
action was a self-inflicted wound, which proved to be fatal. 'I

was very anxious to keep the Cabinet together – and I deferred to him as much as I possibly could,' Salisbury wrote to Lord George Hamilton (25 December). 'The result was a rather composite policy'. 'To my own eyes, I have been incessantly employed for the last five years in making things smooth between him and others, both by word and act,' he explained to Fitzjames Stephens. 'But after all, coldness of manner may be an excuse for an erring wife, but not for an overbearing colleague.' Salisbury admired Churchill's glittering political talents, but he was not prepared to let his government be torn apart by the wayward and erratic behaviour of a man who appeared to lack emotional stability and any sense of proportion. Later myth-makers like to suggest that the clash between Salisbury and Churchill arose over the fundamental differences between Salisburian Conservatism and Tory Democracy. There is no truth in such a simplified judgement. It was Balfour who perceptively pointed out that Lord Randolph disappeared into the wilderness, not as a frustrated Tory Democrat, but as a thwarted Chancellor of the Exchequer, who was unable to convince his colleagues of the virtue of Cobdenite economies.

Our national fault is that too much softness
has crept into our councils;
we imagine that great national dangers
can be conjured away
by a plentiful administration of platitudes
and rose-water.
Salisbury to the National Conservative
Club, London, 7 March 1887

7

DEFENCE OF THE UNION:

AT HOME

January 1887–June 1892

Churchill's abrupt departure brought a political
crisis. Delighted Liberals predicted the government's early fall.
Another general election was expected within a few weeks. Chamberlain jumped to the wrong conclusion that the 'old reactionaries'
were in the ascendancy in the Cabinet and had forced Churchill out
of office. He lost no time in holding out an olive-branch to the
Gladstonians for a Liberal reunion. Conservatives feared that
Churchill would play havoc on the government back benches with
wounding attacks on his former colleagues. Many questioned how
the frail Commons front bench could hope to withstand the ferocious
opposition of the Liberals and Parnellites for very long.

The Liberal Unionists were proving uncertain, wayward allies. Although Chamberlain's effort to mend fences with his old party came to nothing at the round-table conference in January and February 1887, the Birmingham Radical still aroused suspicion in Conservative ranks. Nor did Hartington strengthen his support for the government. Although he responded to Salisbury's urgent telegram on 23 December and returned home from his Italian holiday, Hartington was not ready to change his mind and accept either Salisbury's offer of the premiership or a place in the Conservative Cabinet, despite the Queen's entreaties. All he was prepared to do was persuade Goschen to become Chancellor of the Exchequer. Salisbury was rather taken aback to discover, when Goschen met him at Hatfield to talk over his appointment, that the moderate Liberal was a bigger Tory than himself. Goschen did not relinquish his old party ties. He continued to call himself a Liberal. At the Treasury he gave the government a sound business-like image with his handling of national finance. Attempts to bring other Liberal Unionists like Northbrook and Lansdowne into the Cabinet failed. Both men refused to help Salisbury broaden his ministry. Liberal Unionist scruples and hesitancy were a constant puzzle and irritation to the Prime Minister. Their equivocal attitude made his ministry look vulnerable to defeat in the Commons.

Churchill was not the only leading Conservative to vanish from the Cabinet. Salisbury decided to take the opportunity and move into the Foreign Office himself. The hapless Iddesleigh was promised no more than the sinecure of President of the Council. All the same, his sudden collapse and death in an anteroom at Arlington Street deprived Salisbury of a trusted, loyal colleague. More seriously, less than two months later, Hicks Beach was forced to give up his tenure at the Irish Office. Doctors warned him of his failing eyesight, but after a few months in the Cabinet without a portfolio and then on the back benches, Hicks Beach returned to the government in April 1888 as President of the Board of Trade. His temporary withdrawal from the government's inner counsels came as a blow to Salisbury.

In the spring of 1887, with the threat of war between France and Germany and the disruptive Plan of Campaign in Ireland, Salisbury's government looked incapable of resolute action. But Salisbury was not ready to throw up his hands in despair and run from office at the first opportunity. He was determined to carry on governing with the mandate for Union he had won at the 1886 general election.

In fact, Churchill's eccentric gesture of despair was an unforeseen boon to the government. A decisive cohesion was introduced into Cabinet discussion. Salisbury's ministers developed a sense of collective purpose and a noticeable toughness in action. They were relatively free of the kind of petty intrigue and mutual jealousy which often afflict Cabinets. As Edward Hamilton noted, Salisbury's Cabinet was composed of 'men who were willing to be led and defer to their superiors'. It was made up of what Salisbury called 'straight men'. The Prime Minister provided a loose rein. Ministers were left very much to their own devices in shaping the policy of their departments. Inevitably a small group stood apart as the inner junta, 'the holy of holies'. It was they who gave the government its overall strategy. Salisbury apart, his nephew, Arthur Balfour, became the government's most important figure once he rose meteorically from the obscurity of the Scottish Office to take on Ireland in April 1887. Balfour's appointment at first aroused a good deal of sarcasm. This was not confined to Liberal critics. There were strong doubts whether he had enough physical stamina to withstand the pressures of the job. 'Your Lordship knows his temperament very well and his habits. No one has a greater opinion of his abilities and character than I have, but a man who does not get up before twelve and does not read a paper and hardly ever answers a letter, however quick and acute, cannot face the continual drudgery involved in answering the unceasing Irish questions in the House and doing other business of that kind so undulating and disconcerting,' H.H.Howorth explained to Salisbury from Manchester. Ashbourne recalled that Salisbury's sudden disclosure to the Cabinet of Balfour's promotion to the Irish Office brought 'hesitation, concern, dismay'. To most contemporaries, Balfour looked nothing more than a rather cynical dilettante. It did not take him long to change that misleading impression. Balfour soon showed the fist beneath the velvet glove. He stamped his personality onto the 1886 Parliament. For the next sixteen years he was to become Salisbury's indispensable political confidant.

W.H.Smith took over as Leader of the House of Commons on Churchill's resignation. He proved to be a surprisingly resilient and effective politician, despite ill health. This staid and loyal moderate Conservative, who made his fortune as a bookseller, was an admirable complement to the Prime Minister. 'The combination between Salisbury and Smith was a happy mixture of the most worthy influences of Toryism,' recalled Lord George Hamilton. It was Salisbury who provided 'the patriotic, self-denying, exceptional industry and ability', while Smith provided 'common sense and perception (amounting to genius)'. These qualities supplied

Salisbury's deficiency for he 'did not know or come sufficiently into contact with influences, movements and aspiration of classes other than his own'. During the long, bitter parliamentary sessions from 1887 to 1891 Smith proved to be a tough Leader in the Commons. On his death in October 1891 Salisbury spoke warmly of his colleague as 'a most lovable man'.

Salisbury's tenure of office was entirely dependent on how the Liberal Unionists responded to his government. Salisbury treated their leaders – Chamberlain and Hartington – with uncharacteristic candour and concern. In later years, many Conservatives were resentful of the plentiful supply of patronage which Salisbury provided the Liberal Unionists. He presented their leaders with the drafts of important Bills prior to publication for their detailed comment and advice, and he also kept them fully briefed on what the government was thinking. Salisbury still suspected Chamberlain's ultimate intentions, but he made no attempt to antagonize the Birmingham Radical unnecessarily. On the contrary, he went out of his way to reassure Chamberlain that the Conservatives were not going to take any reactionary course.

In the autumn of 1887 Chamberlain agreed to go to Washington as Britain's chief commissioner and negotiate a settlement of the fishery dispute with the United States. His political opinions were eagerly sought by Salisbury and his colleagues. The government was strongly influenced by Chamberlain's fertile ideas, particularly over local county government and free education. In return, Chamberlain became a powerful defender of the Conservatives on the public platform. In March 1889 John Bright died. The question of his successor in the Central division of Birmingham sparked off a furious row in Unionist ranks. Local Conservatives wanted Churchill to have the Unionist nomination. After Salisbury's intervention however, Chamberlain's nominee was given an unopposed run. The personal *entente* between the two leaders was symbolized by Salisbury's triumphant visit to Birmingham in November 1891. There, the two men who had once called each other 'the pinchbeck Robespierre' and the representative of the class 'who toil not, neither do they spin' respectively sat down to dinner in the Town Hall. Chamberlain recalled that during the early difficult years of the Unionist alliance, his relations with the Conservative leaders were 'cordial, frank and satisfactory'. He was astonished at how 'broad and liberal' a view of political issues Salisbury took. Salisbury refused to countenance the disestablishment of the Anglican Church in Wales, and Chamberlain was sensible enough to shelve that particular item on the Radical agenda. On the other hand, it was on a Conservative platform at the Aston by-election in March 1891 that Chamberlain first raised the question of old-age pensions. Two months later Salisbury appointed him chairman of a parliamentary committee to investigate the subject.

There was nothing inevitable about the longevity of the Unionist alliance. At the beginning its survival was due to the persistence of Ireland as the main dividing issue in British politics. Home Rule's defeat at the polls in July 1886 settled nothing. It was the first round in a long and bitter struggle. During the 1887 parliamentary session the Opposition fought the Irish coercion bill tooth and nail through the Commons. This kept up Irish spirits, but it failed to split the Unionist ranks. On the contrary, Gladstone's 'raging, tearing' campaign helped to solidify the new alliance. If Irish questions ceased to be of overwhelming importance, it is more than likely that the Liberal party would have re-established an uncertain but workable unity. In the late 1890s Salisbury was often to worry over the cohesion of the Unionist alliance, when Home Rule was no longer a pressing issue.

Salisbury once likened the Irish question to 'an evil dream', to 'a nightmare' where 'a danger or a horror' pressed on the mind, 'fettering the limbs and paralyzing the energies'. Yet there was never any suggestion that he might want to rid himself of that apparition by granting Ireland a measure of Home Rule. Salisbury practised a hard-headed pragmatism as Prime Minister but on Ireland he was firm and uncompromising. His detestation for Home Rule was total. This attitude was not the result of any crude calculation of party self-interest. It stemmed from the belief that Gladstone's political panacea was quite unworkable. There is a common opinion nowadays on both sides of the Irish Sea that the creation of a separate but subordinate legislature for the Irish people would have solved Ireland's problems. This would have provided the Irish, so the argument goes, with a sense of national self-respect within the broader framework of the United Kingdom. Shortsighted and stubborn Unionism blocked the path to its fulfilment. But Salisbury's objections to Home Rule were not based on any diehard prejudice to stop the onward march of progress. He simply did not believe that Home Rule would bring Ireland either a stable or a lasting political settlement. In his view, no measure of internal self-government could ever succeed if it was imposed from the outside on a society deeply divided by fundamentals. Ireland was in such a condition. To Salisbury, Ireland was inhabited 'by men of different

E

races and antagonistic traditions'. 'Representative government answers admirably as long as those who are represented desire much the same thing, and have interests tolerably analogous, but it is put under intolerable strain when it rests upon a community divided into two sections, one of which is bitterly hostile to the other and desirous of opposing it on all occasions.' Salisbury's argument over the relations between Hindus and Moslems in a debate on the Indian Councils Bill in 1890 was applicable equally in his eyes to the deep division between Roman Catholic and Protestant Irishmen.

There was a deep and unbridgeable gulf between the two Irish communities on the question of political sovereignty, which the Liberals refused to recognize. A 'half-way house' solution would not have satisfied anybody for long. Home Rule was unlikely to be an effective method for administrative devolution, nor would it prove a satisfactory moral atonement for all those centuries of alleged Anglo-Saxon oppression. Ireland's mutual antagonisms, hatreds, prejudices could be reconciled only within the larger unit of the United Kingdom. The creation of an all-Ireland assembly would mean the tyranny of a Roman Catholic majority, whatever the paper guarantees might be to safeguard the rights of Irish Protestants. The Stormont experiment in devolution between 1921 and 1972 demonstrates the harsh truth of Salisbury's analysis. That Home Rule measure, ironically imposed on the six north-eastern counties of Ireland which were most hostile to Gladstone's original proposals, enabled the Protestant majority to enjoy an uninterrupted monopoly of political power for half a century, despite sporadic outbreaks of sectarian violence by the alienated Roman Catholic minority.

Salisbury once remarked that Ireland awoke the 'slumbering genius of English imperialism'. There is no direct connection between the Irish problem and the extension of imperial supremacy in Africa and Asia during the 1880s and 1890s, but the threat to the cohesion of the mother country did bring a more strident note into British politics. A government's capacity to deal with Ireland became a vital test of its will-power in international diplomacy. At a time when other states such as Germany, Italy and the United States were going through a process of 'consolidation', it was unthinkable to many Englishmen that the country should decide to loosen, if not break, the ties with Ireland. As Salisbury wrote to Canon MacColl in 1889: 'Nations do not change their political nature, except through blood. It would require a subordination of all ordinary motives, a resuscitation of traditions and prepossessions, a far-reaching and disciplined resolve which is never engendered by mere persuasion, and only comes after conflict and under the pressure of military force. To ask the British nation in its present moral and political condition to execute such a transformation would be like making the doctor's cob win the Derby. The forces are not there.'

Salisbury, like other Unionists, refused to accept the existence of Irish nationalism. In his eyes, the respectable gloss of political idealism thinly disguised the economic roots of Irish discontent. Salisbury believed that Parnell's strength as a leader arose not from his political appeal as a nationalist, but through his unscrupulous exploitation of the genuine grievances of the Irish peasantry. 'To teach the debtor how he shall not pay his creditor – that is their heroic gospel.' This was Salisbury's verdict on the Parnellite programme. In his opinion such a doctrine was 'inconsistent' with 'the most rudimentary morality'. It was 'fatal to the existence of any civilized society'. Catastrophe would surely follow if political power was ever handed over to men who knew 'no better standard than an appeal to the lowest instincts of cupidity'. This would mean renouncing 'a sacred trust' and condemning millions of fellow countrymen to 'misery and ruin'. Even a limited degree of local self-government was not to be lightly granted to those who 'accepted robbery as part of their creed'. Salisbury believed that Home Rule meant Rome Rule. The superstitious priest and the corrupt, drunken machine politician would dominate a self-governing Ireland. This was a recipe for civil war. Ulster Protestants would fight rather than tolerate 'the subjection of their prosperity, their religion, their industry, their lives to the absolute mastery of their ancient and unchanging enemies'.

Salisbury also believed that a Home Rule Ireland would be a permanent threat to national security. Once more that unhappy country would become 'a haven for the enemies of the Empire as in the days of the Wars of the Roses, the Reformation and the Jacobite threat'. In a forceful speech in April 1892 to Exeter Conservatives, Salisbury gave articulate expression to that inner nagging fear which lay at the heart of the Unionist cause: 'What is it that gives to this little island its commanding position?' he asked. 'Why is it that fleets from every nation, from every quarter of the globe, come into your ports; that the product of countless regions are subject to your industry; and that the manufactures which the industry of your people complete are carried to the furthest corners of the globe? What is it that gives to you this privileged position? It is that your flag floats over populations far more numerous and regions far vaster than your own and that upon the dominions of your sovereign the sun never sets [loud cheers].

'But when they see that, under the pressure of Irish disaffection, you have lost the nerve, or the fibre, or the manliness to uphold the integrity of your Empire, will they not apply the lesson to themselves and many of them say, "Now is the time for us to shake off this connection and stand alone and independent in the world"? Remember, there are vast regions and vast populations over which you rule by force, because your rule is mild and gentle, and over which you would not rule if your force was not believed in [cheers]. I cannot conceal the deep apprehension with which I look to any failing or flinching on the part of this people during the trial which destiny has appointed to them. We are now at a point where, if we show qualities by which our ancestors attained the Empire, we may be thought worthy to retain it and hand it on.

'But if we are deceived, if we allow ourselves to be deceived by hollow sentimental follies which are in reality only excuses for weakness and want of courage, the day of our power will be set, and slowly we shall recede from the great position that was handed to us. If you fail in this trial, one by one the flowers will be plucked from the diadem of Empire and you will be reduced to depend on the resources of this small, over-peopled island.'

Behind the natural excess of platform rhetoric, Salisbury exposed Unionism's raw nerve. To him, it was not a self-confident ideology binding together the ruling class, but far more a desperate recognition of the essential fragility of imperial power. The vulgar outbursts of jingo fury, which Salisbury so much deplored, were not proof of a vibrant, complacent national mood, but of the feverish uncertainty of public opinion. It was Gladstone's avowed mission to pacify Ireland by giving that country justice; Salisbury's was to reinforce the feeble, crumbling pillars of the Empire from inevitable decay and the growing threats to its position from an increasingly hostile outside world.

What was to be done for Ireland? Salisbury occasionally expressed a regret that his government could never be allowed to enjoy the autocratic power of a Tsar, but he knew the British people would not stomach a regime of permanent, bloody coercion in Ireland. Such a negative, unyielding policy was doomed to fail, because it could not rely on the steady, solid support of the country. The dismal record of Unionist by-election defeats from 1887 to 1891 was proof enough that no government could hope to retain popular approval for long in the face of aggressive domestic opposition. Salisbury blamed much of the Irish agitation on indecisive Westminster, where successive governments – both Conservative and Liberal – slid backwards and forwards between coercion and conciliation. This was the inherent weakness of democratic government that Salisbury spent a political lifetime fighting. Salisbury was sure that 'any steady, unvarying, consistent policy' would soon reduce Ireland's problems to manageable proportions. It was the perpetual party battle that destroyed a government's ability to push a coherent strategy through to a successful finish. Bipartisanship at Westminster was crucial in finding a solution to the Irish problem, but the discovery of a common policy was impossible after 1886 when the Liberals embraced Home Rule. This hardened party divisions. In the past, important national issues, such as the franchise or Free Trade, were settled across the floor at Westminster without any threat to constitutional government. Ireland was a question which the British political system found hard to digest.

Salisbury was no believer in panaceas. His prescription for Ireland was 'steady persistence in a sound policy'. This would 'teach the Irish the political wisdom which the rest of our race has in great measure acquired', he remarked in May 1892. Time was to be the common arbitrator. The trouble was, this was precisely what the British system of government could not provide.

Salisbury wanted a 'just, discriminating and firm government' in Ireland. He recognized that 'whole centuries of hesitating government' were not to be erased by a few years of power. Unionist policy for Ireland was the programme for at least a generation. Respect for the rule of law had to take root in Irish society. Until Ireland enjoyed 'ordinary fidelity to a pledged word', it could expect neither prosperity nor social stability. What Salisbury called 'the life of industry' would never come of its own free will to a society which lacked any confidence in its own future. He believed that if Ireland could experience a period of sustained economic growth, then the seductive charm of Home Rule would lose its appeal to Catholic Irishmen. Salisbury assured a Primrose League meeting in May 1889: 'As prosperity returns and order resumes her sway and men find there is not only more peace but more profit in tranquillity than in outrage and disorder, we shall see the forces of the Nationalist party desert them and nothing will be left but the hollow sentiments from which we have nothing to fear.'

Under Balfour's regime in Ireland from 1887 until November 1891 coercion, or the restoration of respect for the law, became the major priority. Salisbury accepted that the Irish must 'take a licking' before they could be satisfied with the material largesse of economic improvement. By the twentieth-century standards of European tyrannies,

Unionist 'repression' in Ireland during those years was fitful and limited, although it was quite enough to provide a place for Balfour in the pantheon of Irish demonology. Salisbury, for all his harsh words, did something to temper Balfourian excess. He disliked executive action in the suppression of Irish newspapers, and he stood out against the continual prosecution of Irish nationalist leaders like Dillon and O'Brien. Resolute efforts to quash the National League pleased Conservative back-benchers, although it provided numerous propaganda victories for the Union of Hearts forged between the Gladstonians and Parnellites. In fact, the Salisburian recipe proved a singular success. A few relevant statistics make the point. In 1888 1,475 people were prosecuted under the Crimes Act, 1,082 of whom were convicted. By 1891 only 243 were prosecuted and 186 convicted. By June 1892 only four men still remained in Irish jails for offences under the Crimes Act. At the same time incidences of boycotting and agrarian violence fell sharply. It was estimated that 4,901 landlords were under a boycott by their tenants on 30 June 1887. By 31 May 1891 the number had dropped to 403.

Salisbury was far less successful in his efforts to discredit Parnell and his party. In the spring of 1887 a series of articles in *The Times* suggested that the Irish Nationalist leader had been involved with the assassins who murdered Lord Frederick Cavendish and the Irish Secretary of State in Phoenix Park in 1882. When Parnell unaccountably took no legal action against the newspaper, his omission looked to many Englishmen as proof of his guilt. During a trial in which an Irish ex-member sued *The Times* for libel, counsel for the defence and the Attorney General, Sir Richard Webster, produced other letters which incriminated Parnell in open court. The Irish leader now felt compelled to take action to clear his name. He demanded that a House of Commons select committee should ascertain the authenticity of the letters. The government turned down his request. Instead, the Cabinet decided to set up a special commission of three judges to investigate all the charges made in *The Times* articles. It is clear that Salisbury and Balfour were out to destroy Parnell and his party through judicial exposure as collaborators with the men of violence. However it was discovered in February 1889 that *The Times* letters were a forgery. Although the Commission made grave charges against some of the Irish leaders when it finally reported in February 1890, Parnell was triumphantly acquitted. His vindication was not to last very long. On 17 November 1890 the divorce court granted Captain O'Shea, Liberal M.P. for Co. Clare, a decree nisi in a suit against his wife. Parnell was quoted as

her co-respondent. The Irish leader offered no defence. Under pressure
from Gladstone and Cardinal Manning, the Irish party split irretriev-
ably when Parnell refused to relinquish the leadership. He died a year
later. It is often suggested that it was Chamberlain who encouraged
O'Shea into taking action through the courts. Whatever the truth
might be, the Unionist alliance enjoyed a short lease of life, free from
the cares of Irish obstruction in the Commons. This enabled it to
recover a good deal of its lost momentum.

Even during Balfour's early years at the Irish Office, the government did not strike an entirely negative attitude towards Ireland.
In the spring of 1887, Lord Cowper's commission recommended that
Irish rural distress should be remedied through the extension of the
benefits of the 1881 Land Act to all leaseholders, and the reduction
of the contractual term for judicial rents from fifteen to five years.
More important, the commission called for the adjustment of rents
in Ireland in accordance with the rise and fall of agricultural prices.
At first, Salisbury and his Cabinet were hostile to such a proposal.
It was a clear threat to the sanctity of contract. Salisbury refused to
accept that the majority of rents fixed since 1881 by the Land
Courts were either 'obsolete or unfair'. But it soon became clear that
the proposed Land Bill would never win the vital support of the
Liberal Unionists unless it made provision for a revision of all
rents hit by the fall in prices over the previous five years. Despite a
Conservative outcry, the Cabinet, in Cranbrook's words, 'submitted
to rather than approved' that proposal. 'It is a price which we have
to pay for the Union and it is a heavy one,' Salisbury lamented.

Salisbury was also unenthusiastic about Balfour's 1891 Land
Purchase Act. He believed that it had become necessary to intervene
in the operation of the Irish land system in order to ensure the
ultimate safety of the Act of Union. He wrote to an irate Ulsterman
in May 1890: 'The Bill is not a good thing in itself. It is only a
remedy for worse evils, rendered necessary by the improvident and
disastrous legislation of the last quarter of a century. I do not in
the least anticipate that it will put an end to the class of landlords.
But what we hope for from it is not that it will fill the country with
peasant proprietors, but that it will establish them in greater or less
numbers in various parts of the country, scattered all over it, so
that the present uniformity of condition and feeling which enabled
agitators to turn the whole political and social force of the occupiers
against the landlords will be arrested and broken and will lose its
formidable effect.' Salisbury also gave his blessing to the extensive
outlay of public expenditure on relief of economic distress in Ireland.

He supported Balfour's decision to form Congested District Boards in 1891, designed to channel assistance to the more depressed areas of the country. In the following year Balfour introduced a bill in the Commons which extended a limited form of local self government to Ireland, but the summer dissolution of Parliament ensured that the measure did not reach the statute book.

Ireland did not entirely preoccupy Salisbury and his colleagues between 1887 and 1892 to the exclusion of any other domestic issues. The Irish question is often said to have proved a useful issue in diverting the attention of the English electorate from social reform. Certainly Ireland consumed much parliamentary time during that period, but Salisbury's legislative record does not suggest that his government was entirely unsympathetic to cautious, worthy legislation. The Prime Minister was embarrassed by Chamberlain's claim during the 1892 general election that the Conservatives had implemented his entire 'unauthorized programme' of 1885. It is more plausible to argue that Conservative dependence on Liberal Unionist support compelled Salisbury to take a far broader view of domestic questions than perhaps he would otherwise have done. Certainly Salisbury had lost none of his old pessimism about the future. 'We are in a state of bloodless civil war. No common principles, no respect for common institutions or traditions unite the various groups of politicians who are struggling for power,' he confessed to Smith in February 1889. 'To loot somebody or something is the common object under a thick varnish of pious phrases.' Salisbury still spoke of the 'great conflicts', 'vast controversies' that threatened society. He was troubled by that scourge of industrialism – unemployment. To Salisbury the vision of men without work was 'one of the greatest evils' of a 'closely compacted and highly developed civilization'. 'A body of half-sustained labourers, a body who can hardly find sufficient field for their industry' were in Salisbury's opinion 'a constant anxiety to the benevolent and a constant peril to the state'. The spread of Socialist nostrums in the Labour movement of the late 1880s, highlighted by the growth of New Unionism among unskilled workers and the 1889 London dock strike, worried Salisbury, but he was not unmindful that such developments arose from genuine hardship. Socialism was no cure, but it was 'a great mistake', not 'an irremediable evil'. 'When you see quacks gathering round a bed, however deeply you may despise the quacks, it is probable that the patient lying on the bed is suffering from a serious illness or a deep disease,' Salisbury argued.

He was also alarmed by the social evils of the time. 'We have come upon an age of the world when the action of industrial causes, the great accumulation of populations and many other social and economic influences have produced great centres of misery,' Salisbury argued. 'They have added terribly to the catalogue of evils to which the flesh is heir. It is our duty to do all we can to find the remedies and even if we are called Socialists, in attempting to do it, we shall be reconciled if we can find these remedies, knowing that we are undertaking no new principle but pursuing the long and healthy tradition of English legislation.' Salisbury could offer no attractive remedies. The state could not be expected to provide much comfort, if it meant an infringement of individual freedom or the need for 'confiscatory' doses of direct taxation. Salisbury doubted whether the comfortably-off voters would tolerate any vast public expenditure to rid the country of social distress. He retained a conviction in the virtues of self-help. 'No man and no class of men ever rise to any permanent improvement in their condition of body or of mind, except by relying upon their own personal efforts,' Salisbury claimed. He told his Exeter audience (1 February 1892): 'The wealth with which the rich man is surrounded is constantly tempting him to forget that truth, and you see in family after family men degenerate from the habits of their fathers because they lie sluggishly and eat and enjoy what has been placed before them without appealing to their own exertions. The poor man, especially in these days, may have a similar temptation offered to him by legislation, but the same inexorable rule will work. The only true benefit which the statesman can give to the poor man is so to shape matters that the greatest possible liberty for the exercise of his own moral and intellectual qualities should be offered to him by law. It would be a very sound exercise of the powers of government and could do nothing but good, if we could, without interfering with the existing institutions that work well, put within the reach of every poor man the power of making effective provision for the days of darkness, the days of helplessness and of old age and keep himself from the possibility of having to apply to the workhouse for relief.'

Salisbury was reluctant to give his blessing to the popular agitation for a statutory eight-hour working day. Nevertheless by the standards of late Victorian England, the legislative record of his second ministry was impressive. Even the 1887 session, despite its prolonged wrangles over Ireland and reform in parliamentary procedure, was not entirely barren of domestic achievement. C. T. Ritchie at the Local Government Board proved to be a reforming minister, in the mould of previous Tory legislators like Sir James Graham and

Sir Richard Cross. He piloted a Labourers' Allotment Bill through the Commons, which was designed to 'elevate' the working classes 'into a position of manly independence by industry and society'. The measure was to supplement voluntary effort, giving local authorities the power to acquire land for allotments. The Mines Regulation Act was another useful addition to the statute book in 1887. This provided an extension of statutory protection for miners in their work and it won the approval of the Trades Union Congress.

The showpiece of the 1888 session was the Local Government Bill for England and Wales, promised by Salisbury in his Newport speech. 'Representative bodies are the fashion of the day and against a fashion it is almost impossible to argue,' he wrote to a doubting Tory, Sir John Dorington (18 August 1886). 'I do not believe that they will govern better than the existing county governing bodies have done. But I see no reason for apprehending that their section will be injurious.' Salisbury was apprehensive that the creation of democratic county councils would antagonize the party's squire-archy with doleful results at the next general election. However, he refused to believe that the bill would spell the defeat of the landed interest in local politics. In his opinion, the new system would provoke neither 'any social change or subversion'. Salisbury accepted that there might be more political activity in the shires with 'a multiplication of caucuses and wire-pullers', but he believed that these 'evils' were 'matters of very slight importance'. The purpose of the Local Government Bill was 'to make institutions more acceptable to the people'. In the past the gentry had established a supremacy, not through the exercise of any statutory privilege, but because of 'their essential qualities, their circumstances, and their ability'. Salisbury could see no reason why they should not continue to hold sway over the new county authorities. When Carnarvon suggested that the measure was a sign that the country was 'running down hill with the reins hanging about the horse's heels', Salisbury angrily rebuffed him. The only aspect of the Act which Salisbury grew to dislike was the arrival of the Progressive party in charge of the London County Council, but he refused to believe that this damage would prove irreparable. 'I may be wrong – but I rather look to the new London County Council to play the drunken Helot for our benefit,' he wrote to Goschen (26 January 1889). 'Such a body at the outset must make some portentous blunders and I am not sorry that, as luck will have it, they will be carried to the account of the Radicals.'

Despite Opposition obstructionism in the Commons, a fair amount of legislation reached the statute book during the 1889 and 1890 sessions. A Board of Agriculture was established in 1889. Salisbury hastened to warn the aggrieved farmers that the new department should not let them rush to the conclusion that it would make a dramatic difference to their economic plight. The Prime Minister's son, Cranborne, piloted the Cotton Cloth Factories Act through Parliament. A measure was passed to provide local authorities with the power to protect the poor from fraud in shops. In 1889 a Local Government Act gave Scotland the same system as England and Wales. A bill was also placed on the statute book to deal with the prevention of cruelty to children and another to root out corruption in the public services.

However, in the following year's session the government came to the brink of collapse. Smith's health was under strain with the constant parliamentary battle. The Unionist cause had suffered continuous defeats in by-elections. Many Conservative back-benchers disliked Goschen's Local Taxation Bill. By June the timetable in the Commons was blocked with unfulfilled measures. 'Passing bills will soon be a lost art,' Salisbury complained to the Marquis of Lansdowne, the Indian Viceroy. 'The explanation always given is the blundering of those who have the management of the House. But during the past fifteen years no one has succeeded who has not had an over-whelming and homogeneous majority and no majority, even much more homogeneous than ours ever was, has stood the disintegrating influence of four years' existence' (27 June 1890). The Cabinet was compelled to consider shelving legislation until the next year. Salisbury argued with his harassed colleagues that this would bring 'discredit' on the government if they abandoned any of their pro-gramme, but he was over-ruled. The Prime Minister confessed to the Queen that 'so grave a difference of opinion' would in normal circumstances lead to a dissolution of Parliament. However, Salis-bury assured her that the government would 'get on as well as they could' because the alternative was the return of the Gladstonians and the inevitable attempt to legislate Home Rule.

Parnell's downfall in November 1890 brought a fall in the amount of parliamentary obstruction. For the next two years, the govern-ment's legislative efforts were relatively trouble-free. A shoal of measures reached the statute book. The Tithe Bill was passed in the 1890 autumn session after three years' delay. This made the landlord and not the occupier responsible for tithe payments, and resolved an issue which caused friction in rural areas. The 1891 Education Act brought free education within the reach of almost every family in the country. Along with the 1890 Education Code, which removed the iniquities of the payment-by-results method of teaching, this brought a major advance in the schools. There were also measures to improve protection for the worker in industry, to consolidate working-class housing legislation, and to provide small-holdings for agricultural labourers.

However, there was one major issue on which Salisbury was unable to satisfy many of his party followers. Fair Trade had not lost its appeal to many of the rank and file. However, Salisbury refused to contemplate any return to a modified form of protection. The agricultural interest was suffering from economic distress but, other than attempts to lower the burdens of taxation on the land, there was nothing else that Salisbury felt the government could do to help. 'In my belief the economical arguments in favour of Free Trade are very strong,' he argued (12 March 1888). 'If protection were introduced, it would be introducing a state of division among the classes of this country which would differ very little from civil war.' Salisbury ruled any duty on corn as 'out of the bounds of political possibility'. 'We are a community peculiarly situated. We have vast artisan populations, whose interest is in manufactures and not in the land. Would you raise the price of their food merely for the purpose of giving benefit to one particular industry?' he argued in a speech at Derby (20 December 1887). Although he was ready to consider the virtue of taxing foreign luxury imports more heavily or even introducing a limited form of retaliation against countries who were penalizing British exports, Salisbury maintained that there could be no major change in the country's trading system, unless both major political parties were agreed on its necessity. He was equally doubtful whether imperial preference would win much support in Britain, even if it was a way of strengthening ties. 'It is very difficult to bring home to the constituencies the feeling that the maintenance of our Empire in its integrity may depend upon fiscal legislation,' he explained (21 March 1891). 'It is not that they do not value the tie which unites us to the colonies. On the contrary, it is valued more and more in this country. But they do not give much thought to political questions and they are led away by the more unreasoning and uncompromising advocates of free trade.'

By the summer of 1892 the government had recovered some of the momentum which it had appeared to lose through the late 1880s. Salisbury in his long period of power had shown that the Conservatives were capable of governing the country. In retrospect, his ministry has a far more impressive legislative record than either

Disraeli's between 1874 and 1880 or any of Gladstone's administrations. A natural diffidence about self-advertisement might explain the lack of credit which went to a government with an achievement equal to that of Peel's famous ministry between 1841 and 1846. During the 1892 election campaign, Chamberlain's boast that the Conservatives had carried through his old 'Unauthorized Programme' brought an entreaty from Salisbury: 'To say that the Tories have supported measures whose liberalism you approve, will only be interpreted by them as showing that knowing them better you do them more justice. But if you say that they have given in on all points on which you differed from them in 1885 – you give them an uncomfortable feeling that they have deserted their colours and changed their coats. I do not think there is any ground for such self-reproach – though I believe it is true that they have proved – and that you have found them – more liberal on many points than in 1885 you could have imagined.'

*Is it our destiny
to be always making bricks without straw?
Without money,
without any strong land force,
with an insecure tenure of power,
and with an ineffective agency,
we have to counterwork the efforts
of three Empires,
who labour under none of these disadvantages.*
Salisbury to Queen Victoria,
29 August 1886

8

DEFENCE OF THE UNION:

ABROAD

January 1887–June 1892

Salisbury always preferred to run the Foreign Office rather than be Prime Minister. He often assured his colleagues that he would have gladly given up the premiership to concentrate his mind and energy on international diplomacy. This abiding interest in foreign affairs is partly explained by Salisbury's distaste for what he once called the 'sham' of politics. Lady Gwendolen recalled that domestic intrigue was 'a source of constant irritation to him and he hailed with a recurrent sense of relief an escape into the pure air of diplomacy'. It was at the Foreign Office that Salisbury could indulge in his 'instinctive reverence for facts', that 'constant impulse towards building upon an empirical foundation'.

The department also provided Salisbury with an opportunity to exercise an independence of authority. During his second spell at the Foreign Office, Salisbury was hardly troubled by dissenting counsels either in the Cabinet or among his permanent advisers. He tended to by-pass normal diplomatic procedure and conduct his policy through interviews and private correspondence with ambassadors and consuls. Salisbury devoted his whole time to the minutiae of foreign affairs. Those red dispatch-boxes followed him everywhere.

Yet Salisbury never had much faith in the lasting value of Foreign Office work. 'Nothing matters,' he once remarked to a startled civil servant in the middle of an international crisis. In Salisbury's view, the diplomat bequeathed an ephemeral legacy, as he explained in his perceptive essay on Castlereagh:

> There is nothing in his [the diplomat's] achievements which appeal to the imagination: nothing which art can illustrate, or tradition retain, or history portray. A military commander is more fortunate in his vocation. All his achievements are a succession of dramatic effects; each of his advantages is gained by one sudden and skilful blow; the effort by which the destinies of whole nations are decided, and which puts to the uttermost test every quality of mind and heart, is concentrated into a few hours. The excitement is contagious to his countrymen who are spectators of his deeds, and to the posterity which reads of them. But there is nothing dramatic in the successes of a diplomatist. His victories are made up of a series of microscopic advantages; of a judicious suggestion here, of an opportune civility there; of a wise concession at one moment, and a far-sighted persistence at another; of sleepless tact, immovable calmness, and patience that no folly, no provocation, no blunders can shake. But there is nothing exciting in the exercise of excellences such as these. A list of such exploits lends no fascination to a narrative. Writers will not encumber their pages with a throng of minute circumstances, which are individually trivial, though in aggregate they effect results of vast importance; and readers would not be found to read them if they did. The result is that while the services of a commander are celebrated with almost undiminished enthusiasm from age to age, the services of a diplomatist fade rapidly away from a nation's memory. (January 1862)

Salisbury rarely divulged the principles of his foreign policy, but he did sum them up on one occasion as 'to perform our own part with honour, to abstain from meddling diplomacy, to uphold England's honour steadily and fearlessly, and always to be prone rather to let action go along with words than to let it lag behind them'. Salisbury believed that the English people were 'trustees for the vast populations with whose interests they are charged'. He maintained that they would be found 'deeply culpable if those interests' were 'neglected'. Salisbury saw that his task was to pass on 'that trust with all its strengths, all its glory, all its traditions untarnished' to his successors. He placed severe limitations on the objectives of British foreign policy, believing that while the Empire was vital to England's future as a world power, there was no need to expand its frontiers. As Salisbury warned in the late 1890s when there was pressure for annexation beyond India's North-West Frontier, 'However strong you may be, whether you are a man or a country, there is a point beyond which your strength will not go. It is courage and wisdom to exert that strength up to the limit to which you may attain; it is madness and ruin if you allow yourself to pass it.'

Salisbury believed that Britain should acknowledge that if it was not prepared to construct a vast military machine, but intended to carry on its old tolerant, passive ways, then the country's foreign policy could not afford to be too ambitious. He wrote to Lord Roberts (6 July 1885): 'We cannot reconcile ourselves to the truth, that if we will not provide cloth enough for the coat we want, we must cut down our coat to the cloth we have got. Our people require to have it driven into their heads that if they will not submit to a conscription, they must submit to a corresponding reduction of their exploits.'

Salisbury hated war. He regarded it as 'the final and supreme evil'. In his eyes, bloody conflict was the nadir of diplomacy. His major purpose was to avoid such conflagration. 'All the great triumphs of civilization in the past have been in the substitution of judicial doctrine for the cold, cruel arbitration of war,' he maintained. 'We have got rid of private war between small magnate and large magnate in this country; we have got rid of the duel between man and man, and we are slowly, as far as we can, substituting arbitration for struggles in international disputes.' Salisbury never shared the liberal optimism of the Manchester school. By the turn of the century, he was filled with apprehension at the galloping arms race and the new spirit of aggressive, selfish nationalism which was sweeping through the major European powers. 'Science has done much for the massing of armed men,' he told the Lords (27 May 1889). 'All the refined and subtle machinery of war which a nation may possess may now be concentrated and directed at the building of a single will upon a single point in an incredibly small space of time.' Salisbury predicted that when the danger came it would arrive like 'a thief in the night' and give the government 'little time to ward it off'. He was worried that 'the fiscal burden imposed on the masses' in order to pay for armaments might even provoke some country to go to war in order to ease the dangers of internal conflict. Salisbury took a Darwinian view of a death-struggle between

nations. He believed his aim should be to temporize and soften the
ferocity of that conflict and so ensure England was able to keep
her Empire intact and preserve her world trade routes. He told the
Primrose League in a memorable speech: 'You may roughly divide
the nations of the world as the living and the dying. On the one side
you have great countries of enormous power, growing in power every
year, growing in wealth, growing in dominion, growing in the per-
fection of their organization. Railways have given them the power
to concentrate upon any one point the whole military force of their
population and to assemble armies of a magnitude and power never
dreamt of in the generations that have gone by. Science has placed
in the hands of those armies weapons ever growing in their efficiency
of destruction and therefore, adding to the power – fearfully to the
power – of those who have the opportunity of using them. By the
side of these splendid organizations, of which nothing seems to
diminish the forces, and which present rival claims which the future
may be able only by a bloody arbitrament to adjust – by the side
of these there are a number of communities which I can only describe
as dying, though the epithet applies to them, of course, in very
different degrees, and with a different amount of certain application.
They are mainly communities that are not Christian but I regret to
say that is not exclusively the case, and in these states disorganization
and decay are advancing almost as fast as concentration and increasing power are advancing in the living nations that stand beside them.
Decade after decade they are weaker, poorer, and less provided with
leading men or institutions in which they can trust, apparently drawing nearer and nearer to their fate, and yet clinging with strange
tenacity to the life which they have got. In them misgovernment is
not only not cured but is constantly on the increase. The society,
and official society, the Administration, is a mass of corruption so
that there is no firm ground on which any hope of reform or restoration could be based, and in their various degrees they are presenting
a terrible picture to the more enlightened portion of the world – a
picture which, unfortunately, the increase in the means of our information and communication draws with darker and more conspicuous
lineaments in the face of all nations, appealing to their feelings as
well as to their interests, calling upon them to bring forward a remedy.
How long this state of things is likely to go on, of course, I do not
attempt to prophesy. All I can indicate is that that process is proceeding, that the weak states are becoming weaker and the strong
states are becoming stronger' (May 1898).

During his last years at the Foreign Office, Salisbury often appeared to be unsure in which category – of the living or the dying – England stood. On one occasion, he joked with a Chinese diplomat that their two countries were Empires in decline. The main cause of anxiety to Salisbury arose from the quasi-democratic foundations of the British system of government. He feared that the impact of ill-informed and emotional public opinion would make it extremely difficult to pursue any consistent foreign policy. 'An English minister contesting with foreign powers is very much in the position of a player at whist who has got a noisy and talkative friend behind him who insists on discussing, in the hearing of all present, the value of the various cards in his hand,' Salisbury argued (30 June 1898). He believed that the people were a malignant, unpredictable force, who could be easily swayed by demagogy into a mindless agitation. This was something that a Foreign Secretary could ill afford to ignore, as Salisbury explained to his old friend Acland: 'The terrible phenomenon of the time is that nations have a power of irritating each other enormously larger than they ever possessed before. They are ready to fly at each other's throats, not on account of what one nation has said of another, but on account of what one nation has overheard another saying, in its own family circle and in the conduct of its own political business. We have got to the point that we may not speak fully and cordially to the democracy that rules us, lest the report of what we should say should offend a monarchy or a democracy a thousand miles away. Under these conditions the work of the Foreign Office is not light.'

The frequent use of the telegraph annoyed Salisbury, because the immediate impact of an international crisis whipped up patriotic emotions. He was appalled by the yellow-press journalism of the 1890s, even if it did usually support the Unionist cause. Salisbury once described the *Daily Mail* as a paper 'written by office boys for office boys'. The popular press made his task at the Foreign Office more difficult by manipulating public opinion in strident tones. This is not to argue that Salisbury was not prepared to defend the Empire, although he was less than enthusiastic about taking on the white man's burden in Africa and Asia. Experience of the India Office convinced him that white and black could not live happily together. The inveterate racialism of the European was bound to cause friction among native populations and eventual upheaval. Salisbury shared none of the missionary zeal of Joseph Chamberlain for the imperial cause. He doubted whether the insular English electorate would ever agree to support the cause of an imperial Free Trade area if it meant higher food prices. When Chamberlain embraced the programme of

Tariff Reform, Salisbury viewed it from retirement as the 'ultimate calamity' to hit the Unionist alliance. Salisbury did not believe it was possible to manufacture an imperial spirit. He was sceptical of any attempts to draw the far-flung corners of the Empire together into a cohesive political, military and economic bloc. In one of his last public speeches before his retirement as Prime Minster, Salisbury argued that the cohesion of the Empire could evolve only through mutual cooperation. He told the annual meeting of the Primrose League: 'We have no power by legislation to affect the flow of opinion and of affection which has arisen so largely between the mother country and her daughter states . . . We cannot safely interfere by legislative action with the natural development of our relations with our daughter countries. All kinds of difficulties are there before us, difficulties as to the burden of finance, difficulties as to the duty of defence, difficulties as to the right of decision which the mother country should retain and unless feeling is running very strong and we have a great force behind us, I look with some apprehension upon any attempt to anticipate events, or to foreclose the results, which if we are only patient and careful, the future has in store for the Empire' (8 May 1902).

On his return to the Foreign Office in January 1887 Salisbury was faced with a serious international situation. The kidnap by the Russians and eventual abdication of Prince Alexander of Battenburg from the Bulgarian throne was threatening to disrupt the power balance in the Balkan peninsula. It was widely feared that Russia was attempting to transform Bulgaria into her obedient satellite. The British government was trying to encourage Austria-Hungary to take a stronger line against Russian intrigue. At the same time, relations between France and Germany were strained. Imminent conflict looked likely with Bismarck's call to the Reichstag for an increase in the size of the German army, and the meteoric rise of Boulanger in the Third Republic with his call for *revanche*. 'The prospect is very gloomy abroad, but England cannot brighten it,' Salisbury confessed to the Queen (24 January 1887). 'Torn in two by a controversy which almost threatens her existence, she cannot in the present state of public opinion interfere with any decisive action abroad.'

Yet with Churchill's resignation from the Cabinet, Salisbury found himself in a much stronger position to carry on his foreign policy without any danger of serious opposition from his colleagues. In the early months of 1887 Salisbury worked to ensure the containment of Russian influence in the Balkans through the creation of a defensive arrangement with other powers in the area. The Italian government suggested that he should join them in an alliance in case of any war with France. This was something which the British Prime Minister was not anxious to do. However, Salisbury was willing to support Italian interests in the Mediterranean and he was ready to accept Italy's eventual occupation of Tripoli. He informed Robilant, the Italian Foreign Minister, that England could never promise 'material assistance in view of an uncertain war', when neither the object nor cause were known. What Salisbury did agree to was cooperation with Italy in the maintenance of the *status quo* in the Aegean, Adriatic and Black Sea. Bismarck took an active interest in the progress of the Anglo-Italian negotiations and Hatzfeldt was instructed to impress upon Salisbury the necessity for such an understanding. The German government even assured Salisbury that it would back up the British interest in Egypt against French designs. The exchange of letters between Britain and Italy took place on 12 February. Salisbury explained to the Queen that he had not joined any formal alliance with Italy, but it was as close to an alliance 'as the parliamentary character of our institutions permit'. 'Your Majesty's advisers recommend it on the whole as necessary in order to avoid serious danger. If, in the present grouping of nations, which Prince Bismarck tells us is now taking place, England was left in isolation, it might well happen that the adversaries, who are coming against each other on the Continent, might treat the British Empire as divisible booty, by which their differences might be adjusted; and though England could defend herself, it would be at fearful risk and cost.' The Mediterranean Agreement was also signed by Austria-Hungary on 24 March, with Bismarck's eager blessing. The Anglo-Austrian exchange of letters recognized that the two countries had 'the same need of maintaining the *status quo* in the Orient, so far as possible, of preventing the aggrandisement of one power to the detriment of others, and consequently of acting in concert in order to ensure these cardinal principles of their policy'. The *status quo* in the Mediterranean was also guaranteed by Spain. This was a flimsy and informal diplomatic structure to keep Russia in check.

Notwithstanding the Mediterranean Agreements, which drew Britain close to the Central powers, Salisbury wanted to retain his freedom for diplomatic manoeuvre. In the spring of 1887 he made another attempt to resolve the Egyptian dilemma. British occupation of the Lower Nile valley continually poisoned Anglo-French relations and made Salisbury over-dependent on the friendship of Germany and her allies. The Prime Minister called Egypt a 'disastrous inheritance'. 'National or acquisitional feeling has been aroused; it has tasted the fleshpots and it will not let them go,' he lamented. In January 1887 Sir Henry Drummond Wolff was sent back to Constantinople by Salisbury with the job of negotiating England's withdrawal from Egypt. However, the Prime Minister insisted that the country must retain the right of reoccupation, if Egypt slipped back into anarchy. He agreed under pressure with the Turkish demand that the British evacuation should occur within three, not five years. On 22 May 1887 the Turks agreed to sign the convention. It looked as though Drummond Wolff's mission had met with success. Such optimism was, however, premature. Both Russia and France, in unison for the first time, rejected the convention angrily and the Sultan was persuaded not to ratify it. The failure of the Drummond Wolff mission marks the real end of Salisbury's attempt to extricate himself from the embarrassment of Egypt. 'I see nothing for it but to sit still and drift awhile: a little further on in the history of Europe the conditions may be changed. Till then we must simply refuse to evacuate,' Salisbury explained to the British ambassador in Paris, Lord Lyons (20 July 1887). Salisbury was angry with the French attitude and their 'incessant vexation'. 'Can you wonder that there is, in my eyes, a silver lining even to the great black cloud of a Franco-German war?' he confided to Lyons.

The collapse of the Drummond Wolff mission also highlighted Britain's weakening influence over the Sultan. It was beginning to look as though the old Crimea policy was becoming increasingly difficult to uphold. Yet British relations with France and Russia did not deteriorate immediately. An Anglo-French agreement was patched up over the dispute over the New Hebrides islands in the spring of 1887 and the two countries reached a settlement over the Suez Canal in the same year. Nor were relations too strained with Russia. A further agreement was reached over the demarcation of the Afghan border. And Salisbury gave no warm support to Prince Ferdinand of Coburg's claims for the Bulgarian throne, which pleased Russia.

Moreover he was unenthusiastic about any extension of the Mediterranean Agreements. Salisbury distrusted Bismarck's zeal to see a more formal arrangement to defend the Sultan. 'I think the time inopportune and we are merely rescuing Bismarck's somewhat endangered chestnuts,' Salisbury argued with White (2 November 1887). 'If he can get up a nice little fight between Russia and the three powers, he will have the leisure to make France a harmless neighbour for some time to come. It goes against me to be one of the Powers in that unscrupulous game.' Salisbury placed little faith in building up a front to defend the 'sickly, sensual, terrified, fickle Sultan'. Germany's secret reinsurance treaty with Russia, signed in May 1887, ensured only tepid support from Bismarck for British interests at the Porte. Yet pressure for a strengthening of the Mediterranean Agreements grew stronger. 'Whatever happens will be for the worse, and therefore it is our interest that as little should happen as possible,' Salisbury maintained (23 August 1887). None the less he agreed to exchange further letters in November with Italy and Austria-Hungary. The alternative of isolation was something the Prime Minister wished to avoid. The new agreement extended the former *status quo* guarantee to Asia Minor as well as Bulgaria and the Straits. Salisbury was unable to win Cabinet support for this decision, when Bismarck dangled the details of the 1879 treaty between Germany and Austria-Hungary in front of them. This appeared to convince the government that 'under no circumstances could the existence of Austria be imperilled by a resistance to illegal Russian enterprises'.

The new agreement was signed on 12 December. It was kept secret, on Goschen's insistence, from the Sultan, although the whole point of the treaty was to uphold 'the maintenance of the Ottoman Empire and the integrity of its territory'. Salisbury tended to spurn the agreement's importance. 'It is like putting a coarse sieve under a fine one,' he told White (14 December 1887). 'Of course, it may be said that this plan sacrifices the ideal we have pursued since Lord Stratford's days of a leading influence at Constantinople. But is not that idea a chimera? Can anyone have that leading influence for more than a month together?'

During the following year Salisbury found himself having to fend off the Italian Prime Minister, Crispi, who demanded British support in his tariff quarrels with France. But Salisbury was very reluctant to champion Italy's impetuous policies. He viewed the Mediterranean Agreements as an unfortunate necessity to prop up the traditional British position in Constantinople and as a way of keeping Berlin's support for the British position in Egypt. He did not see them as a prelude for Britain's full-blooded involvement with the Triple Alliance. However, Salisbury was unable to say anything too blunt which might upset both the Italians and, more important, Bismarck. Both Berlin and Rome urged British naval support in the Western Mediterranean. Salisbury responded by sending the Channel fleet to Genoa and La Spezia on manoeuvres. But he had no intention of rushing into any precipitate action at the behest of Crispi, who

Salisbury likened to Churchill in his unreliability and excitable nature. The Prime Minister assured Bismarck that Britain would come to Italy's assistance if she was attacked by France without offering provocation and on those grounds alone.

Such a commitment worried British naval circles who doubted the capacity of the fleet to carry out its obligations. The existing forces were no longer enough to stand up to the combined fleets of France and Russia. There were just not enough ships available to bombard Toulon, the main French naval base in the Mediterranean. As France and Russia grew palpably closer together, this problem became more intractable. In the winter of 1888 the Cabinet agreed to launch a massive and expensive naval construction programme of £21·5 million in order to establish a two-power standard for Britain. This would ensure that the navy retained a margin of superiority over any two potential aggressors. It was a way of avoiding any closer ties with the Central powers in combating the possible dangers of a Franco-Russian alliance.

None the less Salisbury's relations with Germany and her allies were warm and close in the late 1880s. In January 1889 Bismarck even made the sudden offer of a formal alliance with England. Herbert Bismarck was told by Salisbury that an Anglo-German *entente* would be 'the best tonic for both countries and for European peace'. But he was unable to take up Bismarck's suggestion. Salisbury explained that it was 'inopportune' because such an alliance would not win a parliamentary majority in the divided Commons where the government lacked an overall majority. Herbert Bismarck reported back to Berlin that Salisbury had explained, 'We live no longer, alas, in Pitt's times; the aristocracy governed then and we were able to form an active policy, which made England after the Congress of Vienna the richest and most respected power in Europe. Now democracy is on top, and with it the personal and party system, which reduces every British government to absolute dependence on the *aura popularis*. This generation can only be taught by events.'

Such constraints did not rule out Anglo-German agreements on colonial matters. By the summer of 1889 Salisbury had reached the conclusion that Britain could no longer leave Egypt whatever the French might argue. The corollary of that decision was that the Upper Nile valley which was still in the Mahdi's hands must eventually be restored to Egyptian control. This meant that the other European powers should not be allowed to extend their influence into the Sudan. Salisbury was unwilling to act on behalf of the chartered African companies or even the missionaries. But from 1889 onwards maps of Africa bedecked the walls of his office. During the next three years he helped to carve up vast territories between the European powers. His aim was not to splash Africa with the red of the British Empire, but to safeguard British interests on the Nile. Bismarck was willing to make sizeable concessions to Britain in East Africa in return for a closer friendship. The German Chancellor's fall from office in March 1890 made no difference. Neither the impetuous Kaiser Wilhelm II nor his new Chancellor, Caprivi, were too upset at the ceding of German territory in East Africa. Salisbury was able to acquire what later was to become Uganda and Kenya, as well as control over Zanzibar and Witu. He also ensured that Britain retained the Stevenson Road, but he was ready to rebuff the jingo enthusiasts of the Cape-to-Cairo-railway idea, by claiming the northern end of Lake Tanganyika for Britain to ensure a thin red line through the continent. Salisbury mocked such an idea when he explained the contents of the Anglo-German treaty to the Lords in July 1890. But the Prime Minister found considerable difficulty in persuading the Queen to accept the loss of Heligoland to Germany in return for the African acquisitions. His agreement with Germany helped to secure Britain's stake in the Upper Nile. A month later Salisbury signed a treaty with France. The French government recognized British control of Zanzibar and Pemba, and in return the Prime Minister gave France a free hand in the central and western Congo and Madagascar. In the Lords, Salisbury airily suggested that the land he had acknowledged to be French was 'very light land, that is to say, the desert of the Sahara', a comment which upset the French ambassador.

The Prime Minister had far more trouble in convincing the Italian government of the need to sign a demarcation treaty in East Africa. But by 1890 Salisbury was tired of the antics of Crispi in the Mediterranean with his claims for Tripoli and exaggerated fears of a French attack on Italy from Bizerta. He disliked Italian activities in northeast Africa, which appeared to impinge onto the Upper Nile valley. 'A good deal of exaggerated language is used in diplomatic conversation and post-prandial oratory as to the value of the Italian alliance to England,' he wrote to Baring (31 August 1890). 'It is desirable; but it is not worth a very great price, even in African square miles.' Crispi's pretensions irritated Salisbury. There was an abortive attempt at a colonial settlement between the two powers at Naples in October 1890. The Prime Minister explained to the British ambassador to Rome, Lord Dufferin (16 January 1891), 'There is a misapprehension in the Italian way of looking at affairs which causes infinite trouble. They imagine that their alliance is a pearl of great price which we would do well to secure; and on the strength of this belief they are constantly hinting that we should show our gratitude by large material concessions. I confess I do not take this view. To my mind the Italian alliance is an unprofitable and even slightly onerous corollary to the German alliance.' It was not until March 1891 that di Rudini, the Italian Prime Minister, signed an agreement with Salisbury over East Africa. It met all Salisbury's demands. The Upper Nile valley was now safe for reconquest when the time became ripe.

With Bismarck's fall Germany's reinsurance treaty with Russia came to an end. France and Russia began to close ranks. In July 1891 the French fleet visited Kronstadt and played the 'Marseillaise'. Salisbury made every effort to placate France. 'It is most important to persuade the French, if we can, that England has no antipathy to France, or any partisanship against her,' he explained to the Queen. Salisbury was ready to give vague assurances to Italy in the Mediterranean over Tripoli and Tunis, but he was anxious not to upset France. He refused to stand up to the French in Morocco, despite Italian insistence.

In early 1892 it began to look as though Salisbury's foreign policy was edging to the brink of collapse. Ever since the spring of 1890 there had been pressure from the naval experts that it was no longer tenable for Britain to expect to continue with its traditional policy of defending Constantinople from Russian attack. The rise of the Franco-Russian alliance made it impossible for the Royal Navy to block the Russians at the Straits and at the same time keep a wary eye on the French in the Western Mediterranean. Salisbury's attempts to mend fences with France and the Sultan had not proved very successful. And yet it now appeared that his bending towards the Central powers was untenable. The report of military intelligence was discussed in the Cabinet in June 1892. The Prime Minister was sceptical of its value. He drew up a powerful memorandum in which he warned that it looked from the report that foreign and military policy had grown divergent, and that 'the most serious disaster' could result. 'At present, if the two officers in question are correct in their views, our policy is a policy of false pretences,' he argued. 'If persisted in, it will involve discomfiture to all who trust in us and infinite discredit to ourselves.' Salisbury was unwilling to accept the logic of the Report, that limited alignment with the Central powers was no adequate counter to French power. Two months later he found himself out of office, so he was spared the difficulty of resolving the question. Salisbury left his successor Lord Rosebery with an account of England's diplomatic position in August 1892. 'The key of the present situation in Europe is our position towards Italy, and through Italy to the Triple Alliance,' he argued. 'While keeping clear of any assurance of material assistance, we have expressed the strongest concurrence in the Italian policy of maintaining the *status quo* in the Mediterranean.' Salisbury warned that if Britain was too cold to Italy the Italian government would pull out of the Triple Alliance and go over to France. This would ensure that Germany and Austria were too weak to withstand a possible attack from Russia and France and mean a Berlin–St Petersburg *rapprochement* with dire consequences for Constantinople. But by the time Salisbury returned to the Foreign Office three years later the diplomatic picture had drastically changed.

Governments can do so little
and prevent so little nowadays.
Power has passed
from the hands of statesmen,
but I should be very much puzzled
to say into whose hands it has passed.
It is all pure drifting.
As we go down stream,
we can occasionally fend off a collision;
but where are we going?
Salisbury to Cranbrook, 1 January 1895

9

UNIONISM TRIUMPHANT:

AT HOME

August 1892–July 1902

Salisbury wanted to dissolve Parliament in the autumn of 1892 but he was over-ruled by the rest of his Cabinet, who preferred a summer general election. Ministers in the Commons argued that Conservative back-benchers would not bother to stay at Westminster if the session dragged on again through July, so that the government's majority might shrink to nothing in the lobbies. Captain Middleton, the party's shrewd national agent, was also a confident champion of an early appeal to the country. Salisbury was unconvinced, but he was reluctant to defy party opinion. Only Chamberlain offered the advice that the government should stick it out until the autumn. 'It would be hazardous to impose a policy profoundly distasteful to them, based on the advice of Mr Chamberlain alone. It might provoke mutiny, or at all events disgust and resentment, and consequently antipathy,' Salisbury explained to the Queen. Parliament, therefore, was dissolved on 28 June.

Salisbury made the threat of Irish Home Rule (if the Liberals won) and the promise of Conservative social reform the major themes of his party's campaign. He tried to convince the voters that the main obstacle to the passage of measures beneficial to the working classes came not from any crusty Tory prejudice, but from Gladstone's single-minded obsession to bring so-called justice to Ireland to the exclusion of anything else. Salisbury believed that his government's domestic record, mainly over the previous three years, was proof enough that Conservatives were not hostile to change. He promised that the party would deal with the problems raised by the conflict between capital and labour and the widespread existence of poverty, if returned for another term. Salisbury explained at length in a letter to *The Times* what the Conservatives proposed: 'The diminution of poverty, the prevention of ruinous disputes in trade, the amendment of the Poor Law, the protection of the lives and health of the industrial community, are matters of which it is not easy to exaggerate the momentous interest. Under our existing constitution the working classes are evidently powerful enough to obtain any measure, which upon discussion, they generally believe will conduce to their welfare. No party will have the power or is likely to pursue the policy, of refusing to listen to their unanimous wish.'

The Prime Minister claimed that Britain's 'sound system of finance based on a pacific policy' should enable the Conservatives to devote their energies to social issues in the future.

All the same, Salisbury was vague about the content of any social reform 'programme'. He was far more intent on concentrating public attention on Ireland. Unionists warned that a Liberal victory followed by the passing of a Home Rule Bill would provoke civil war on the other side of the Irish Sea. They argued that the Protestant majority in Ulster would refuse to submit to any autonomous government established in Dublin. Balfour and Chamberlain were the main platform speakers for the Unionist alliance during the campaign. Salisbury stayed aloof, on the convention that peers did not speak in elections.

The Liberals just managed to nose ahead in a tightly fought contest. Gladstone came back to power without an overall majority. His survival depended on the goodwill and support of the seventy-two Irish Nationalists. The Unionists polled just over two million

votes (47·3 per cent of the total) and 268 Conservatives and forty-
seven Liberal Unionists were returned to Westminster. It seemed
that there was little real movement of political opinion since the 1886
election. In fact, the Liberal share of the vote dropped by 0·7 per
cent to 44·2 per cent. The big difference came with the fall in the
number of uncontested Unionist seats. This went down from 117 in
1886 to a mere forty-one.

Salisbury decided to hang on until the new Parliament assembled
on 4 August. Chamberlain wanted Salisbury to prove Unionist concern for social reform by unveiling an ambitious programme at once.
Such an idea did not appeal to him. 'It implies we have bills ready –
at least in outline – to sustain our programme. We have not,' Salisbury
explained to Balfour. 'It must deal with subjects on which people
are very sensitive on both sides; and though we may use phrases
which will please Joe, we must in so doing alarm a good many people
who have always been with us. I fear that these social questions are
destined to break up our party; but why incur the danger before the
necessity has arrived, and while the party may still be useful to
avert Home Rule?' A week after the Commons reassembled, the
government lost a vote of confidence. Salisbury travelled down to
Osborne and handed his resignation over to a distraught Queen
Victoria.

He sympathized with her plight. Salisbury also feared Gladstone's
return to office would prove harmful to the national interest, although he was sure the old man would have to waste a lot of time
in an attempt to escape from the results of his own 'reckless language'.
But Salisbury was thankful to lay down the unwelcome burdens
of the premiership after six years. He confessed to Lord Henry Cecil
such a length of time was 'about the extreme limit to which the
strength given to men will carry them in the discharge of laborious
offices'. Salisbury was said to have displayed an 'indecent haste' in
his resignation. He left a memorandum on the state of diplomatic
relations behind at the Foreign Office for the new Foreign Secretary,
Lord Rosebery, and then fled to his villa at Puys. Salisbury was
forced to draw up an honours list, a task he found as tiresome and
degrading as ever. 'I think if Dante had known all we know, he
would have created another inferno, worse than all the others, in
which unhappy sinners should be condemned eternally to the task
of distributing two honours among a hundred people so as to satisfy
them all,' he grumbled to Manners. Salisbury did not believe that
he would ever become Prime Minister again, nor hold any other
high office of state. 'I suppose any new Unionist Cabinet must include

Chamberlain and Churchill. I doubt if I am exactly the man to lead them,' he confided to Manners. 'I do not think I could accept any other office than that which I hold. A study of Lord John Russell's career has convinced me that the dowager prime ministers in a Cabinet are nothing but a nuisance.' A few weeks of rest at the Chalet Cecil made Salisbury realize how tired he was. 'The F.O. leaves you no holiday – not for a weekend. After six years one gets to hate the sight of a red box and to feel doubtful whether one is giving the necessary attention and thought,' he wrote to Cranbrook (24 August). 'If a change of men could be affected without a change of policy, it would have been quite desirable. I could see that many of my colleagues were as tired as I was and poor Smith – we know how fatigue affected him.'

The narrow election defeat was not too upsetting to Salisbury. He was sure the Unionist alliance would prove a far 'more united phalanx' on the opposition benches than it would ever have been if the Conservatives had come back with a tiny Commons majority to face 'endless controversies'. Salisbury refused to accept that Gladstone's victory was a mandate for Home Rule. He left no doubts that the Conservative majority in the Lords would be mobilized to destroy any Liberal measures he disliked. 'The object I have in view is to make it evident either that the House of Lords has all the independent right necessary to a second chamber – if it is too weak for that, then to force men to face the fact that a stronger body must be substituted,' he disclosed to Alfred Austin (28 October). 'What I dread is that the House of Lords should be bullied into allowing its independent right to become atrophied, while the name of the second chamber remains to it – thus leaving the House of Commons in unchecked supremacy.'

Salisbury defended the Upper House in a signed article in the November 1892 edition of the *National Review*. He spoke contemptuously of Gladstone's 'motley' majority of thirty-eight, which he claimed was based on the votes of a mere 765 electors scattered through the marginal seats. In his view this was not enough to justify 'the supreme abandonment' of the Irish Protestant community. Home Rule was not the only question that had been put to the voters, Salisbury claimed. In Wales radicals triumphed on the Church disestablishment issue. Up in Scotland and in East Anglia, voters for the Liberal party were 'full of agrarian projects and aspirations'. Coal-miners supported the Liberals because of their demand for an eight-hour working day. Leicester went for Liberalism because of its opposition to vaccination. Salisbury pointed out that in other Western European democracies, constitutions provided checks and balances, such as weighted majorities, to prevent any drastic organic change. In Britain, only the House of Lords could check or question the supreme authority of the Commons which was now highly disciplined by the needs of the party system and obedient to the dictates of the Prime Minister. It was Salisbury's opinion that the success of the British constitution was due to its very illogicality. He believed that the upper assembly should only go against its own collective opinion if the Commons enjoyed the obvious support of the people for a measure, expressed at the ballot box. 'That the Lords is likely to set itself against the will of the nation, when that will has been sufficiently ascertained, is an assumption so much at variance with all that it has done in the past that the hypothesis need not be discussed,' Salisbury argued.

Despite his tiny Commons majority, Gladstone was quite determined to try once again to push an Irish Home Rule Bill onto the statute book. The new measure was given a first reading in February 1893. The session was almost entirely devoted to its passage through Parliament. Balfour and Chamberlain fought every clause of the bill tooth and claw through the committee stage. The government was compelled to resort to the guillotine. The Unionist leaders in the Commons kept in close touch with Salisbury and Devonshire. Salisbury did not retain a prudent silence. He paid a visit to Ulster in May 1893 where his unyielding oratory captivated the beleaguered Protestant community. Twenty years later the Conservative leader Bonar Law was criticized for his militantly Unionist outbursts during the third Home Rule Bill crisis before the Great War. Salisbury provided an eloquent precedent. In Ulster Hall in Belfast, the Leader of the Opposition spoke of Home Rule as 'the insane eccentricity' of one man. It would mean putting 'the most prosperous, the most thrifty, the most advanced province in the United Kingdom' under 'the government of those less advanced and less successful'. Ulster was 'a rampart of the Empire, to beat back the waves of iniquity and darkness'. Salisbury went over to Londonderry and addressed the Apprentice Boys, warning them about 'that ancient, arrogant, hostile, lawless spirit which often hides itself behind a blackened garment and sometimes masquerades in ecclesiastical garments'.

The Home Rule Bill did not eventually emerge from the Commons until 1 September, with a majority of thirty-four on the third reading. The Lords lost no time. Within a week they threw the measure out by 419 votes to forty-one. Salisbury made a powerful contribution to their debate. Some of his tightly structured arguments retain their

F

value today in the debate over power-sharing in Northern Ireland.
Salisbury maintained, 'Ireland is a country which from the first has
been deeply divided to the base by perpetual differences and conflicts.
It is a society in which unity has never existed. I defy you to devise
any system of government that shall be in the true and literal sense
to the satisfaction of the governed, for three-fifths of the governed
will like it and two-fifths of the governed will detest it. It is an
absurdity, because it is impossible.'

What was the answer? Salisbury saw no alternative to Abraham
Lincoln's dictum – 'keep pegging away'. Ireland could hope for rest
and tranquillity only after another two generations. There was no
chance that Conservatives would change their views. He argued: 'It
takes long to change the opinion of a nation, of a people, of a party.
Gladstonian peers imagine that it takes as long to change the
opinions of a party as it takes to change their own, but that is a
lamentable error. The mass of mankind are much stauncher than
that. Men hold to their beliefs and will not desert them, and a
community changes its opinion not in any great degree by a change
in the opinion of the individuals of which it is composed, as by the
fact that the men who have grown up in one set of opinions and
clung to them die off, and others who had no cause to form those
opinions succeed and take their place. That is the history of a change
in the opinion of a community.'

Gladstone wanted to call an immediate general election after Home
Rule's defeat on the issue of the peers against the people. His
Cabinet colleagues dissuaded him from such a step. In March 1894
the old Liberal leader decided to retire. He resigned the premiership
in protest at the spiralling cost of naval estimates. Lord Rosebery
succeeded him. For the next fifteen months he led a divided and
quarrelsome Cabinet continually on the verge of collapse.

The failure to pass Irish Home Rule brought no relaxation from
the opposition of the Unionist alliance. There was now a clear-sighted
resolve to question every major item of the Liberal 'programme'.
In the Lords, Salisbury marshalled his aristocratic forces for battle.
He did not look upon every Liberal bill with a scornful eye. The
measure to establish parish councils in England and Wales caused
him no worries. Salisbury argued that 'this age has a passion for
symmetry – for what we call tidiness in legislation'. He did not
suppose that it was either possible or even desirable to stand out
against such a general tendency. On the other hand, Salisbury
thought Liberal claims for the value of the councils was somewhat
'exaggerated'. He acknowledged that if the Conservatives resisted

the new bodies, then the labourers would think that there was something in them after all, and such a feeling would tend to diminish the loyalty of the labourers 'to the institutions under which they lived'. All the same, Salisbury proceeded to make the Parish Council Bill toothless with a series of crippling amendments.

Other Liberal measures were simply emasculated by the Lords. An Employer Liability Bill was destroyed beyond repair when the Upper House inserted a clause into the measure that allowed working men to contract out of its provisions. An effort to legislate on local option by licensing authorities proved equally abortive. Salisbury never believed that the restrictionism of the law could stamp out demon drink, which he agreed was a 'barbaric vice'. He put his faith for reform on the spread of 'education and enlightenment', not on the imposition of 'a dogmatic theology by force'. Salisbury refused to accept that 'sober people' should be deprived of something that was 'looked upon as harmless, as a salutary indulgence' merely 'to prevent a small minority of drunkards from giving way to their own bestial propensities'. He took up a familiar attitude on the need to safeguard denominational education in the voluntary schools. He explained to the Lords (4 September 1893): 'The notion that there is a religion expunging that upon which men differ, and leaving nothing but that upon which all men can agree, is the wildest chimera that ever entered the brain of a politician. A politician cannot make these things happen as he desires. The religious conviction is much too strong for him. It will have its way and all you will do by this attempt to force an impossible neutrality upon the mind you are attempting to teach the most important things will be undoubtedly to propagate infidelity in the first place and in the next, to promote a bitter, angry religious reaction, from which the education you are trying to press forward will be the first to suffer.'

Salisbury spoke out against the formation of a royal commission to examine the land question in Wales. He took the view that Parliament had 'no right to interfere in the contracts between landlord and tenant'. He was highly critical of the decision to set up a commission on evicted tenants in Ireland because it would teach the tenantry that 'those who defy the law shall be taken care of, and those who obey the law shall be neglected'.

Salisbury was not entirely destructive during his short period in opposition. In November 1894 Chamberlain suggested the Conservative peers should embrace certain social reforms 'as an antidote to the Gladstonian policy of destruction'. This would prevent the government attempting to use the rallying cry of the people against the peers in an early general election. The Birmingham radical wanted Salisbury to bring forward an alien immigration bill, local and trade option for shopkeepers on their hours of work, the creation of industrial arbitration courts, the establishment of labour exchanges, encouragement for local authorities with slum clearance, cheap commuter transport, compensation for industrial injuries, technical education and temperance reform. In a long reply, Salisbury made it clear he did not object to most of the content of reforms that Chamberlain proposed. His only doubts centred on the suggestion of controlling liquor-licensing and 'the largeness of the principle' involved in any state intervention in the fixing of working hours for shopkeepers. What Salisbury really questioned was the tactical sense of trying to hatch a great deal of legislation on the Opposition benches. He was inclined to restrict the number of measures to press from the Opposition benches to only two – artisan dwellings and trade arbitration. Salisbury held no strong objection to the principle of an employer's liability for injuries to his workers, but he did regard the proposal with apprehension from 'a tactical point of view'. 'Parties are always liable to the suspicion on the part of their supporters that the leaders may, in their anxiety to obtain new support, be inclined to hold cheaply the material interests of those whom their legislation affects,' Salisbury argued. 'If by any precipitate adoption of a very comprehensive legislation at this point, we were to alarm the interests concerned, I think we should do ourselves great injury and I do not believe that we should gain any support that would indemnify us for the mistake. Many of our friends are suspicious and are easily shaken off; most of our enemies are implacable and would merely accept our concessions as a confession that we were wrong and a ground for persisting in their opposition to us.'

However, there was one piece of legislation which Salisbury did champion from the Opposition benches. In July 1894 he called for a state restriction on the entry of destitute aliens into Britain, warning of the injury they inflicted on working-class living standards with their depressive impact on wage rates and the burden they imposed on the Poor Law. Salisbury argued that the state had the right 'to say that our system of poor law and our social system is for ourselves'. He wanted to increase health checks on immigrants and revive the power to expel any foreigner 'whose presence in this country is either dangerous to the public peace or is likely to promote the commission of crimes elsewhere'.

By the summer of 1895 the Rosebery government was divided and dispirited. After an unexpected Commons defeat over a vote on the cordite supply Rosebery resigned. Salisbury agreed to become Prime Minister once again. This time he found no difficulty in bringing Chamberlain and Devonshire into the Cabinet. Rows between local Conservatives and Liberal Unionists, notably at Leamington, could not mask the growing cohesion between the two branches of the alliance, strengthened by the tactics of the previous three years in opposition. Salisbury experienced his usual dislike of Cabinetmaking. The need to bring in leading Liberal Unionists provoked some discontent from disappointed Conservatives, who felt they were more entitled to high office. Salisbury was certainly generous to his allies. Devonshire was offered the Foreign Office, but he refused and became Lord President of the Council. The Prime Minister was quite willing to accept Chamberlain in an important domestic post. Salisbury suggested that he might become Home Secretary or Chancellor of the Exchequer. He was surprised to discover that Chamberlain wanted to take the Colonial Office, but agreed to the request. Other Liberal Unionists filled important Cabinet places. Lansdowne became Secretary of State for War and Goschen took charge of the Admiralty. Lord James of Hereford was made Chancellor of the Duchy of Lancaster. Balfour as Leader in the Commons and Hicks Beach, who went back to the Treasury, were the leading Conservatives in the Cabinet.

Salisbury was in a confident, bellicose mood when he addressed the Lords on 6 July as Prime Minister. He called for an end to 'the kind of muffled civil war' in which he claimed the country had lived 'for more than a generation'. The time was now ripe, Salisbury argued, to attend to 'the restoration of prosperity and the decrease of suffering among the poorer classes of the population'. Parliament must turn its attention to the plight of the agricultural interest. There was a need to extend the ownership of small-holdings and take some of the burden of local taxation off the shoulders of the farming community. Then Parliament must look at the urgent problem of the cities where vast populations were 'terribly subject to all the vicissitudes which change of fashion and change in trade might bring among them'. Salisbury was offering no panaceas, but he did suggest that much could be done 'in alleviating the conditions of those who, by no fault of their own, are cast into misery'. The Poor Law's administration required reform. There was a need for more homes for the working classes. Rosebery was so taken aback by the tone of Salisbury's speech that he claimed the Prime Minister had surrendered to the 'Birmingham clique' in his Cabinet.

The 1895 general election began on 12 July and ended on 10

August. It was Unionism's finest hour. The opposition was annihilated, with only 177 Liberals and 82 Irish Nationalists returned to Westminster. In the Commons Salisbury enjoyed a crushing majority of 152, with 340 Conservatives and 71 Liberal Unionists sitting on the government benches. The victory was, however, less decisive in terms of the votes cast. The Unionists managed only to poll 31,000 votes more than their opponents, 49·2 per cent of the electorate. The Liberals helped Unionism by leaving 130 seats uncontested. The election re-emphasized the English character of Unionism. In Wales the Unionists won only 9 out of 34 constituencies, although they did make advances in Scotland, taking 31 out of the 70 seats. In England the Liberals were decimated with 343 Unionists returned out of 456 M.P.s. The Conservatives did spectacularly well in Lancashire where the Liberal party suffered for its weakness over the import duty on cotton goods imposed by the Indian government (48 Unionists were returned and only 7 Liberals and an Irish Nationalist). There was also a Conservative landslide in London, where 54 Conservatives were returned and only 8 Liberals.

What did this result signify? The Liberal historian R.C.K. Ensor believed that England, unlike the rest of the United Kingdom, had been caught up in 'the currents of expansive imperialism'. W.H. Lecky wrote about 1895 in his *Democracy and Liberty*. He believed that it showed 'how enormously men had over-rated the importance of the noisy group of Socialists, faddists, and revolutionaries that float upon the surface of English political thought'. In Lecky's view it was a powerful vindication of constitutional government and meant the end of 'the spirit of feverish unrest'. Salisbury compared the Unionist victory to that won by the Younger Pitt in 1784. He believed that the alliance could look forward with confidence to 'an epoch of continuous rule'. Liberalism had suffered a crushing blow. Salisbury was convinced that he knew the reason why. 'The tinkering at the mechanism of the constitution is at best an evil necessity, and cannot be more than an exceptional proceeding. The Liberal party have committed a fault in believing that for all time they were to uproot and uproot and uproot, and that no other result is to come from the political exertions of their followers. The great lesson of this election is to dissipate that doctrine to the winds,' he told the Lords (15 August 1895).

The historian Halevy spoke of 1895 as 'a turning-point in the history of the English people'. 'No party has ever had such a chance – it remains to be seen what they will make of it,' wrote the young Winston Churchill. 'To my mind they are strong – too brilliant altogether.' Chamberlain believed that the government was in a position to do something which would make it 'memorable'. But Salisbury was uncertain of what lay ahead. Unionism had proved to be a formidable defensive alliance, against the threats of disintegration. After thirty years of prophecy and argument, Salisbury now found himself at the head of a constitutional block, dedicated to national cohesion and moderate social reform, which he had argued for in the days of Palmerston. For the most part, Unionism was a pragmatic, cautious political force, but Salisbury was acutely aware that the coalition needed the existence of a formidable common threat like Home Rule to bind its divergent interests together. The 1895 election was such a decisive defeat for the Liberals that issues like Home Rule, abolition of the House of Lords, the disestablishment of the Church of England and local veto disappeared from the forefront of British politics. The coalition could therefore no longer be nurtured by a sense of national crisis. Salisbury began to worry that his government would consequently break up. 'We have been very fortunate. But though our majority will probably be larger and more homogeneous than in 1886, the difficulties that lie before us are greater,' he explained to Balfour (22 July 1895). 'To some extent we shall be invited to enter upon a legislative ocean that is unknown to us – and the steering may be difficult. However, it is all in a day's work. Whatever happens to us, I think that the position of the House of Lords is very considerably strengthened.' 'Yes, the united national party will have to make mutual concessions and there will be plenty of carping critics in and outside of it,' he wrote to Cranbrook.

For the remaining seven years of active political life, Salisbury was almost wholly preoccupied with foreign policy, but a concentration on international diplomacy should not lead to a neglect of his government's domestic record. It is not often realized that Salisbury regarded social reform as the most important single issue in 1895. He did not see his mandate as one for imperial expansion, even if this was later to be seen as the most notable achievement of his ministry. 'The most interesting feature of these times is not in my department,' he wrote to Cranbrook (12 December 1896). 'I mean the labour wars. I can hardly doubt that the labourers will get the worst of it – but I fear they will not give way till they have organized the employers into federations and trusts and such vile things – and then where will the poor consumer be?'

Salisbury believed that, within circumscribed limits, governments should do what they could to mitigate the excesses of industrial strife and poverty. 'It is the improvement of the daily life of the struggling millions and the diminution of the sorrows that so many are condemned to bear, which is the blessed task that parliaments are called into existence to perform,' he informed the Lords. What the victory of 1895 meant was the end of 'the age of reform' and the beginning of 'the question of social amelioration'. 'We have got, as far as we can, to make this country more pleasant to live in for the vast majority,' he told an enthusiastic crowd in Watford in October 1895.

'Is it not more important that we should save men, well-to-do men from ruin and working men from starvation, instead of bringing forward measures whose only effect can be to hound class against class, and creed against creed in our country?' Salisbury questioned.

He was, however, imprecise and vague on what governments could do about social reform. Salisbury disliked 'programmatic' politics throughout his life, even if he did accept that the working classes were now the arbitrator of the country's electoral fortunes. Nor did he accept there was any panacea to conjure away the evils he so acutely analysed in his speeches and writings. 'We do not live in a despotic country, where a vast change, like the freedom of the serfs, can be affected by the signature of an autocrat,' he argued. 'We have to persuade the people of the excellence of every considerable change which we introduce into their institutions.' Consequently, measures must be 'circumspect and tentative in character'. Governments would have to abstain from any legislation which alarmed men and 'cast doubt and disquiet'.

Salisbury was convinced that the real answer to poverty and unemployment lay through a revival of business confidence in government policy. 'All the measures which the Socialists preach, even if they could, which they cannot, be carried into effect, would not confer one half the benefits which could be conferred if capital, under the influence of unbroken confidence, could flow easily from employer to employed,' Salisbury argued. 'That is the vital thing. That is the life-blood of the body politic and the body commercial. Where confidence is, there is prosperity and civilization. Where confidence is not you are on the rapid road to anarchy and ruin.' The purpose of government was to overcome 'the black, impassable stream of distrust' which lay between 'the overflowing coffers of capital and the half-starved suffering labourer'.

Salisbury believed that one way of achieving this was to extend the boundaries of individual freedom, not in a crude *laissez-faire* way, but through the encouragement of diversity and the removal of constraints on human action. Salisbury wanted 'to free the energies and support the efforts of an intelligent and industrious people'. He was no doctrinaire, warning against the dangers of 'ethereal doctrines and high-flying theories'. 'We think that human affairs must be carried out on the principle of experiments, finding out by actual trying how much good can be done and how much harm can be avoided,' Salisbury explained. But he was not prepared to accept that social reform should involve any massive increase in public expenditure that would require additional direct taxation. 'However much you may desire to benefit your neighbour, do not benefit him by taking money out of the pockets of another man.' In Salisbury's view this would destroy confidence. He was no less hostile to any suggestion that there should be a revival of protection. As a land-owner, he sympathized with the agricultural interest, suffering from the long economic depression, but Salisbury refused to accept that a tariff on food imports was a way of either helping the farmers or providing the means of raising the necessary revenue for paying for urgent social reform.

These constraints on the raising of more government income made sure Salisbury's government did not embark on any ambitious domestic legislation to benefit the working classes. Although Hicks Beach was able to achieve a number of handsome budget surpluses during the late 1890s, these were mainly swallowed up either in an increase in the size of the navy or helping to pay for overseas military expeditions, notably in the Sudan and South Africa.

All the same, Salisbury's government was not entirely without domestic achievement. In 1896 there was the Conciliation Act, which empowered the Board of Trade to appoint arbitrators in industrial disputes if both sides of industry were agreeable. In the following year, Chamberlain piloted through a bold measure to provide com-pensation to workers who sustained injuries while at work as long as they were not due to the worker's own negligence. This was a far more sweeping proposal than the abortive bill which the Liberals had tried to put on the statute book in the previous Parliament. Salisbury raised no objections to it. On the contrary, he came to the bill's defence, when it was attacked in the Lords by that incorrigible champion of free enterprise, the Earl of Wemyss, who suggested that workmen's compensation was socialistic.

As Salisbury told the Lords: 'There is a great danger of Socialism in the present day. It is an inclined plane down which we are tending to move. It is a snare which we should avoid in all our legislation; but it is impossible to cry "wolf" when there is no wolf there and if you perpetually cry out "Socialism" whenever an Act for the benefit of the people is introduced. You do not weaken the Socialistic propaganda by doing so. On the contrary, you destroy the argument which will be used against it and you give to every Socialist reasoner a basis for saying that the arguments against his views are simply imaginary and pointing to your extravagance as proof. To my mind the line which is to be drawn in dealing with state interference is largely affected, if not entirely governed by the question whether you are saving property or life. Where property is in question I am guilty, like him [Wemyss] of erecting individual liberty as an idol, and of resenting all attempts to destroy or fetter it; but when you pass from liberty to life, in no well-governed state governed according to the principles of common humanity, are the claims of mere liberty allowed to endanger the lives of the citizens. The state has a right and it is the duty of the state to see to those interests which are represented by safety of life and limb for all its citizens' (29 July 1897).

Salisbury remained as concerned as ever during his final years as Prime Minister that the Conservatives should not neglect social reform. 'There is no surer guide to the party in trying to maintain and to improve their hold over public opinion in London than that they should devote all the power they possess to getting rid of that which is really a scandal to our civilization – the sufferings which many of the working class have to undergo, in the most moderate, I might say the most pitiable, accommodation,' he told the National Union (19 December 1900). 'They have been created quite as much by economic laws as by any conscious human agency . . . You must not allow yourselves to be frightened away from the remedies for social evils by the fact that they are made a cover or pretence for attacks upon property and other institutions.'

Yet in retrospect the legislative record of the 1895 ministry does look feeble. Salisbury's government went some way to help the ailing agricultural community. An act was passed in 1896 to reduce rates payable on farming land by half. Greater safeguards were established to stop the import of diseased livestock into Britain. And in 1899 a bill tightened up controls on the quality of food and drug imports. There was also the 1900 Agricultural Holdings Act to simplify land-transfer procedures.

The 1898 Vaccination Act led to a sharp increase in the number of children vaccinated against infectious diseases. There were some modifications in the administration of the Poor Law after a parliamentary select committee reported on the subject in 1896. The 1899

London Government Act aroused a good deal of controversy, with the establishment of twenty-eight London boroughs, under the county council structure. Liberals denounced the measure as a Unionist attempt to divide and rule radical County Hall. A number of measures reformed the law on criminal evidence, infant life protection, the running of the prisons, vagrancy and money-lending. A bill was passed to amend the Factory Acts and improve health standards at work. In both 1899 and 1900 modest measures amended previous working-class housing legislation. Salisbury's government also passed bills to improve the working conditions of coal-miners, cotton-operatives and shop assistants. None of these domestic reforms were particularly earth-shattering, and they aroused no bitter divisions at Westminster.

Education was a different matter. Here, Salisbury's Cabinet nearly tore itself apart. A bill was brought forward in the 1896 session. It was mainly designed to reorganize the education system by making the local authorities broadly responsible for the administering of the schools. Under pressure from Chamberlain, who refused to desert his Nonconformist convictions, the Cabinet agreed to drop the intended provision for the direct-rate aid of the voluntary schools. None the less, the bill suffered a rough passage in the Commons during the committee stage. Balfour came to the conclusion that the measure would have to be abandoned. Salisbury did his best to persuade his Commons front bench to press on with the bill. He pointed out 'in the strongest language' of 'the great danger of the decision' as 'an unexampled triumph to obstructionism'. The Queen was so furious with the Cabinet that she insisted Salisbury should recall his colleagues and make them change their minds. But the Prime Minister was still unable to convince the Commons ministers of their mistake and he had to yield to their opinion. Salisbury won a bare Cabinet majority with Chamberlain's support for the introduction of two smallish measures in the 1897 session to provide additional grant aid to both voluntary and board schools without any reorganization of the system.

There was one particularly glaring matter on which no progress was made during Salisbury's rule, despite earlier hopes. The Unionists dragged their feet over old-age pensions. Chamberlain did not press the subject on which he spoke with such vigour in the early 1890s. A royal commission came to no positive conclusions over pensions in 1893. A parliamentary committee spent two years mulling over the problem, but its report in 1898 did not progress matters any further. A Commons select committee under the chairmanship of

Harry Chaplin, President of the Local Government Board, recommended in 1899 that all needy and deserving poor over the age of sixty-five should receive five shillings a week under strict conditions. A further committee was set up to find out how much this would all cost but it did not come up with any report until 1900. By that time the Boer War ruled out any faint chance of helping the aged. 'We ought to make in the first instance only tentative proposals, which will not commit us to a very large undertaking beyond recall,' Salisbury assured Hicks Beach (31 August 1899). Salisbury envisaged paying pensions to the over-seventies. 'It is very easy to go further afterwards,' he explained to a doubting Chancellor of the Exchequer. 'I am sceptical of the possibility of any large measure and I think any measure in favour of those who are not in real poverty would be very unjust,' Salisbury told Hicks Beach (18 December 1899). 'Some relaxation of the rigour of the Poor Law in favour of old people would be (within the limits of financial feasibility) both just and wise. But that is not urgent just yet.'

There was, however, substantial and lasting achievement in one area of domestic policy. Gerald Balfour's work at the Irish Office 'to kill Home Rule by kindness' may not have weakened the political grip of the Nationalists over the Irish electorate, but it brought comparative quiet and prosperity to that turbulent country after decades of unrest. The government no longer had to resort to the use of the Crimes Act anywhere in Ireland during the 1895 ministry. Sustained efforts were made to improve Irish agriculture, with the creation of a Department of Agriculture and Technical Instruction in 1899 and an increase in the income and responsibilities of the Congested District Boards. Horace Plunkett's cooperative movement brought economic benefits to Irish agriculture with the government's blessing. The 1896 Land Purchase Act aroused the fury of the Irish landlords, but it stimulated the gradual creation of that conservative peasant proprietor class which was to be the social backbone of the new Ireland. After the bitterness of the 1880s, there was very little anguish on the Unionist benches when Salisbury's government gave Ireland local self-government in 1898 on the English model. This gave a valuable opportunity for Irish politicians to exercise power at the local level. It was one more sign that Salisbury and his Cabinet were ready to preside over a social revolution in Ireland just as long as it did not destroy the Anglo-Irish Union. Further concessions were to enflame right-wing opinion after 1903, but they took most of the sting out of the Home Rule issue which the divided Liberals preferred to ignore during the late 1890s.

During his final spell as Prime Minister, Salisbury was unable to enjoy his old freedom in the running of the government. Although he retained much of his reputation for sagacity and common sense, his word no longer went unquestioned in Cabinet. Salisbury continued to preside over his colleagues with a genial tolerance. There was 'a tacit understanding' that ministers should only speak out in Cabinet on the work of their own departments, but by the end of the 1890s it was clear that Balfour, Chamberlain and the Duke of Devonshire were exercising far more influence over Cabinet proceedings than Salisbury himself. The Prime Minister was willing to accept his self-effacement. He withdrew even more than ever into his own private family world. Although Salisbury's prestige was relatively unscarred outside the government, there was a steady, growing flow of criticism within, as his hold over public affairs became frail and uncertain. 'I have great sympathy for Salisbury and his practice of holding few and far Cabinets but this enhances his difficulties, as he nurses a policy until the time comes for an expression in action and he then finds his Cabinet against him, and has to retrace his steps. This for a strong and proud man must be very unpleasant,' Lord George Hamilton wrote to Balfour (12 January 1896).

Salisbury's ideas and attitudes appeared exasperatingly mid-Victorian to the impatient 'new men' of the Unionist alliance. There was the feeling that he was out of step with the aggressive spirit of the times. This did not just apply to foreign policy. It appeared to affect his whole outlook. Yet in his response to domestic politics, Salisbury had not really lost his sureness of touch. It is true that his comments on poverty and unemployment provoked no major intervention by government in social and economic life. But, on the other hand, there was no popular pressure for such change either. The philosophy of self-help was still strong among the working classes. Collectivism was a middle-class preoccupation. In old age, Salisbury was perhaps more cautiously aware of the obstacles to change, but he was far more eloquent than most other politicians of his time on the evils of urban society. It is true that he did not attach much value to legislation and placed far more merit on administration. Salisbury believed that the cure to a specific problem could often irritate or inflame. He tried to avoid any measures which divided classes, or bred mutual mistrust, jealousy, malice and hatred.

But by the turn of the century there were widespread doubts throughout the political world about whether the country would be able to survive as a great power for much longer unless there were fundamental social and economic changes. This brought sweeping

criticism of the country's institutions under the banner of 'efficiency'.
Could Britain carry on in the traditions of what was loosely called
Gladstonianism – of a belief in free trade, balanced budgets, economy
and government by politicians responsible to Parliament and the
people? Salisbury was never complacent about the future. Throughout his political life, he warned of the dangers of democracy. But he
was unwilling to swallow the paternalistic, anti-democratic opinions
of the 'efficiency' school of thought. Salisbury was convinced that
the country could not afford to throw away prudence, self-restraint
and circumspection. It is something of an irony that the man who
owed his eventual political success to the collapse of Gladstonian
Liberalism should become in the eyes of many of his contemporaries
the most faithful follower of many of the Grand Old Man's sacred
tenets. This was perhaps more obvious in his work at the Foreign
Office, but it was also clear in his defence of Free Trade and balanced
budgets. Salisbury was no orthodox economic Liberal, but he was
always convinced that any resort to protection to aid either the
farmers at home or the cause of imperial unity would be disastrous
for the Conservative party. He was to look with anger and dismay
at Chamberlain's self-destructive Tariff Reform campaign after 1903.

The early disasters for the British forces in the Boer War intensified the demands for a reappraisal of the state of Britain. The
amateurism of government was attacked. There was a call for more
expertise and professionalism in the corridors of Whitehall, for a
civil service grounded, not on the classics, but in science and
technology. Salisbury too had always been a critic of the Gladstonian
examination methods of entry, but he was unlikely to look with any
more favour on the kind of advice that would come from so-called
technical experts. The aristocratic ideal was also coming under
critical scrutiny. Salisbury was willing to accept some of these
criticisms. He was himself particularly scathing at the negative
attitude of the Treasury to public spending. In October 1899 Hicks
Beach threatened to resign because of rising expenditure. Salisbury
talked him out of it in a philosophical vein. 'You do not sufficiently
allow for the peculiar position given by our system to the Treasury
and which is very galling to other departments. That the Treasury
should say that any expenditure is excessive or thriftless, in regard to
the objects for which it is intended, is obviously within its functions.
But in practice the Treasury goes much further. It acts as a sort of
Court of Appeal on other departments. Because any policy at every
step requires money, the Treasury can veto everything and can do so
on proposals which have nothing financial in their nature and pass

judgement upon which it has no special qualifications. The line I admit is hard to draw – but it is natural for the head of a department to feel annoyed if, by applying the financial brake, the Treasury hampers a policy in which it does not concur. Of course, in wartime when decisions must be taken promptly any such impediment to prompt action is very keenly felt. It is much more keenly felt if the interference of the Treasury wins, not at arresting a policy which it disapproves, but at securing sufficient delay to enable it to disapprove if it wishes' (18 October 1899).

As the blunders continued in South Africa, Salisbury did not confine his criticism to private correspondence. He expressed the opinion in the Lords that the British system of government was not 'a good fighting machine'. 'It is unequalled for producing happiness, prosperity, and liberty in time of peace,' Salisbury argued (30 January 1900). 'But now, in time of war, when great powers with enormous forces are looking at us with no gentle and kindly eye on every side, it becomes us to think whether we must not in some degree modify our arrangements in order to enable ourselves to meet the dangers that at any moment may arise.' The Prime Minister accused the Treasury of 'taking away the freedom and diminishing the initiative' of other government departments. 'I quite agree that the questions of large measures go to the Cabinet, and if the Cabinet think the Treasury wrong, the Treasury is over-ruled,' he said. 'Just as a wall is built of bricks, reforms – salutary reforms – are built up of a long succession of useful changes, but it is in those smaller changes, which individually are small, but in the aggregate are large, that I think the exaggerated control of the Treasury has done harm.'

In early September 1900 Salisbury decided to dissolve Parliament and go to the country. He explained to the Queen that the government could act 'with much more confidence and effect' if it was 'fully acquainted with the views of the electors and assured of their support' over its handling of South Africa and China. As usual, Salisbury kept aloof from the electioneering. This time he even refused to issue any kind of manifesto. Chamberlain was the star of the Unionist platform, with his charge that every vote for a Liberal was a vote for the Boer cause. The khaki election results did not produce any further swing to Unionism on top of the 1895 landslide. The Liberals and Labour together managed to make a net gain of nine seats. At the same time, the Unionists won an absolute majority for the first and last occasion in Scotland. Further Unionist inroads were made into working-class England, notably in Sheffield (with the loss of Brightside) and the radical Potteries. A noticeable feature of the election was the return of 163 Unionist M.P.s without any contest. This contrasts with only twenty Liberals who went back to the Commons without a fight. The Unionist alliance won 51·1 per cent of the poll and 402 seats.

Salisbury was strangely unimpressed by the victory. 'I'm not sure whether I can consider the omens as altogether favourable,' he confessed to Cranbrook (19 October 1900). 'The phenomenon is without example that a party should twice dissolve at an interval of five years, and in each case bring back a majority of more than 130. What does it mean? I hope the causes are accidental and temporary. But it may mean that the Reform Bills are digging down deeper into the population, have come upon a layer of pure combativeness. If this is the case I am afraid the country has evil times before it. Of course I recognize the justice of the verdict the country has given: but that the love of justice should have overborne the great law of the pendulum I confess puzzles and bewilders me.' Salisbury's Cabinet reconstruction provoked some unrest on the government back benches. Under pressure both from his doctor and family, Salisbury agreed reluctantly to stand down from the Foreign Office. The Marquis of Lansdowne became Foreign Secretary, although the Queen insisted that Salisbury should keep a close eye on his activities and make sure that no telegrams or dispatches were sent out without his scrutiny. Goschen's decision to retire from active politics meant a new man for the Admiralty. Salisbury decided to appoint his son-in-law, Selborne, to the post. St John Brodrick became Secretary of State for War in place of Lansdowne. The other Cabinet changes were few. Ritchie succeeded Ridley at the Home Office. Gerald Balfour went into the Cabinet as President of the Local Government Board. Another Salisbury relative, George Wyndham, became Irish Secretary. The Prime Minister's eldest son, Lord Cranborne, was given his first office as Under-Secretary for Foreign Affairs. Chaplin was not given another job. The Wiltshire squire, Walter Long, succeeded him at the Local Government Board.

A disgruntled Tory back-bencher, Bartley, moved an amendment to the Address complaining at the number of the Cecil family in the government. Salisbury was undisturbed by such party discontent. He explained to Balfour: 'Please note that exactly the same number of "relations" minus Jim [Cranborne], were in the government in July 1895, as there are now. The arrangement has therefore been before the country during two general elections without provoking any adverse comment. No doubt one or two have been promoted.

But they cannot be treated as a class apart who can be employed but not promoted, like Second Division clerks' (9 December 1900).

The Prime Minister was now seventy-one; his health was becoming more unreliable. The Boer War troubled him. His absent-minded behaviour and short-sightedness were making him less and less effective. His ignorance of who was in his own Cabinet became proverbial. On one occasion at a Hatfield garden party, he regaled the African explorer and administrator, Sir Harry Johnston, believing that he was talking to the army chief, Lord Roberts, back from South Africa. 'Salisbury is no more than when Foreign Secretary an effective Prime Minister; the ingrained habit of leaving the premiership to look after itself keeps him as reluctant as ever to undertake its burdens,' grumbled Sir Almeric Fitzroy. Yet the Prime Minister soldiered on until the successful conclusion of the war in South Africa. He waited until 11 July 1902 before handing in his resignation to King Edward VII. 'I have contemplated taking this step on grounds of health for some time; but have been deterred from it by the fear that, so long as the war continued I might give an impression that there was a division in the Cabinet,' he explained to Halsbury, the Lord Chancellor.

We are near some great change
in public affairs in which the forces which
contend for the mastery among us
will be differently ranged and balanced.
The large aggregation of human force
which lies around our Empire
seems to draw more closely together,
and to assume almost unconsciously
a more and more aggressive aspect.
Their junction,
in menacing and dangerous manner,
may be deferred for many years –
or may be precipitated
with little notice at any moment.
Salisbury to Lord Curzon, 9 August 1902

10

UNIONISM TRIUMPHANT:

ABROAD

August 1895–June 1902

On his return to the Foreign Office in the summer of 1895, Salisbury soon discovered that he could no longer enjoy a free hand in the making of policy. Increasing old age and recurrent bouts of ill-health were to ensure that he exercised a frail grasp over the running of his Cabinet. An added difficulty, which he faced during the late 1890s, arose from the very nature of his government. This time, it was a coalition, and with Liberal Unionists taking a prominent part in Cabinet. Joseph Chamberlain at the Colonial Office was a dynamic and forceful colleague with strong views, not just on the future of the British Empire, but on the conduct of international diplomacy as well. Lansdowne at the War

Office and Goschen at the Admiralty were also men with firm opinions, who were quite ready to contest Salisbury's line of thinking. With his predisposition to rule with a loose rein and bend to the pressure of others, Salisbury was less able to exert his authority and influence over the Cabinet. Consequently, its meetings meandered on, often indecisively and without any coherence. 'The Cabinet is a funny body and this Cabinet collectively an effete organization,' grumbled Lord George Hamilton to the Indian Viceroy, Lord Curzon (12 September 1900). 'This is mainly the chief's fault. He won't press for a decision. He does not keep people to the point and all sorts of irrelevant trivialities are discussed *ad nauseam* to the exclusion of affairs of real importance. If it was not for the general regard felt for him by his colleagues and their departmental efficiency, the whole concern must long ago have tumbled to pieces.' Salisbury often gave the impression that he was tired of the cares of office. Lord Esher spoke of him sitting 'in a crumpled heap like Grandpa Smallweed – evidently wearied out'. It was not just Salisbury's short-sightedness and forgetfulness which aroused concern. By the end of the 1890s it was quite clear that his cautious policy of no entanglements and limited liability no longer enjoyed the support of most of the Cabinet. Only the economy-minded Chancellor of the Exchequer, Hicks Beach, was ready to throw his weight behind the Prime Minister. Even Balfour joined the 'new men' of the Cabinet in questioning whether Britain could continue for very much longer to stand aloof from formal alliances with other European powers. There was a growing school of influential opinion that was alarmed at what it saw as Britain's dangerous isolation in world diplomacy. Salisbury fought hard, if unsuccessfully, against such thinking through most of his last spell at the Foreign Office.

In August 1895 he was faced with a thankless task in the Balkans. The outbreak of Turkish atrocities against the Armenian population of the Empire in 1894 shocked liberal opinion. Under Rosebery's guidance, Britain joined Russia and France with the intention of imposing urgent internal reforms on the unwilling Porte. However, it did not take Salisbury long to discover that there was no enthusiasm for any decisive action against the Sultan from either Russia or France. The Prime Minister was genuinely horrified by the behaviour of the Turks. 'Words are quite inadequate to describe these horrors,' he confessed to the Queen (15 January 1896). The real trouble was that Britain could not act alone against Constantinople. 'Our ships will not surmount the mountains of Taurus,' Salisbury explained to the House of Lords (30 April 1896). The Prime

Minister doubted whether Turkey could hold together for much longer, and he was sceptical of the Sultan's capacity to change his autocratic system of government. During the winter of 1895–6 Salisbury even gave the German ambassador in London, Hatzfeldt, the impression that he was willing to let Constantinople fall into Russian hands and contemplate the Turkish Empire's partition.

Whether this was a genuine suggestion or not, it failed to convince the German government nor did it upset the Sultan. Other attempts at applying pressure on Turkey to reform its ways were equally unsuccessful. Salisbury contemplated a diversionary military expedition into Arabia. 'You cannot cook so very unsavoury an omelette as that which has been bequeathed to me by my predecessors without breaking a monstrous number of eggs,' he explained to Sir Philip Currie, the British ambassador in Constantinople (13 September 1895). Salisbury was ready to admit that the old anti-Russian Crimean policy had been a mistake, but he continued to believe that British 'fame and prestige' were tied up with keeping Constantinople out of Russian hands. 'For near half a century, if not more, it has been a vital article of our political creed,' Salisbury argued with Goschen. Yet was it any longer possible for any British government to prop up the oppressive and corrupt Turkish Empire, if the Sultan refused to accept internal reform?

Salisbury's eloquent appeals for collective action through the 'Concert of Europe', 'the federation of mankind', fell on deaf ears. The Prime Minister believed that there was not a soul from 'Archangel to Cadiz' who cared 'whether the Armenians are exterminated or not', except in England where the feeling approached 'frenzy in its intensity'. Salisbury suggested that Currie in Constantinople should be given the power to call in the fleet, if necessary, to overawe the Sultan, but such a proposal found no support in the Cabinet. The Admiralty experts maintained that the Franco-Russian alliance of 1894 had tipped the naval balance of power in the Mediterranean decisively against Britain. Salisbury's instinctive suspicion of expert opinions was revived, but other ministers did not share his scepticism. The Prime Minister, to his chagrin, found himself without Cabinet support. 'The Cabinet's refusal to give *carte blanche* to Currie means, or at least may mean, the surrender of Constantinople to Russia,' he pointed out to Goschen. 'If Russia gets there much before we do, so as to be able to man the Dardanelles forts with her own men, I take it that the place is impregnable. On the other hand, if we get there first we are a good deal the strongest and our voice will be at all events very weighty to the ultimate arrangements that are made' (3 December 1895). Salisbury was taken aback by his Cabinet defeat over sending the fleet to Constantinople. He could not hope to keep the old Crimea policy alive for much longer. In the winter of 1896–7 Austria-Hungary insisted that the Mediterranean Agreements, which required renewal, should be rewritten to make it clear that Britain would defend Constantinople from Russian attack. To his obvious regret, Salisbury felt unable to agree to such a change, because it would have brought a severe discrepancy between Britain's obligations and the country's physical power to uphold them. Salisbury outlined other cogent reasons why it was impossible for his government to accept such a commitment in Constantinople. 'The institutions under which we lived entirely prevented Her Majesty's government from making any engagement with respect to the military or naval action of England upon contingencies which had not yet arisen,' he explained to Currie (20 January 1897). 'When these contigencies arose, they would be fully considered by the Parliament and public opinion of this country, and no influence of any government, and probably no promise into which any government might have entered, would in such case avail to prevent this country from acting upon its own views of what was right and expedient in such a matter.' The lapse of the Mediterranean Agreements was the start of Britain's gradual drift away from 'leaning' towards the Central powers. This was the direct consequence of the change in the power balance in the Eastern Mediterranean.

In August 1896 there were further massacres of hapless Armenians in Constantinople in full view of foreign ambassadors. Salisbury made a final, determined attempt to rally active support against the violence. When the Tsar visited Britain in the autumn of 1896, Salisbury journeyed up to Balmoral and urged him to join in demanding the recall of all the powers who had attended the Congress of Berlin. The Prime Minister insisted that the Concert of Europe should draft a reform programme and force it on the Sultan. Salisbury argued that if the Porte refused to swallow the proposals, the Sultan should be dethroned and his Empire partitioned. The Prime Minister hastened to assure the Tsar that the British interest at the Straits had become much less and was 'not so large as others and purely maritime'. He even suggested that if Austria, France and Italy were favourable to Russian control of the Straits in the event of Turkey's disintegration, then 'England would not maintain her objection alone, but would seek for some arrangement by which it could be met'. The Tsar refused to go along with Salisbury's argument, but on 20 October the Prime Minister proposed the calling of an ambassadorial conference at Constantinople to draw up a reform programme to force on the Sultan. The Russians, after some hesitation, agreed to this suggestion. The conference met in December and reached agreement on 2 February 1897. But the proposals were shelved with the outbreak of the Greco-Turkish war in April 1897.

Salisbury agreed to join with the rest of the Concert of Europe in February to crush the revolt in Crete against the Sultan's rule and to land an army of occupation. But despite some Cabinet opposition, he was unwilling to dispatch British forces to blockade Greek ports. The war between Turkey and Greece lasted no more than a month and the Greeks were soon crushed. On his return from a convalescence in France in May 1897, Salisbury urged Greece to accept mediation from the great powers. During the peace talks, he fought hard to defend Greek interests. He was able to prevent any Turkish annexation of Greek land and to ensure that the size of the indemnity that the Greek government had to pay the Sultan was reasonable. This was to bring a virtual end to British long-term involvement in the Balkans until the First World War. Salisbury explained to Currie (19 October 1897), 'Since, some two years back, the Cabinet refused me leave to take the fleet up the Dardanelles, because it was impracticable, I have regarded the Eastern question as having little serious interest for England. We have no other way of coercing the Turk . . . On the other hand, our interest in Egypt is growing stronger . . . the idea that the Turkish Empire is on the verge of dissolution has been dissipated and the Concert of Europe has conclusively shown that it can never be trusted with even the slenderest portion of Executive authority . . . The only policy which it seems to me is left to us by the Cabinet's decision to which I have referred is to strengthen our position on the Nile (to its source) and to withdraw as much as possible from all responsibilities at Constantinople.'

During 1897 Russia and Austria agreed to put the Balkans 'on ice'. Germany was rapidly to replace Britain as the major foreign influence in Turkey. Salisbury was the last man in the Cabinet to accept, reluctantly, that his government could no longer hope to prop up the Turkish Empire. His attention was gradually forced to turn to the second line of defence on the route to India. This was Egypt.

It was not until as late as January 1898 that Salisbury and his Cabinet gave the final go-ahead for the reconquest of the Upper Nile valley. He was very much 'a reluctant imperialist'. On his return to power in 1895 Salisbury had been quite content to let the

Mahdi keep possession of the Sudan. At least the Dervishes kept other European powers out of the region, he reasoned. Salisbury contemplated an eventual expedition against the Mahdi from the south through Uganda. This could not occur until the railway from the East African coast at Mombasa to Lake Victoria had been built. 'For the next two years there is no remedy, we must trust to our luck,' Salisbury maintained. Even in late February 1896 he was quite willing to ignore Italian entreaties and accept the Italian loss of their fortress town of Kassala to the Dervishes. 'The power of the Khalfifa tends steadily to diminish and a waiting game is an obvious policy. Whenever we are masters of the Nile, Kassala will be easily dealt with. Till then it is of little value,' he argued (29 February 1896). However, the Italian defeat at Adowa on 1 March changed his mind. Under pressure from both Berlin and Rome, Salisbury agreed finally to launch a diversionary move up the Nile as far as Dongola and thus take some of the pressure off the Italians trapped at Kassala by the Dervishes. The Cabinet took a long time to make up its mind to act. Memories of Gordon's fate still haunted government counsels. Moreover, Cromer in Cairo was desperately anxious that any proposed expedition should not add to Egypt's already crippling financial burdens. Salisbury instructed Kitchener to advance his army as far as he could go without any 'undue effect on the power of Egypt'. Yet it was no temporary foray to be followed by a retreat. Salisbury decided to 'kill two birds with one stone, and use the same military effort to plant the foot of Egypt rather farther up the Nile' (13 March 1896). Salisbury assured the Queen that 'the ultimate object and intention was to go to Khartoum and restore it to Egypt, but time was needed for that' (8 April 1896). He told the House of Lords that Egypt would not have been restored to a position of safety until the Egyptian flag flew over Khartoum. Kitchener made satisfactory progress, defeating the Mahdi's forces at Firket, and retaking Dongola in September 1896. But his success was not enough to convince Salisbury that it was wise to go any farther up the Nile immediately. The Prime Minister feared that financial difficulties alone ruled out such a step. Salisbury continued to doubt the popularity of imperialism, if it meant the Commons had to sanction any large outlay of public money. Salisbury's aim was to push ahead with the railway to Uganda, and in July 1896 Parliament voted £5 million for the project by large majorities.

The Prime Minister realized that his eventual reconquest of the Sudan would precipitate friction with the French government, which continued to oppose the British occupation of Egypt. He made a determined effort to placate the Third Republic in other parts of the world. In March 1896, for instance, the two countries reached agreement to recognize Siam's independence and Britain abandoned its presence in the Upper Mekong valley. Discussions were also conducted on the reconciliation of Anglo-French differences in West Africa. Salisbury was quite willing to make substantial concessions to French colonial ambitions on the Niger, which he believed was an area chiefly made up of 'malarious deserts', of value to nobody. He was scornful of the prospects of any Empire-building there. 'If we are to send British or Indian troops in the hope of fighting another Plassey with Lugard as Clive and Sokota as our Bengal, the prospect becomes very much more serious,' Salisbury argued sarcastically with Chamberlain (3 June 1898). 'Our Clive will be in no danger of being astonished at his own moderation. There is no loot to get except in Goldie's dreams.' The Prime Minister did not relish the imposition of direct imperial rule over West Africa. He explained to Hicks Beach, 'Ever since I recommended the restoration of Mysore thirty years ago, I have always been of the opinion that the condition of a protected dependency is more acceptable to the half-civilized races and more suitable for them than direct dominion. It is cheaper, simpler, less wounding to their self-esteem and spares them the unnecessary contact with white men.'

However, Salisbury's view was not shared by Chamberlain, who visualized West Africa as one of the Empire's 'undeveloped estates'. The Colonial Secretary was determined not to let the French get their own way in the Niger negotiations. Salisbury found himself forced to beat a retreat. He grumbled to the Queen that Chamberlain was 'a little too warlike' and unable to see the other side of the question. However, the Prime Minister was unable to ease French *amour propre* in the west of Africa to compensate for British reoccupation of the Upper Nile valley. The June 1898 Anglo-French Niger Convention was to give Chamberlain most of what he wanted.

From the autumn of 1896 Salisbury began to grow concerned at French intentions in the Sudan. In June the French government had ordered Captain Marchand to advance to Fashoda on the Nile above Khartoum. The British Cabinet agreed to seek parliamentary approval for £800,000 to help Egypt to pay for railways and gunboats to back up Kitchener. By the end of August 1897 the expedition had reached Berber. On a visit to Ethiopia, Cromer's assistant Rodd discovered that French influence was considerable there. The Ethiopian ruler, Menelek, was in no mood to compromise with Britain. In June 1897 MacDonald, the army commander in Uganda, was instructed to form an expedition for an attack on the Sudan from the south as soon as he could launch it. Unfortunately an army mutiny wrecked this plan. Consequently, the British Cabinet decided to sanction a northern offensive under Kitchener. On 3 September 1898 he routed the Mahdi's forces at Omdurman and he entered Khartoum three days later. 'A slaughter of 16,000 ought to satisfy our Jingoes for at least six months,' Salisbury wrote to Cranbrook (12 September 1898). 'Some people say that the strange outburst of unreasoning desire for war which showed itself last winter and spring was due to the intoxication of the Jubilee. If that was so, the victory at Omdurman may even do harm.'

Kitchener and Marchand confronted each other at Fashoda on 19 September. From the start of the crisis, Salisbury refused to countenance any negotiations until the French government had agreed to withdraw Marchand. War fever rose on both sides of the Channel. In the Cabinet Chamberlain and Goschen were resolute for an immediate showdown with the French. Salisbury's room for manoeuvre was severely limited. His public reputation had already suffered during the spring of 1898 over the Far East. Now the Cabinet was restive. Chamberlain went round telling colleagues that Salisbury's 'policy of peace at any price could not go on any longer and that England has to show the whole world that she can act'. The French government was forced to bow to the inevitable. Her ally Russia could do nothing to help. The British fleet in the Eastern Mediterranean emphasized France's strategic weakness. In November, Marchand was told to leave Fashoda. The Anglo-French declaration of 21 March 1899 recognized the boundary between French Africa and the newly established Anglo-Egyptian condominium in the Sudan. There was much rejoicing at the successful outcome of the crisis in England. Salisbury's apparent firm handling of France had helped to revive his tarnished image. But the Prime Minister disliked the whole business of confrontation, which ran counter to his own cautious ways. 'The dangerous temptation of the hour is that we should consider that rhapsody can be made an adequate substitute for calculation,' he informed Lansdowne (17 December 1898).

By this stage, Salisbury's power in the government was already crumbling. As early as the winter of 1895 he had been over-ruled by his colleagues over the Venezuela dispute with the United States. Salisbury wanted to stand up to the United States and refuse to accept President Cleveland's demand for arbitration in the boundary dispute between British Guiana and Venezuela. But the Cabinet insisted that he should agree to the American request. The eventual arbitration in October 1899 came down mostly in England's favour. A far more serious check to Salisbury's authority in foreign affairs came in the Far East. The Prime Minister was anxious to maintain the traditional 'open door' policy in the Manchu Empire, which had suffered defeat at the hands of Japan in 1894–5. He was willing to support the economic penetration of China with the creation of 'spheres of influence' as long as this did not encroach on China's political independence or territorial integrity. Salisbury did not wish to see China suffer partition at the hands of the European powers. In his opinion, fear of Russian intentions in Manchuria was misplaced in the late 1890s. Salisbury wanted to placate Russia as much as possible. With the pressure of events in Sudan and South Africa, Salisbury did not relish the prospect of any further theatre of armed conflict. However, his policy was upset by the Kaiser's sudden decision to seize Kiachow on the North China coast in November 1897. This looked like the start of a dismemberment of China. The dispatch of the Russian fleet to Port Arthur for the winter suggested that the Tsar wanted to join in the act. In January 1898, therefore, Salisbury made a direct overture to Russia. He promised British support for her commercial interests in North China. 'Our idea was this. The two Empires of China and Turkey are so weak that in all important matters they are constantly guided by the advice of foreign powers. In giving this advice Russia and England are constantly opposed, neutralizing each other's efforts much more frequently than the real antagonism of their interests would justify; and this condition of things is not likely to diminish but to increase. It is to remove or lessen this evil that we have thought that an understanding with Russia might benefit both nations,' he wrote to the British ambassador in St Petersburg, O'Conor (25 January 1898). The problem was that Salisbury was adamant that there should be no interference with China's territorial integrity. He had nothing to give the Russians that they could not already get themselves. The British fleet moored near Port Arthur was a bluff. On 27 March the lease agreement for Port Arthur and the near-by town of Talienwan was signed by China and Russia. Salisbury was convalescing at the time. It was left to Balfour, as acting Foreign Secretary, to sound the retreat. With great reluctance and with Chamberlain dissenting, the Cabinet agreed to accept the Russian *fait accompli* and take Wei-hei-wei as compensation from China. It looked as though Britain was also throwing over the 'open door' policy. Russia's triumph at Port Arthur was regarded as a personal defeat for Salisbury. Chamberlain

rushed to the conclusion that the debacle in China required a fundamental review of the whole basis of British foreign policy. The
Colonial Secretary was alarmed at what he saw as Britain's decline
in world politics. He called for an alliance with Germany. Balfour
gave his blessing to his talks with Hatzfeldt, the German ambassador
in London, during the spring of 1898, while Salisbury was recupera-
ting in France. The Kaiser and his chief diplomatic adviser, Holstein,
drew the wrong conclusion that Britain was bargaining from a
position of weakness. Germany had no wish to stand in the way of
Russian ambitions in the Far East.

This was not the first occasion during Salisbury's last spell at the
Foreign Office that talk of an Anglo-German alliance had been
mooted. In the autumn of 1895 Salisbury was convinced that the
Kaiser was trying to 'frighten' Britain into joining the Triple
Alliance. The famous telegram to Kruger after the abortive raid by
Jameson into the Transvaal demonstrated the German capacity for
mischief. The Prime Minister was not opposed to friendly relations
with Germany. Despite his well-founded suspicion of the Kaiser's
highly emotional attitudes, he was ready to 'bend towards' the
Central powers. But this position was to fall far short of any formal
entanglement in any alliance. He explained to the Queen (15 January
1896): 'It is almost impossible for an English government to enter
into such an alliance as this because when the crisis came, and the
decision of war and peace had to be taken, the Parliament and the
people would not be guided in any degree by the fact that the
government had some years before signed a secret agreement to go
to war, but entirely by the cause for which it was proposed to go to
war, and their interests and feelings in respect to it. Their fury
would be extreme when they discovered that their ministry had
tried to pledge them secretly beforehand. The secret agreements
which were signed with Italy and Austria some years ago contained
no sort of promise to go to war.'

On his return from France in April 1898 Salisbury lost no time
in putting an end to the Colonial Secretary's activities. 'The one
object of the German Emperor since he has been on the throne has
been to get us into war with France. I never can make up my mind
whether this is part of Chamberlain's object or not,' he wrote to
Balfour (9 April 1898). In a stirring speech to the Primrose League
on 4 May Salisbury asserted that 'we know we shall maintain against
all comers that which we possess, and we know in spite of the jargon
about isolation, that we are competent to do so'. On 11 May the
Prime Minister met Hatzfeldt and left the German ambassador in

no doubt that any alliance was out of the question. 'You ask too much for your friendship,' Salisbury remarked.

Although the Prime Minister was able to make sure that Chamberlain's efforts at creating an Anglo-German alliance came to nothing, he was unable to withstand the pressure for a 'new course' which was growing in the Cabinet. The situation in South Africa was a cause of growing concern. Chamberlain was anxious to re-establish imperial authority over the Transvaal. There the Boers were intent on breaking away from the remaining ties with Britain and restricting the rights of the Uitlanders (English settlers) who had come into the state since the middle 1880s to work in the goldfields. In 1895 Salisbury allowed his Colonial Secretary to carry on his own policy in Southern Africa without check. In fact, there was no disagreement between the two men on the necessity for an eventual restoration of imperial suzerainty over the Transvaal. Salisbury accepted that 'sooner or later' the state would 'be mainly governed by Englishmen'. The Prime Minister wanted to see this happen not just through external aggression, but as a 'result of the action of internal forces' (30 December 1895). After the Jameson raid fiasco, Chamberlain drifted between appeasement and threats of coercion to bring Transvaal round to its senses. The initiative was increasingly seized by the Cape Commissioner Lord Milner on the one side and Kruger in the Transvaal on the other. Salisbury did not seek trouble in South Africa. 'I should look with something like dismay to a Transvaal war,' he warned Chamberlain (16 April 1897). 'It might mean a necessity of protecting the north-east of England as well as the south.' Salisbury worried over the 'European inconvenience' of such a conflict, which might provoke an anti-British continental coalition. None the less he was ready to agree to Chamberlain's request for a doubling of troop strengths in the Cape in the spring of 1897. 'I came to the conclusion that as Chamberlain based his demand principally on the effect of inaction upon colonial opinion it was hardly possible for us, who have not had his opportunities of watching that opinion, to refuse him the reinforcements he requires.'

The Colonial Secretary wanted to block Transvaal's main outlet to the sea at Delagoa Bay in Portuguese Mozambique. An opportunity to attempt this came when Portugal went bankrupt in January 1897 and sought a loan from Britain. Salisbury supported Chamberlain's suggestion that Britain should only pledge financial aid to Portugal if this country could have virtual control of Delagoa Bay. The Anglo-Portuguese talks broke down in the summer of 1897, but they were resumed in the following spring. This time, the German government demanded to contribute to the loan to Portugal in return for a share of Portuguese colonies, if Portugal defaulted on her loan repayments. Salisbury did not want to agree to such a proposal, but on 22 June he was once more over-ruled by the Cabinet. 'I could not help telling His Excellency [Hatzfeldt] that we were like two Jews in the bazaar at Constantinople bargaining over property which did not belong to either of them,' Salisbury exclaimed (23 June 1898). Yet he was forced to go through the motions with talks with Hatzfeldt on the proposed loan. The settlement was not concluded until Salisbury was once more convalescing in France. The Prime Minister disliked the whole business. 'I am not to be held to have given my consent definitively to anything. Germany is trying to induce us to join in putting the knife into Portugal,' he pointed out to Balfour (19 August 1898). However, his nephew hastily signed the Anglo-German Agreement over Portugal three days before Salisbury's return to London. Whatever its morality, this ensured German neutrality during the Boer War, although it brought British control of Delagoa Bay no nearer. It was not until the summer of 1899 that Salisbury was able to persuade the Portuguese to stop arms shipments through the port *en route* to the Transvaal. Portugal offered Salisbury an alliance in the event of conflict in South Africa. A secret treaty was signed between the two countries on 14 October 1899.

Salisbury and the Cabinet drifted into war with the Boers. In the final months before the outbreak of fighting, he accepted its inevitability and backed up Chamberlain. None the less he was unenthusiastic. He blamed Milner for the conflict. 'We have to act upon a moral field prepared for us by him and his jingo supporters,' Salisbury explained to Lansdowne (30 August 1899). 'And therefore I see before us the necessity for considerable military effort – and all for people whom we despise and for territory which will bring no profit and no power to England.' With his wife dying, the Prime Minister was in a sad, depressed mood. He regarded the Boer War as 'a bad investment' which would 'represent another penny on the income tax in perpetuity'. 'If it has the effect of teaching our countrymen that they cannot have the moon whenever they cry for it, the money may not altogether be thrown away,' he wrote to Curzon. Nor did Salisbury like the ruthless way the generals fought the war, which soon turned out to be no 'side show'. When his old friend Canon MacColl protested at the 'methods of barbarism', Salisbury was half inclined to agree. He replied, 'War is a terrible thing. The Boers should have thought of its horrible significance when they invaded the Queen's dominions – without a cause. The detailed measures of the war must be adopted in conformity with the opinions of the generals to whom we trust our policy. I agree with you that the horror of the concentration camps followed on this decision almost of necessity. The huddling together of so many human beings, especially women and children, could not but cause a great mortality – particularly among a people so dirty as the Boers. The question whether it will dispose the election against us in 1905 or 1906 is not a question which can aid us now – though I dare say you are right' (18 November 1901).

Salisbury had become a tired and lonely man. 'Only those in his most intimate circle knew how distasteful office had become to him in his later years,' wrote his son Lord Robert (*Monthly Review*, October 1903). 'He hated war and his hatred of it grew as he grew older.'

The Boer War demonstrated British isolation, and to many in the government it no longer appeared 'splendid'. While the Kaiser stayed neutral over the Boer War and refused to join any anti-British European coalition, he insisted that Britain should pay a price for his good behaviour. Once more, Salisbury was over-ruled by his Cabinet and forced to agree with the ceding of the British interest in Samoa to the Germans in November 1899.

British preoccupation in South Africa weakened Salisbury's already frail hand in China. The outbreak of the Boxer rising in the summer of 1900 compelled international action. The Prime Minister was reluctant to intervene, despite the entreaties of Britain's representative in Peking, Sir Claude MacDonald. 'One of the demonstrating powers will take the opportunity of appropriating something nice – and we with our engagements in South Africa will have to give and look pleasant,' Salisbury argued (11 March 1900). The Cabinet was forced to apply considerable pressure on Salisbury to make him appreciate the seriousness of the Chinese crisis. Eventually he agreed to send British reinforcements to China and also called on the United States and Japan to provide troops. Yet Salisbury was anxious to keep discussion on the matter to a minimum. He even enforced an hour-long Cabinet argument on whether the third reading clerk of the House of Commons should keep his job or not, in order to divert attention away from China. On 14 August 1900 the siege of Peking was lifted by the international expedition.

The development of the China crisis alarmed Germany and the Kaiser made an overture to Britain to support the 'open door' policy. Salisbury's colleagues believed that the German government was willing to reach an understanding in China in the face of Russian and French interests. The Prime Minister was unimpressed. 'I should like to consider the matter carefully, but at first blush I am averse to giving special assurances to the German Emperor. I do not see what he has got to do with it, and his observations look very much an attempt to make a quarrel between France and us,' he argued (23 August 1900). Nevertheless, the Cabinet insisted on pressing ahead with negotiations, and an Anglo-German China Agreement was signed on 16 October 1900. Both countries recognized Russia's special position in Manchuria, and they promised to uphold the 'open door' policy as far as they could exercise influence. But the Agreement meant different things to Germany and Britain. Bulow, the German Chancellor, believed that it was to apply strictly to the Yangtze valley; the British Cabinet were under the impression that they had signed an Anglo-German *entente* in the Far East. Salisbury did not relish the arrangement, but he was on the point of leaving the Foreign Office, with the Cabinet reshuffle following the 1900 general election.

On 3 January 1901 the text of the Sino-Russian Agreement on the future status of Manchuria was published in *The Times*. It immediately provoked an international crisis, for it virtually amounted to the Russian annexation of Northern China. The Kaiser, who happened to be visiting England at the end of January 1901 to attend Queen Victoria's funeral, appeared anxious to establish closer relations in the face of Russian intentions in the Far East. Japan too was in a bitter mood at the behaviour of the Russian government. The new British Foreign Secretary, Lansdowne, was determined to fashion a Far East alliance to check Russian influence. In early March 1901 he even proposed a secret understanding with Germany over China. This was to involve British and German naval support for Japan, if that country was attacked by Russia. The Germans were uninterested in such a proposal. Bulow made it clear in a Reichstag speech that Germany was 'indifferent' to Manchuria's future. But the *coup de grâce* for any Anglo-German alliance came from Salisbury. He produced yet another formidable Cabinet memorandum in which he spelt out the reasons why such a formal alliance with Germany was unwise. 'The liability of having to defend the German and Austrian frontiers against Russia is heavier than that of having to defend the British Isles against France,' he argued. 'Even, therefore, in its most naked aspect the bargain would be a bad one for this country. Hatzfeldt speaks of our "isolation" as constituting a serious danger for us. Have we ever felt that danger practically? It would hardly be wise to incur novel and most onerous obligations, in order to guard against a danger in whose existence we have no historical reason for believing.' Salisbury's objections to the proposed alliance went much deeper: 'The fatal circumstance is that neither we nor the Germans are competent to make the suggested promises. The British government cannot undertake to declare war, for any purpose, unless it is a purpose of which the electors of this country would approve. If the government promised to declare war for an object which did not commend itself to public opinion, the promise would be repudiated, and the government would be turned out. I do not see how, in common honesty, we could invite nations to rely upon our aids in a struggle, which must be formidable and probably supreme, when we have no means whatever of knowing what may be the humour of our people in circumstances which cannot be foreseen. A promise of defensive alliance with England would excite bitter murmurs in every rank of German society. Several times during the last sixteen years Count Hatzfeldt has tried to elicit from me, in conversation, some opinion as to the probable conduct of England, if Germany and Italy were involved in war with France. I have always replied that no English minister could venture on such a forecast. The case of the English government in such a crisis must depend on the view taken by public opinion in this country, and public opinion would be largely, if not exclusively, governed by the value of the *casus belli*.'

It was characteristic of Salisbury that he should do nothing to interfere directly in Lansdowne's handling of foreign policy, even though it was on the Queen's insistence that he was shown every dispatch and telegram flowing out of the Foreign Office. Salisbury clearly disapproved of Lansdowne's search for formal allies, but when the Foreign Secretary proposed an alliance with Japan in the autumn of 1901, Salisbury put up only a half-hearted defence of his old policy of no entanglements. Not that the Prime Minister approved of the Anglo-Japanese Alliance, which promised reciprocal assistance in the Far East if either was attacked by more than one power. On 7 January 1902 he drafted his last Cabinet memorandum to point out the dangers of the 'new course'. Salisbury argued that the proposed treaty with Japan pledged Britain to defend Japanese action in Korea and in the whole of China against France and Russia, 'no matter what the *casus belli* may be'. 'There is no limit: and no escape. We are pledged to war, though the conduct of our ally may have been followed in spite of our strongest remonstrances, and may be avowedly regarded by us with clear disapprobation,' Salisbury argued. He doubted whether Parliament would sanction

G

such a step. Salisbury concluded that he thought it unwise to give Japan the right of committing Britain to war, 'unless the policy which Japan is pursuing has been approved by the British government'.

Despite its doubts, the Cabinet agreed to sign the Anglo-Japanese treaty on 30 January 1902. Salisbury retired a few months later at the conclusion of the Boer War. The Prime Minister had spent his last years of active political life in attempting to put out bush fires that threatened Britain's position as a world power. In Persia and Afghanistan, as well as in the Far East and Turkey, Salisbury was troubled by British military and financial weakness in holding back the forces of disintegration which threatened the Empire. Far more than his colleagues, the Prime Minister was acutely aware of the severe limitations which were placed on the conduct of British foreign policy. He believed that there was no easy escape from isolation, which would not gravely threaten the stability of constitutional government. It is one of the major paradoxes of Salisbury's life that he became the civilized defender of the old mid-Victorian values, which he used to castigate in his youth. His admirers now lay among Little Englanders like John Morley and Sir William Harcourt, not with the other leaders of the Unionist alliance. Yet Salisbury's main reason for doubt about overseas entanglements with foreign powers stemmed from his life-long suspicion of the power of public opinion. In the 1890s, in an unguarded moment, he made the observation that the policy of the British government was decided by the working classes. It is certainly true that Salisbury often appeared to introduce the question of what the state of public opinion might be on a particular issue in order to buttress his own argument for a certain course of action. But the Prime Minister sincerely believed that the new electoral system made it extremely difficult for any government to commit its successor to formal alliances with other states. Salisbury exaggerated the importance of public opinion, but his belief that it was fickle and unpredictable brought a natural caution into his conduct of foreign policy. Neither of his successors – Lansdowne and Sir Edward Grey – followed his principles of limited liability. They sought to combine influence with commitment, and by so doing they displayed a contempt for Parliament, which Salisbury never did. Salisbury became a resolute opponent of the ways of secret diplomacy. During his last ministry he kept both Cabinet and Parliament fully informed about what he was doing. His annual November Guildhall speeches became the major occasion for an account of his stewardship abroad as well as at home.

Salisbury's suspicion of public opinion was combined with a

personal hatred of war. He disliked jingoism and militarism intensely. It was his apprehension of the effects of modern technology on the conduct of war which ensured that his foreign policy was prudent and defensive. His much-admired handling of foreign affairs, however, owed a good deal to his own pessimistic nature and his deep distrust of the emotional moods of *la populace*. The terrible carnage of the Great War was amply to justify Salisbury's grim prophecy of the international future.

That strange, powerful, brilliant, obstructive
deadweight at the top.
Lord Curzon on Salisbury

CONCLUSION

Salisbury lived for only just over a year after his retirement from the premiership. He died at Hatfield House on 22 August 1903. Lady Frances Balfour wrote to a friend: 'I wish you were looking out of this window with me. Below me the brilliant West garden, surrounded by its pleached alley of limes. On the right the Bishop of Ely's Palace and Banquet Hall. A little below the Church spire cutting the wide western horizon, and on it the half-masted flag. On the left, a towering mass of copper beech whose dark purple leaves look like a pall today. Beyond under the quiet sky stretches Hertfordshire and its woods for miles. Nothing sad or unhopeful can live in such a scene. The family life goes on, with

G*

the laughter of children, and all as if there was no break in the home life. So it should be.'

With Salisbury's departure, the Unionist alliance, which he had patiently built up, disintegrated with a devastating election defeat in 1906. Under the influence of Chamberlain, the Conservatives embraced protection, which Salisbury had resisted for twenty years. By doing so, they lost the vital middle ground of politics which they had captured in the 1880s. Radicalism was revived triumphant. All the familiar enemies who Salisbury had fought successfully returned once more. The House of Lords came under political siege. Home Rule became again a burning issue. The left wing of the Liberals pursued domestic policies with a sharp class bias, symbolized by Lloyd George's Budget of 1909. There was an increase in labour militancy. In the eyes of Salisbury's dwindling band of aristocratic disciples, the Conservative party was turning into a capitalist conspiracy, a sordid alliance of industry and commerce held together by material self-interest. Perhaps none of these developments were avoidable. Certainly it is by no means clear that Salisbury's continuation in office would have made any difference. His Cabinet was already riven by disagreement over the 1902 Education Bill before his retirement.

Salisbury remains the unknown Prime Minister, despite his long, eventful life at the centre of British politics. In his early years he won a well-deserved reputation as an acidic, vigorous Ishmaelite, the abrasive defender of Church and state from Radical attack, the prophet of class war and national decay. By his old age, Salisbury had become the prudent, hesitant sage, the last formidable champion of the mid-Victorian values of government. With a reputation for impulsive behaviour and unstable judgement, he was transformed into the epitome of restraint and wisdom, the civilized aristocratic *seigneur* out of sympathy with the more turbulent passions of his time. Salisbury is far too complicated and fascinating a figure to suffer the fate of a brief summary. His work as a diplomat for nearly a quarter of a century has received the sympathetic attention of the historians, but his importance in British politics has not yet been fully appreciated. There is still a tendency to either ignore or denigrate his achievement. Paul Smith has suggested that Salisbury's ultimate success was the result of a fortuitous series of events, which lay outside his influence or control:

If Joseph Chamberlain had succeeded in the early 1880s in capturing the Liberal party for his Radical programme, Salisbury might have got something approaching the overt politics of class which he had so long been heralding, and how, in such a juncture, the Conservative party would have fared, under a leader of his provocative outlook and record, is an interesting speculation. Far from being the most successful of Conservative leaders, Salisbury might have turned out one of the most disastrous.

Smith has argued that the Unionist triumphs of the 1880s and 1890s owed little, if anything, to Salisbury. Apparently they 're-flected trends and circumstances with which he had little to do, though his personal reputation for integrity, wisdom and knack in foreign policy certainly helped'. Electoral studies have revealed that the foundations of Unionism at the polls were built on fragile ground. J.P.Dunbabin, for instance, maintains that its dominance was 'more fortuitous and insubstantial than it has seemed in retrospect'. Liberal decline – a compound of bitter personal division at the top and genuine differences over doctrine–is used to explain Salisbury's long tenure of office. No one was more aware of the dangers of the electoral 'pendulum' than Salisbury himself, but this does less than justice to his own personal contribution to the success of the Unionist cause.

It was Irish Home Rule that made Salisbury. This was the single, urgent issue which split the Liberal party apart and drove many moderates into the arms of a revived Conservatism. Yet those anti-Gladstonians would not have deserted their old home in such numbers if the Conservatives had simply remained a collection of incorrigible reactionaries. Salisbury made himself acceptable as their leader. It was he who divided the forces of Unionism the least. The depths of trust and loyalty, the mutual respect which Salisbury forged with his party were all-important. Those attributes took time to grow. Salisbury's tenure as a party leader was uncertain until he became Prime Minister. But even since his days as a vitriolic journalist, Salisbury had been intellectually a fusionist, although his emotions often led him astray. His constant ideal was the creation of a comprehensive bloc of consolidation covering the political centre. Salisbury remained a pessimist all his life. He continued to pour scorn on the dogmas of the age and peer gloomily into the future, whether in government or opposition. 'Come the revolution' was a favourite Salisburian remark within the intimate Hatfield family circle. Salisbury's fear of the coming of class conflict was paralleled by apprehension about the forces of military technology and modern nationalism. However, his underlying melancholy was never allowed to paralyze his will to act. Whatever his doubts and reservations over particular decisions, he was always imbued with a sound common sense.

Far more than Disraeli, and even Gladstone, Salisbury was a shrewd, though unwilling, practitioner of the arts of party management. He left the Commons to its own devices, but he was a frequent visitor to Central Office keeping in close contact with party feeling in the constituencies. Those boxes of correspondence from local party leaders in his papers testify to that important side of his political activity. The 1880s witnessed the spread of extra-parliamentary politics. Salisbury did not hesitate to use the platform. In the early half of the decade, he spoke in almost every major urban centre in the country where he expressed his pungent opinions and propagated his faith in Conservative principles, which were designed to appeal, not to any particular class or interest, but to the nation as a whole. Some of those views might have been expected to arouse anger, but his eloquent defence of the House of Lords or his scarcely disguised scepticism of programmes and manifestos did not appear to offend his audiences.

Despite his interest in elections and party organization, Salisbury's concept of party was highly traditional. The purpose of the party machine was to mobilize support for the Conservative cause. He once explained this in a speech to the Constitutional Club in May 1887: 'The Conservative party has no ordinary organization at its command, unlike the Liberals. The chapel is the centre of political organization. The Non-Conformist pastor is the leader of the Radical advance. The danger of the Conservative party up till a very recent time has always been to under-rate the value of careful and exact organizations and our power in the state has never been equal to the real extent and even predominance of our opinions among the people . . . because it seems that the very effect of Conservative opinions is to induce people to let things take their course and trust to accidental circumstances or to the course of events to give the victory to the convictions to which they are attached.'

Salisbury deplored the professionalism of political life. The wire-puller and the machine boss were always the object of his venom. Yet Salisbury valued the discipline and loyalty of the party tie, which he believed brought an essential coherence and harmony to the parliamentary system. He abhorred the idea of unity for its own sake in a party, but he also disliked the tendency to faction and grouping. Salisbury believed that men should serve the interests of the nation through the party, but not use party as a means for their own self-advancement. Despite his low opinion of human nature, Salisbury believed that politicians should be guided by a sense of national pride, genuine conviction, a feeling of duty and honour.

Lady Gwendolen argued that her father was 'quite without party sentiment; and that was why his convictions were of such a thorough-going and uncompromising character. He championed causes; not a tradition, not a name or a party cockade; he fought a battle, he never played a game.'

Salisbury was often accused of placing party before country in his opposition to Irish Home Rule. J.L.Hammond in his study of Gladstone and Ireland suggested that Salisbury lacked 'moral judgement' in his treatment of the subject. It is often claimed that Salisbury held back on Home Rule because he refused to split the Conservatives. In the words of Winston Churchill: 'He always sought to obtain and use power through the party and by the party. No English statesman of the nineteenth century was less likely to split his party or lead some forlorn, uncalculated crusade of enthusiasm or adventure.' This is a misunderstanding. There were times when Salisbury was ready to defy the party or lead his reluctant followers into unknown territory, notably during the 1884 Reform Bill crisis. After the first Home Rule crisis, there were numerous occasions when Salisbury was ready to ignore his party's feelings or prejudice, if it was necessary to do so to preserve the Union with Ireland.

Salisbury was unyielding over the Irish question, because he refused to believe that Home Rule would provide a lasting political settlement of the issue. He believed that Ireland was too intractably divided into two by race, religion and politics. After the bloody events of the last six years in Ulster, is he to be blamed for reaching such a conclusion in the 1880s? What is often overlooked is that Salisbury was the grudging initiator of a quiet social revolution in the Irish countryside. Under the Unionists, the Irish tenantry were gradually transformed into peasant proprietors. Salisbury was sure that his party's objections to Home Rule were unpopular with the electorate. Nor did he accept that the issue was a cunning diversion away from urgent social reform. On the contrary, Salisbury used to argue that it was Gladstone's mission for Ireland which was blocking the way to legislation beneficial to the working classes. Salisbury believed that the way to save the Union was to make sure that Conservatism became an empirical creed which could appeal to national sentiment across class and regional barriers. Under Salisbury the Conservatives became even more predominantly the English party and they have remained so ever since. It is the paradox of Unionism that it owed eventual success to the highlighting of national differences between England and the Celtic regions.

Salisbury never sought political place for himself. High office came to him without any personal effort, intrigue or struggle on his part. He rose to the premiership through sheer intellectual ability. Salisbury was a reluctant Prime Minister. He was always willing to assume that somebody else was quite capable of taking his place. Even his long periods at the Foreign Office were mainly due, in the first instance, to the refusal of other men to undertake the job instead of him. Salisbury had no relish for political power. He regarded the distribution of patronage as a degrading task. Salisbury took only a limited view of the importance of government. He once remarked that a politician was 'no higher in the scale of things than a policeman, whose utility would be gone if the workers of mischief disappeared'. He was detached from the cares and burdens of office. Despite his inner doubts, however, Salisbury gave an air of serenity and firmness. He had a personal and lasting devotion for Queen Victoria, but he was contemptuous of the ways of Court. He had no romantic attachment to the pomp and glory of Empire, but he dedicated himself to its defence.

Salisbury believed that his primary task was essentially a holding operation. Abroad, he faced the dangers to British power with the military and economic rise of other major European countries notably Germany. Within the Empire, there was the spreading problem of insurgent native nationalism, whether in India, South Africa or Egypt. The 1890s is still in popular imagination the decade of imperialism, the high summer before the long decline. Salisbury, who was responsible for an enormous extension of British political control in Africa, believed that what he was doing was not carrying the Union Jack across the globe, but holding back the forces of disintegration. His actions stemmed from fear and not confidence. Salisbury was always suspicious of jingoism. He doubted the popularity of imperialism. Memories of Midlothianism never faded. It is a strange but understandable paradox, that the anti-democratic Salisbury should take so much notice of the unpredictable, volatile moods of the public in the making of his foreign policy. 'I agree with you that "the public" will require some territorial or cartographic consolation in China,' he wrote to Chamberlain in December 1897. 'It will not be useful and it will be expensive; but as a matter of pure sentiment, we shall have to do it.' Salisbury was hostile to secret diplomacy. He sought friendship and understanding with other countries, but not formal alliances. He was no isolationist. There was a strain of high idealism in his approach to international affairs, which never completely clouded his most pragmatic actions. 'We often think ill of the proceedings of Parliament – we do not in that see any reason for abandoning Parliamentary government,' he explained to Curzon. 'The same with respect to the Concert of Europe. In spite of constant defects and errors, it is on the whole a beneficent institution.'

At home too, Salisbury believed he was on the defensive. He once joked bitterly that he had spent a lifetime in politics, suffering defeat. However, in 1903 the foundations of Church and state appeared to stand as firmly as ever. The power and independence of the House of Lords was at its height. The monarchy had deep popular roots of affection throughout the country. Salisbury's worst fears of class war had not come to fruition. There was no large working-class party. Political loyalties were still based on vertical and not horizontal divisions in society.

He recognized the dangers of corruption in modern politics. He feared an increase in the size of the electorate would make politicians promise instant solutions to complicated problems and attempt to manipulate public opinion for their own ends. Salisbury also hated race prejudice. He feared that the 'posture of superiority', what he called the 'damned-nigger attitude' was not 'merely offensive' but 'a political peril'. 'It belongs to that phase of British temper which has led detachment after detachment of British troops into the most obvious ambuscades – mere arrogance,' he explained (8 June 1900).

Salisbury had a healthy distrust of experts. He once remarked of the army chiefs: 'If these gentlemen had their way, they would soon be asking me to defend the moon against a possible attack from Mars.' When Lytton swallowed the views of his civil servants in India, Salisbury explained the dangers of the specialists: 'No lesson seems to be so deeply inculcated by the experience of life as that you never should trust experts. If you believe the doctors, nothing is wholesome: if you believe the theologians, nothing is innocent: if you believe the soldiers nothing is safe. They all require to have a strong wine diluted by a very large admixture of insipid common sense.'

Salisbury was a hater of humbug. 'There is a political cant that is worse than any other – the use of vague general phrases which the person who uses them has not taken the trouble to think out and which he offers to his countrymen as a solution for real practical problems' (24 May 1889). He championed the liberty of the individual to pick and choose, to make mistakes as well as the right decisions. He warned of the dangers of the over-centralized state. This was no soulless freedom of the *laissez-faire* school. Throughout his political life, Salisbury opposed the intolerant who sought to impose their moral opinions on others. On one occasion, the Bishop of Hereford wanted a select committee to inquire into betting. 'You are going against the feelings and desires of a vast mass of people – and I doubt very much whether the results of this crusade will be satisfactory to the minds of those who undertake it,' Salisbury argued. 'Will it not produce, by the opportunities of annoyance and conspiracy which it will give, evils infinitely greater than those you desire to arrest?' (20 May 1901). On the drink issue, Salisbury opposed the temperance fanatics. He disliked attempts to restrict the freedom of people to drink alcohol if they wanted to do so. 'It is the habit, when you wish to prevent an offence, to direct your punitive efforts on the person who commits it,' Salisbury observed. 'But here, you wish to prevent a certain number of people from getting drunk – therefore you are asked to prevent four, five and six times as many, who are sober consumers, from having an opportunity of the indulgence and sustenance to which they have a right. Why are you to punish the innocent in order to save the guilty?' Salisbury suggested that such legislation was of 'a class character' because while the upper classes could stock up their wine-cellars, the working classes were deprived of the liberty to drink. Salisbury believed that the solution to the evils of alcoholism were to be found in 'the gradual growth of intelligence and education', which would enable men to make the choice. 'We have been induced in the past by advisers who, I think, were not wise, to take upon the shoulders of Parliament a responsibility which belongs to the individual and the community themselves.'

Lord Robert Cecil recalled of his father:

He had an almost fanatical belief in personal liberty. Discipline by one human being over another was extremely repugnant to him. He recognized, of course, that where common action was necessary, obedience to orders was essential. In the fighting services or in party politics disciplinary action could not be avoided. Even then, when he was Prime Minister of a Cabinet or leader of a party, he would explain to his followers his view as to what should be done as clearly and forcibly as he could, but if some of them were recalcitrant, it was only in extreme cases that he thought it right to proceed further. He carried the same principles into family life, and so did my mother.

It was in the family circle at Hatfield that Salisbury practised his personal freedom.

Salisbury tried to delay change and dilute its impact. As Canon MacColl once remarked, 'He was a pessimist at heart; he fought a losing battle well.' Salisbury was to leave no school of admirers. His name means little to present-day Conservatives. Yet his patriarchal sense of public duty, his belief in integrity in politics, his willingness to compromise but contempt for opportunism are still of lasting value. Moreover, there is a modern ring about Salisbury, even if most of the political issues of his time have long since vanished. He was remarkably detached from the popular attitudes and assumptions of his day. His scepticism for the future, his questioning of the complacent and widespread belief in the onward march of progress, both material and spiritual, his contempt for the fancies of the moment, and his deep respect for the old and well-tried methods of doing things remain worthy of study. Salisbury deserves to be remembered, not merely as one of Britain's most effective Foreign Secretaries, but also as a successful party leader and an intellectual Conservative, who was able with some success to blend theory with practice.

SELECTIVE BIBLIOGRAPHY

The following collections of papers were consulted in the preparation of this short biography: Acland papers, Bodleian Library; Ashbourne papers, in private possession; Balfour papers, British Museum; Carnarvon papers, Public Record Office; Lord Robert Cecil papers, British Museum; Joseph Chamberlain papers, Birmingham University Library; Lord Randolph Churchill papers, Churchill College, Cambridge; Cranbrook papers, East Suffolk Record Office; Cross papers, British Museum; Disraeli papers, Hughenden, National Trust; Gladstone papers, British Museum; Edward Hamilton papers, British Museum; Hartington papers, Chatsworth, Derbyshire; Hicks Beach papers, Gloucester Record Office; Layard papers, British Museum; Lytton papers, India Office Library; Northbrook papers, India Office Library; Northcote papers, British Museum; Richmond papers, East Sussex Record Office; Salisbury papers, Christ Church Library, Oxford; White papers, Public Record Office

Lady Gwendolen Cecil's splendid biography of her father is unsurpassed and remains the definitive work. Its four volumes (Hodder & Stoughton 1921, 1931 and 1932) cover Salisbury's life up to the 1892 general election. The biography remains an unfinished masterpiece. The typescript of the unpublished fifth volume lies with Salisbury's papers in Christ Church library in Oxford. There is a shorter, but slighter and less informative life of Salisbury: A.L.Kenny, *Salisbury: Portrait of a Statesman* (John Murray 1953). Two books deal with the younger Salisbury: M.Pinto-Duschinsky, *The Political Thought of Lord Salisbury* (Constable 1967) and *Salisbury on Politics*, edited by Paul Smith (Cambridge University Press 1972). Both books examine Salisbury's vast output of articles in the *Quarterly* and *Saturday Reviews*, mostly written in the 1850s and 1860s. Those essays are still well worth reading. A number of them were republished in book form in *Essays Biographical* (John Murray 1905) and *Foreign Policy* (John Murray 1905). There is a perceptive, privately printed portrait of Salisbury by Lady Gwendolen, *Biographical Studies of the Life and Political Character of Robert, Third Marquis of Salisbury* (n.d.). His Antipodean journey is partially retold in Lord Robert Cecil's *Gold Fields Diary* (1935). Glimpses of family life can be discovered in Viscountess Milner, *My Picture Gallery* (John Murray 1951); Blanche E. Dugdale, *Family Homespun* (Hodder & Stoughton 1940); Viscount Cecil of Chelwood, *All The Way* (Hodder & Stoughton 1949) and Lady Frances Balfour, *Ne Obliviscaris*, two vols. (Hodder & Stoughton 1930).

For Salisbury's early life up to his accession to the leadership of the Conservative party the following books are of importance: Robert Blake, *Disraeli* (Eyre & Spottiswoode 1966); Monypenny's and Buckle's six-volume life of Disraeli (John Murray 1910–20). There are two scholarly accounts of the Second Reform Bill crisis, throwing light on Salisbury's attitudes: Maurice Cowling, *Disraeli, Gladstone and Revolution* (Cambridge University Press 1967) and F.B.Smith, *The Making of the Reform Bill* (1967). A number of important references to Salisbury can be found in Paul Smith, *Disraelian Conservatism and Social Reform* (Routledge & Kegan Paul 1967) and E.J.Feuchtwanger, *Disraeli, Democracy and the Tory Party* (Oxford University Press 1968). For Salisbury's period at the India Office, see S.Gopal's *British Policy in India 1858–1905* (Cambridge University Press 1965) and Edward C.Moulton, *Lord Northbrook's Indian Administration 1872–1876* (1969). For Salisbury's first spell at the Foreign Office the following are of particular value: C.J.Lowe, *The Reluctant Imperialists*, Vol. 1 (Routledge & Kegan Paul 1967); W. N.Medlicott, *The Congress of Berlin and After* (1938); R. W. Seton Watson, *Disraeli, Gladstone and the Eastern Question* (1935); D. W. Lee, *Great Britain and the Cyprus Convention* (1934) and M.S.Anderson, *The Eastern Question* (Macmillan 1966).

Biographies of leading ministers provide glimpses of Salisbury as party leader after 1881. The following are worth looking at: Blanche E. Dugdale, *Arthur James Balfour*, Vol. 1 (Hutchinson 1936); A.Balfour, *Chapters of Autobiography* (Cassell 1930); D. Judd, *Balfour and the British Empire* (Macmillan 1968); J.L.Garvin and J.Amery, *Joseph Chamberlain*, four vols. (Macmillan 1935–51); P. Fraser, *Joseph Chamberlain*

(Cassell 1966); W.S.Churchill, *Lord Randolph Churchill*, two vols. (Macmillan 1906) and R.Rhodes James, *Lord Randolph Churchill* (Weidenfeld & Nicolson 1959); Viscount Chilston, *W.H.Smith* (Routledge & Kegan Paul 1965) and his *Life of Akers-Douglas, Chief Whip* (Routledge & Kegan Paul 1961); Lord Newton, *Lansdowne* (Macmillan 1929). The best study of Unionist policy in Ireland remains L.P.Curtis Jr, *Coercion and Conciliation in Ireland 1880–1892* (Princeton University Press 1965). See also J.L.Hammond, *Gladstone and the Irish Nation* (2nd edition, Cass 1964) and C.H.Hardinge, *Life of Carnarvon*, three vols. (Oxford University Press 1925).

There are brief accounts of Salisbury as a party leader in R.T.McKenzie, *British Political Parties* (Heinemann 1955) and M.Ostrogorski, *Democracy and the Organization of Political Parties*, Vol. 2 (Macmillan 1902). There is a study of the third Reform Bill crisis: A.Jones, *Politics of Reform* (Cambridge University Press 1972). Robert Blake's *Conservative Party from Peel to Churchill* (Eyre & Spottiswoode 1970) is helpful. There are also two important articles by J.P.Cornford: 'The Parliamentary Foundations of the Hotel Cecil' in *Ideas and Institutions of Victorian England* (Bell & Sons 1967) and 'The Transformation of Conservatism in the Late Nineteenth Century' in *Victorian Studies*, Vol. vii (1963–4), pp. 35–66. Henry Pelling, *Social Geography of British Elections* (Macmillan 1967) provides a wealth of information on grassroots Conservatism. Psephology is to be found in J.P.D.Dunbabin, 'Parliamentary Elections in Great Britain 1858–1900: A Psephological note', *English Historical Review*, Vol. lxxxi, 1966.

Salisbury's foreign policy is densely covered by books, articles and monographs. The following are the more essential, which need to be consulted: J.A.S.Grenville, *Lord Salisbury and Foreign Policy* (London University Press 1964); L.Penson, *Foreign Affairs under the Third Marquess of Salisbury* (London University Press 1962); C.J.Lowe, *Salisbury and the Mediterranean* (Routledge & Kegan Paul 1962); R.Robinson and J.Gallagher, *Africa and the Victorians* (Macmillan 1965); Colin L. Smith, *The Embassy of Sir William White at Constantinople* (Oxford University Press 1957); G.N.Sanderson, *England, Europe and the Upper Nile 1882–1899* (Edinburgh University Press 1965); C.W.Monger, *End of Isolation* (Nelson 1963); Z.Steiner, *The Foreign Office and Foreign Policy* (Cambridge University Press 1969); W.L.Langer, *European Alliances and Alignments 1871–1890* and his *Diplomacy of Imperialism 1890–1902* (Vintage Books, New York 1951 and 1956).

Both parliamentary *Hansard* and *The Times* are invaluable sources for any study of Salisbury's speeches and writings.

INDEX